FORGIVENESS

A Time to Love and a Time to Hate

Helen Whitney

Published by FastPencil, Inc.

Published by FastPencil, Inc.
3131 Bascom Ave.
Suite 150
Campbell CA 95008 USA
(408) 540-7571
(408) 540-7572 (Fax)
info@fastpencil.com
http://www.fastpencil.com

All photos in this book: Paul Sanderson, Old Town Films

CONTENTS

ACKNOWLEDGMENTS

As this book is inextricably connected to the film upon which it is based, my gratitude extends to people involved in both the creation of the film and of the book. The title is the same for each: *Forgiveness: A Time to Love and a Time to Hate.*

Above all, I owe a particular debt to my executive producer, Paul Dietrich, who approached me four years ago with an offer to make a film and a companion book about forgiveness. His passion for the subject was an inducement. Equally so was his willingness to give me complete artistic freedom. I am also grateful to his business partner and executive producer, Ian Watson. He shared Paul's passionate engagement with the subject and offered his encouragement throughout the long period it took me to bring both projects to completion.

My friend Monsignor Lorenzo Albacete was my primary consultant on the film and book, providing invaluable insights about what became its central theme: the existential, as opposed to the religious, roots of forgiveness. He was present throughout the years, whether late at night on the phone or over dinner, always encouraging, listening, and willing to review the material in all of its iterations.

My other key consultant, Thane Rosenbaum, was similarly involved. Our first conversation was unforgettable for it came at a discouraging period midway through the research. He understood immediately what I wanted to do, believed in its importance and shared his deep knowledge generously.

I am grateful for my other consultants:

Charles Griswold was finishing his own, soon-to-be acclaimed book on forgiveness when I approached him. His enthusiastic support and appreciation, along with his authoritative text was immensely important. Arthur Magida, ever practical, always seemed to be able to find entrés for me into inaccessible worlds, or to suggest fresh voices. Phyllis Tickel, wise and witty, provided decisive help at the very beginning. Her resounding, "Yes, make this film, you are on the right track!" put needed wind in my sails. My close friend and co-writer on previous projects, Jane Barnes, was an essential sounding board for my thinking as it evolved. Nir Eisikovits raised important questions and illuminated vital distinctions between forgiveness, sympathy, and empathy.

While forgiveness is of theological concern within all the major religions, there are differences within and between the traditions. I appreciate the many people who shared their knowledge about this subject. Rabbi Irvin Kula and Rabbi Brad Hirshfeldt helped clarify the importance of forgiveness within the Jewish tradition. Jeff Jacoby was willing to discuss the different emphasis on forgiveness within Christianity and Judaism. My close friend Hillel Levine provided me with essential Jewish texts along with his own readings.

In the opening part of the book that focuses on forgiveness in the personal realm, I received invaluable help, sometimes from a variety of sources:

Amish forgiveness is difficult to comprehend because of the reluctance of its members to be interviewed. Professor Ray Gingerich, formerly Amish, provided an important perspective from a sympathetic, but not uncritical insider. I am also grateful to Tim Messler for his reporting on the Amish community. Janet Landman, the biographer of Katherine Power, provided me with essential insights about Power's ethical transformation. My close friend David Harris guided me through the history of the anti-war movement and provided an essential political frame to Power's story. Rebecca Wexler reviewed all the material in the book relating to the emerging field of science and forgiveness and her suggestions for the chapter on Judith Shaw-McKnight were especially helpful. Terri Jentz was not only the subject of one of the stories of the film but a valuable guide to my thinking about the importance of anger in healing. My friend Leslie Karsten provided important psychological insights into Don Robeson and the Glick family as well elegant editing for these and other chapters.

Political forgiveness, the subject of the second part of the book, is elusive, complicated, baffling, even counter-intuitive. Here I owe a special debt of gratitude to Donald Shriver. His book, *An Ethic for Enemies: Forgiveness in Politics*, was a revelation. I am also grateful to Walter Reich, Geoffrey Hartmann, and Elisabeth Young-Bruehl in sharing their erudition and reflections about the Holocaust and the controversy surrounding Bitburg. Ben Nienass, the reporter for the Germany shoot, carefully reviewed the chapters on Germany's penitential journey and South Africa's TRC. His ideas immensely improved the text.

I am grateful to my conversations with Rhoda E. Howard-Hassmann and Mark Gibney. Both of them, along with their excellent book, *The Age of Apology*, affirmed the growing importance of public apology. Nicholas Tavuchis, a pioneer in the studies of apology, generously spent hours with me detailing how his thinking had changed over the years—all of this in the middle of a violent thunderstorm. Without the insights of Antoine Rutayisire and Alison des Forges the chapter on Rwanda would not have been possible. Alison's lenses were of a darker hue than Antoine's, and both were indispensable. My gratitude extends to my friend Mia Farrow who opened her vast rolodex when I asked for help in finding Rwandan survivors of the genocide. Through Mia we discovered Beatha Uwazaninka who, along with Antoine, became a central voice of the Rwandan chapter. My friend Katherine Kurs led me to Father Petero Sabune, whose insights into the minds of the Rwandan killers were uniquely valuable. I am grateful to Peter Balakian who, along with

Robert Jay Lifton, became the touchstone for my thinking about the Armenian genocide and its place in the book and film.

Personal friends not only gave their time reviewing the manuscript but they also offered their talents as writers and thinkers. David Berlinski reflects on adultery in chapter five about the Longs. His insights have a depth and originality about infidelity—"this unfathomable injury"—that I believe are unmatched by any other writer on the subject. Peter Hawkins, the esteemed expert on Dante, discusses why the poet, in a startling reversal of the traditional hierarchy of sins, describes betrayal as the worst of all. Novelist Michele Zackheim wrote an inspired introduction to chapter six: The Last Taboo. Author Lesley Karsten's reflections on the corrosive effects of anger in chapter four, Don Robeson were equally enlightening. Ben Nienass added important comments in the chapters about South African and Germany. Professor Richard Neugebauer offered provoking ideas about the complexities of forgiveness in Rwanda, in particular how the dead make powerful claims upon us.

There were many excellent articles and books that provided invaluable insight and did much of the hard work that made my overview possible. I would like to single out several whose thinking truly altered the course of my thinking: Patricia Haynor's comparative study about the growing number of truth commissions in Third World countries provided an essential framework to understand them. Paul Van Zyl's articles and on-camera interview offered wisdom and appropriate caution about the role of forgiveness and reconciliation in the political realm. Mahmood Mamdani's article, *Reconciliation without Justice,* and our subsequent interview both complicated and deepened my thinking about South Africa and Rwanda. Antije Krog's memoir, *Country of My Skull: Guilt, Sorrow and the Limits of Forgiveness in the New South Africa*, was arguably the best—and most bracing—work on this subject that I have yet read. Pumla Gobodo-Madikizela's memoir, *A Human Being Died That Night: A South African Story of Forgiveness,* is a more positive interpretation of the TRC and, along with her interview, provided another layer to my own thinking. Piers Pigou's article, *The Murder of Sicelo Dlomo*, helped me understand the vast differences of opinion in South Africa about the legacy of the TRC. Brandon Hamber's article, *Forgiveness and Reconciliation in the 21st Century; Paradise lost or Pragmatism,* marked a decisive moment in my research. He raised questions that refined my own: Why is forgiveness in the air today? What does it say about us and the times we live in?

I am especially grateful to my editors Ed and Deb Shapiro, who are the award-winning authors of *Be The Change: How Meditation Can Transform You and The World* and *Your Body Speaks Your Mind*. While I was finishing the film, they organized my writings for the book into a rough assembly that was extremely helpful. We had a pressing deadline and their work enabled me to write quickly and efficiently. In addition they devoted long hours both before and during the Christmas holidays to carefully reviewing each chapter. Their manner was unfailingly gracious and their editorial suggestions consistently improved the manuscript.

I am very thankful for our literary agent, David Nelson, for all his tireless efforts on behalf of this book.

I owe special thanks to all the friends and acquaintances who generously offered their most intimate memories of their own struggles with forgiveness. My daughter Christina Schmidt and stepdaughter Betsey Schmidt never ceased to encourage me when my spirits flagged. And, of course, my companion Kent Carroll, who graciously and for the most part uncomplainingly allowed me to disrupt our lives by devoting inordinate hours—and even years—to the film and the book it is based upon. To him, my deepest gratitude.

FOREWORD

THE DALAI LAMA

Why is it so important that we forgive and why do so many of us find it so difficult to forgive?

Forgiveness is difficult and complex. It can involve issues of justice and reparations and of course deep seated anger and the wish for revenge. Forgiveness is not a question of forgetting the wrong done; if you've forgotten what was done, there is nothing to forgive. Forgiveness involves refusing to allow yourself to give in to anger and the desire for revenge. This is why forgiveness ultimately brings peace.

This book and the PBS documentary it accompanies present a powerful exploration of this most important subject.

All of us carry memories of things that we have done that we are not happy about. There isn't anyone who hasn't wounded someone else's feelings, or physically hurt someone, or in some extreme cases even killed someone. The problem is we tend to think we live in isolation; you in your separate world and I in mine. These notions of separateness and isolation are what give rise to fear, suspicion, and mistrust.

Human beings need to live together and are dependent on each other in many essential ways. We are deeply connected, in fact, interdependent. Science tells us very clearly that nothing exists in isolation, powered by itself. But because we can't see it, we mistakenly cling to our separate identities. All that concerns us is me, my family, my village, my people, my religion, my nation. And the next thing we know, we're in conflict. Out of a narrow vision of the world, we've all committed acts that we are not proud of. We've all hurt each other deeply, even within the circle of our own families and friends. And often we're not even concerned about how we've hurt those outside our protected circle.

The basic feature of society is kindness, for it is only through kindness and compassion, caring for others, that society can succeed. If it is correct that qualities such as love, patience, tolerance, and forgiveness are what happiness consists in, and if it is also correct that compassion is both the source and the fruit of these qualities, then the more we are compassionate, patient, and forgiving, the more we provide for our own happiness. Thus, any idea that concern for others, though a noble quality, is a matter only for our private lives, is simply short-sighted. Compassion and with it, forgiveness, belongs to every sphere of activity.

Someone once asked me if there was anything I thought was unforgivable? And I think the answer is that the only thing I might find unforgivable would be if I myself were unable to forgive. In fact, in Mahayana Buddhism, not to forgive, especially when someone has offered you an apology, is considered a serious transgression of the bodhisattva's altruistic pledge.

Forgiveness may be difficult, and it sometimes takes time to achieve, but in the end, it will always bring a measure of peace to ourselves as individuals and to our relations with others.

January 24, 2011

PREFACE

I remember vividly the first time I considered forgiveness as a subject for my next project. It was not a moment of blinding clarity, an on-the-road-to-Damascus event that would provide material for a dramatic preface. Instead, I experienced a range of conflicting emotions: confusion, fascination, of course, but fear as well. In truth, flight was the dominant impulse.

It happened five years ago on a luminously clear day in Salt Lake City where I was surveying Temple Square trying to find the perfect closing shot for my PBS series, "The Mormons." I needed an image that could be the last word about this rapidly growing religion born on American soil. I was exhausted. The four long years involved in completing the series were worthy of the epic struggles of the Mormons crossing the plains. There had been the usual logistical and financial problems of any production, but in addition I'd had serious conflicts over questions about the meaning of Mormonism and its place in American religious history.

The spiritual landscape is my beat; I had put down my flag on this territory thirty years ago when I produced my first and still favorite film for ABC about life in a Trappist monastery. It had been a life-changing experience. Others followed. But after a series of documentaries focusing on religion, I came to realize that while this territory is fascinating, provoking the deepest questions, it is not always a land of milk and honey. These subjects could also be contentious, fractious, filled with land-mines and exhausting.

So, at the moment when my cell phone rang, I was dreaming of rest in a small Umbrian town to be followed by a small project, richly layered of course, but narrowly focused. Perhaps a biography of an artist—ideally someone who lived in my hometown, New York City. I was bone tired of life on the road so if I could shoot and write everything in my living room, that would have been perfect. I was looking forward to recovering my life.

The phone kept ringing, insistently, while I was staring at the odd surreal beauty of the Mormon Temple trying to find my shot. When I finally answered, a stranger, Paul Dietrich, introduced himself as a global investment manager, a spiritual seeker, and an admirer of my work. Without any small talk, he immediately made a passionate pitch why forgiveness should be my next subject. Barely pausing, Dietrich offered me a fully funded two-hour film and a companion book to be based on it.

He concluded with his assurance of complete artistic freedom. A bolt out of the blue. Not the usual way projects are launched.

Given my intense engagement with spiritual themes, the subject was a perfect fit but it was also perfectly wrong. It was everything I had vowed not to do at this point in my life. Forgiveness was larger than the mood I was in after so many epic battles about the Mormons. It was larger than my film about 9/11, "Faith and Doubt at Ground Zero." It was even larger than my most ambitious film about Pope John Paul II, a man whose life intersected with every major event in the twentieth century. Forgiveness was vast, shapeless, emotionally and psychologically scarier than any of my earlier films. The intellectual and geographical boundaries seemed infinite. Where do I begin? How do I structure it? I saw myself back on a road that might take me far from New York City, across the world, around the globe.

Moreover, while forgiveness evokes mystery and power, it also comes with an aura of sentimentality, of hushed reverence and of unexamined New Age pieties. The most egregious: it is always better to forgive than not and someone who remains angry is the lesser for it, a spiritual underachiever.

Before I take on a project, I have an unvarying ritual. I talk to friends, colleagues, and strangers. I roam through libraries and the Internet. I have long lunches with experts. I dream day and night about the topic's possibilities and its pitfalls. This process allows me to ease into the water gradually—or to get back on shore before it is too late. Such caution is appropriate given that these projects can take years. But with forgiveness, surprisingly, the exploratory process was unusually brief; after only a few weeks I jumped in.

Sometimes I look back on this period, mystified. What was it that I discovered that overrode my reservations so quickly and decisively?

To say that I discovered that forgiveness mattered deeply, urgently and sometimes dangerously to many of the people with whom I spoke sounds banal and obvious, but it wasn't so to me. Of course, I was no stranger to the strong emotions that surround forgiveness and unforgiveness. I had my critics and I had judged them in turn. I had experienced betrayal as well, and I too had caused emotional injury to those I loved. I knew the pleasure of forgiving and the pain of asking for forgiveness. I knew the corrosive effect of hanging on to resentment. I was also well acquainted with the great works of art informed by forgiveness, where broken relationships are mended in a spirit of humane, even supernatural tolerance. The final scene of Mozart's "The Marriage of Figaro" is possibly the most sublime expression of forgiveness ever expressed in music. The Count has been caught seducing the servant girl and his wife forgives him half-knowing that he will betray her again. Peace returns to their community and all of this underscored and heightened by Mozart's ravishing shifting harmonies.

However, I had never thought about forgiveness in a disciplined way. I had never taken its measure philosophically and psychologically. I hadn't talked about it with friends—nor they with me—even though my circle is highly expressive, intimate, and open.

But the minute people knew that I was making this film, the floodgates opened. Friends and strangers would approach me; they would call and write, unburdening themselves. Sometimes, people would pretend they were speaking on someone else's behalf because the pain and embarrassment of their experience was too much to reveal. In one memorable week at a hospice, while sitting by the bedside of dying patients, I sometimes felt there was no other subject but forgiveness. Of all the topics I had chosen over the last thirty-five years, forgiveness seems to resonate at the deepest and most intense level.

I wondered about this. And then, late one night talking to my friend and advisor Monsignor Lorenzo Albacete, an eloquent priest straight off the pages of a Graham Greene novel, Lorenzo identified it: "The hunger for connection and the terror of going into the night unconnected, unreconciled, is that fundamental." And then, in words that ultimately were defining for the film and the book, "Forgiveness is a primordial ache in the human heart that precedes all religions, it precedes everything. No matter what the theologians and the religious folks will tell you, religion arrives late on the scene; we provide, at best, structures for this existential ache."

By the end of two years of research I—along with my team of researchers—had spoken to over eight hundred people across the world. From Rwanda and the killing fields, to truth commissions in Liberia; from the Holocaust Museum in Berlin, to its counterpart in Washington D.C.; from frat houses at Yale to backstage at the MET; from the Amish community in Pennsylvania to Mormon wards in Utah. We had conversations with people in extremis: grieving widows, HIV patients, the angry unemployed, betrayed spouses, defiant genocidaires, survivors of atrocities, repentant criminals, sixties radicals, Vietnam War veterans, Third World truth commissioners, repentant politicians, internet bullies. We also came to know many ordinary men and women grappling with these issues in the most intimate ways. We spoke with scholars in various disciplines: philosophers, psychologists, theologians, anthropologists, evolutionary biologists. I also read (and discounted) much of the ever-growing forgiveness literature brimming with optimism, uninflected by complexity. More fruitful research concentrated on pioneering work in restorative justice, human rights, and reconciliation commissions

Throughout most of these conversations, I detected a powerful undersong of urgency. Forgiveness mattered; it was more than a subject out there—to be found in another country, at academic conferences, in a neighbor's house or on the front pages. It was searingly personal, and for some it was a matter of life and death. Most startling to me was the realization that personal betrayal, while on a whole other scale compared to mass atrocities, nonetheless could cut as deeply as a machete. There were mini-holocausts, a phrase I use carefully, in the private as well as the public realm. I witnessed domestic feuds that poisoned generations and whose source seemed, at least to an outsider, breathtakingly trivial. Sometimes the original injury had even been forgotten.

Another surprising discovery that richly complicated forgiveness was that there is virtually no consensus about what it is and what it is becoming. As complexity and contradiction is my signature style, this was invigorating. Forgiveness had become a 'perfect fit' after all. There is a virtual stew of sharply contested meanings, both religious and secular. The elusive quality of forgiveness brings to mind Justice Potter Stewart's memorable quote while he struggled—unsuccessfully—to define "pornography." His solution: "I know it when I see it." Obviously, the comparison only goes so far. Pornography is concrete, tangible, and arbitrary, while forgiveness is abstract, intangible, and essential. We may see the former but the latter is invisible and certainly of a very different character and value. While unseen, forgiveness is, nonetheless, real and one might rightly say, "I know it when I experience it." But to even say that, belies its complexity.

And then the ubiquity of forgiveness gave the film and the book a timeliness and a relevance I had not expected. To be honest, I had mixed feelings about this new forgiveness that had migrated into the political sphere, claiming to heal political leaders, institutions, corporations, even nations. It seemed immodest, promiscuous, cheapening. To live in this era of public apology is to experience more often the ridiculous than the sublime. The sight of yet another disgraced politician clutching his wife in front of a bank of microphones is ludicrous; a mass murderer asking for forgiveness in front of a truth commission sometimes seems obscene; Tony Blair apologizing to the Irish for the potato famine, or the Pope for the Crusades, however well intentioned, is questionable. Our Senate apologizing for not apologizing for lynching is absurd. I wondered, along with Theodore Dalrymple, whether all this apologizing "is a form of moral exhibitionism that subverts moral thought."

Admittedly, the instances of authentic public apology and true political reconciliation are rare, but there have been shining moments and one of them converted me. Early in my research I learned that the most discussed and universally admired public apology in the twentieth century occurred when Willy Brandt fell to his knees in front of the Warsaw Ghetto Memorial in 1970. I studied the footage and the photographs for days; it was a revelation. I could see the shock and awe of the crowds staring at him; I could see luminous sincerity on Brandt's face as he expressed his spontaneous wordless penitence; I could understand, as historians confirmed, why the power of this symbolic gesture changed the history of Polish German relations.

These ideas brought me into this project. They are at the heart of the film and shaped the book. They resonate in my life today. Ultimately, the making of the film was a three-year journey, with sharp turns, dark valleys, and stunning vistas; it was arguably the most meaningful film in my professional career

However, writing the book has, in some respects, brought even greater satisfaction. Both the film and the book are rooted in stories that illumine the heart of forgiveness in all of its facets. I chose these stories for their dramatic power and intellectual richness—for their ability to evoke the contradictions of 'the new forgiveness.' But the constraints of time of the documentary form did not allow me to plumb their depths.

I had to relinquish material because of the time limit for the television series. Filmmakers describe this painful process as "throwing your babies overboard." While the book still takes as its starting point the interviews, I have now been able to expand the voices, to rescue some of my 'lost babies' and even to include new material. I returned to brilliant intellectuals whose insights shaped my thinking but who were uncomfortable in front of the camera. In the new introductions and conclusions to each chapter, I have been able to move away from the minimalist haiku style of television narration into my new voice—fuller and more textured, allowing me to provide essential context and analysis.

Writing up these interviews and going back through the printed materials gave me a chance to walk my own walk, talk my own talk about "the ache for connection." All my films have changed me. This one has been no different. It has taught me how much I had to learn about my own subject. It has sent me on errands of penance and reminded me of my own snares of pride. When penance has been offered to me, I have struggled to practice a deeper humility. And now, more than ever, I try to be alert to "the rumor of angels" that so often goes unnoticed in our own lives.

My hope for the book, *Forgiveness: A Time to Love and a Time to Hate*, is to inform but not dictate, to raise questions but not answer them. If this encounter results in a radical rethinking of what one understood about forgiveness, I will have succeeded.

Helen Whitney, January 3, 2011

INTRODUCTION: THE CHANGING FACE OF FORGIVENESS

Director Helen Whitney

Forgiveness is not something in the other world that we are looking for—it is an experience in this world, an experience of healing broken relations without which we cannot live. It is that fundamental. — Monsignor Lorenzo Albacete

Forgiveness is elusive, mysterious yet primal; it is both an idea and an ache. The giving or withholding of it touches us at the most profound level of our being. Over the last two hundred years it acquired the aura of a uniquely religious word, but forgiveness is now changing and there is no consensus about what it is or what it is becoming

For centuries, forgiveness has been expressed in prayer and meditation. Though the religious practices vary, it is embedded in all sacred texts. "All religions have some kind of structured forgiveness mechanisms that are rooted in fundamental existential concerns," says theologian and Roman Catholic priest Monsignor Lorenzo Albacete.

Muslims pray five times a day asking for forgiveness. During the month of Ramadan there is a ceremony called the Night of Power, when they stay awake praying for forgiveness so that the scroll of their actions is cleansed of their sins.

The Day of Atonement, the most important Jewish holiday, is centered on forgiveness and repentance. Judaism teaches that if one causes harm to another but then genuinely apologizes and attempts to right that harm, then the wronged person should offer forgiveness. "We believe that just as only God can forgive sins against God," explains Chief Rabbi Jonathan Sacks, "so only human beings can forgive sins against human beings."

By its long attachment to the Catholic sacrament of penance, forgiveness has become synonymous with a hushed and privately whispered exchange between priest and sinner. "With all its faults, you go into a secret little room with a curtain and a screen that separates you from the confessor," says Monsignor Albacete, who explains that we may or may not know who the confessor is. But that really doesn't matter. "The confessor is just there as a representative, an envoy of the transcendent presence from whom you want the possibility or experience of forgiveness."

For Christians, Christ's final words on the cross asking God to forgive those who crucified him, are the defining text. In God's eyes, nothing is beyond forgiveness and it is available to all without limitation. In that same light, while recognizing that forgiveness is not always easy, it is something that each Christian strives for.

"God says, behold, I make all things new—not patched, not repaired, but new. And I think that's what forgiveness does." Kathy Power was a sixties anti-war activist who lived undercover for twenty years while being on the Ten Most Wanted Fugitives list for the murder of a policeman. Eventually she turned herself in, knowing that she would have to atone for her actions. During her time in jail she had an epiphany. "I was sitting in my cell when suddenly these words came to me: 'Forgive us our trespasses as we forgive those who trespass against us.' I realized I could never forgive myself until I was also able to forgive the people I opposed."

For the Amish community, who immediately and absolutely forgave the man who shot ten of their children, killing five of them, forgiveness is uncompromising, complete, and unconditional. Such unquestioning forgiveness reflects their ability to, "forgive the perpetrator without having to forgive the act," as one Amish woman explains. "When I saw the bodies of the little girls it just made me real mad, but mad at the evil, not at the shooter." For the Amish, forgiveness comes from God. It is an order, a commandment, and unambiguous. It is absolute and not of this world.

What has changed is that forgiveness is no longer the confine of religion but is in the air as never before. It is ubiquitous: it has left the church confessional and the pulpit, it is in the fractious streets and on the psychoanalyst's couch, it drives the restorative justice movement, it is the subject of scholarly conferences, and it fills the self-help bookshelves. Forgiveness-is-good-for-your health has become the new mantra for a burgeoning field of research, while twelve-step programs around the world incorporate forgiveness as an essential guiding principle for recovery.

Reconciliation, a close relative of forgiveness, is at the heart of truth commissions across Latin America and Africa. It is part of an emotional dialogue between blacks and whites, rich and poor, amputees and their assailants. Far-flung tribal cultures are turning to forgiveness rites and rituals to heal their communities. In Eastern Europe, forgiveness has provoked intense debate among those who collaborated and those who resisted, among those who informed and those who felt betrayed. It has entered the human rights debate about torture, atrocities and genocide.

These contemporary settings for forgiveness present startlingly new realms for transformation and reconciliation, but at the same time, inescapably, they present complexities and problems. As we broaden the range of forgiveness do we deepen or cheapen its power? What does its ubiquity say about us, and the times we live in? Questions are now being asked not only about the power of forgiveness but also its limitations and, in rare instances, its danger.

Traditionally, one of the therapist's roles was to relieve the patient of his neurotic guilt. But in this new forgiving environment is there a risk of robbing the patient of an appropriate sense of sin and authentic existential guilt? Are there times when forgiveness might be in conflict with other values, such as self-respect, self-defense, or allegiance to the moral order? Are there special classes of victims, like abused children or battered wives, where forgiveness could be harmful? Are women so socialized to forgive that they can be considered a danger to themselves? Are victims of atrocities being asked to forgive prematurely, fostering a culture of impunity within their nations?

In the last decade, millions of dollars have been spent on forgiveness research. Provocative new studies suggest it could be good for our health. Fascinating questions are being asked about whether forgiveness is an imperative of biology or even of evolutionary survival. Are we hardwired for forgiveness—and revenge—as some scientists suggest?

And yet, with all this attention on forgiveness as it enters the mainstream, it appears there is little agreement about what it is. For instance, there are profound differences within the religious traditions: Many Christians believe that forgiveness should be bestowed as a free gift without any pre-conditions, while Jews believe that it should be contingent on sincere repentance and, if possible, restitution and reparation. And outside of religious differences, individual experiences of forgiveness are varied, frequently contradictory, and often fiercely contested.

For some, forgiveness means being healed of the hurt and emotional burdens of their past. "Forgiveness means I don't have to carry around this huge weight, this concrete ball of painful, awful suffering and rage," believes Deb Long, who has forgiven her husband for having multiple affairs throughout their long marriage, something many people would find indefensible.

For Judith Shaw-McKnight, forgiveness was a matter of life and death. Without a moment of hesitation she is convinced that forgiving the man who infected her with AIDS saved her life: "When I hold on to unforgiveness it just makes me bitter. If I hadn't forgiven him then I'd still be out there on the streets abusing myself. I would probably have died by now."

This also applied to Abraham Eiboszycz, a Holocaust survivor, who faced an extreme choice when he returned to his hometown in Germany after the war. He was surrounded by people who had looked away as he was being transported to the nearby camp and continued to make the same hate-filled, hurtful remarks about Jews. Decades had passed before he accepted that he could not change them and made a decision: "Either I was going to kill myself and let the neighbors finish off what the Nazis could not do or I was going to forgive them." Forgiveness, he realized, "was not granted out of graciousness, or altruism, but to retain my sanity."

But some wonder whether it might be better to retain our anger and rage as a source of inner strength. Father Michael Lapsley, who was a bombing victim of the apartheid regime when he lost both his hands and an eye, admits that sometimes he feels angry towards the political leaders of the apartheid state and their denial of responsibility for what they did. "And that anger is appropriate. But I am too well aware of the danger of preferring unforgiveness and the negative power this gives us over another human being."

This holds true for Terri Jentz, the victim of an unprovoked and savage axe attack, who refuses to forgive the man for what he did to her. "Unconditional forgiveness," she asks. "No, there are conditions: repentance, contrition, reparations, and ultimately justice." For Terri, forgiveness is inseparable from the reality of evil. "I think we can only talk about forgiveness if we also talk about the existence of evil." She believes that to forgive her perpetrator, who has neither admitted nor atoned for his crime, would just be continuing the violence against herself.

Forgiveness can be an urgent question for those who have already suffered greatly. In South Africa, for instance, years of apartheid have left wounds that may never heal. Gideon Nieuwoudt was a member of South Africa's security forces during that time and established a horrific record of abductions, killings, and torture of activists. While in prison he applied to South Africa's Truth and Reconciliation Commission for amnesty in exchange for telling the truth about his killings. He claimed to have had a religious conversion and was experiencing remorse. Nieuwoudt then asked to meet the family of one of the young men he had murdered. For more than fifteen years he had rebuffed attempts by them to learn of their son's fate. He had tormented the mother, calling her in for questioning and claiming she was hiding her son, knowing all the while that the young man was dead. Now he was seeking their forgiveness.

For the family it was fifteen years too late. During a strained and awkward meeting they rejected his apology and even doubted his conversion to Christianity. Their other son erupted with anger at the audacity to ask for forgiveness and hit Nieuwoudt over the head with a vase, splattering him with blood. This incident illustrates how, if the request for forgiveness comes too late, if it is felt to be false or violates our sense of justice then it can provoke outrage and even violence.

These differences can be raw and unsettling and never more so than when we struggle with the unforgivable. Gary Ridgway admitted killing more than ninety women over a period of twenty years. He pled guilty and received life imprisonment without parole. At the sentence hearing, in a courtroom crowded with the dead women's families who individually rose to speak, he listened to their heart-broken rage and enduring loss and, in rare instances, to their reluctant forgiveness. "I don't know how to describe the pain," said the relative of one of the dead women. "It's inside, there are no words for it, there is no closure, it goes on forever. I can't forgive this man. It is not within my power, that I have to leave up to God."

In contrast, another relative spoke directly to Ridgway: "There are people here who hate you. I'm not one of them. I forgive you for what you've done. God says to forgive you, and so you are forgiven." Ridgway had remained impassive throughout the day's hearing as one bereaved relative after another had confronted him. But at that moment of kindness he broke down and wept. Forgiveness can penetrate the darkest souls, if only for a moment.

There are those who believe that the most important forgiveness has to be for oneself first, before it can be offered to anyone else. This is true for Liesbeth Gerritsen, who left her two young children with their father to create a separate life for herself: "If I can't forgive or atone for the things I've done that were wrong, then how can I expect anybody else in the world to do that for me? I know that the moment I can completely forgive myself is when I will be able to truly ask for their forgiveness."

For others, forgiveness primarily means making amends and repairing relationships, essential for our well-being. "We are made for relationships. The search for forgiveness is the search for the healing of an ache of the human heart," believes Monsignor Albacete. "What is the religious notion of Hell? It is absolute loneliness. It means the incapacity to establish a relationship, or to have anyone establish a relationship with you. So the search for forgiveness is that fundamental, it is an expression of the fear of nothingness." Now in his seventies, his voice is deep and thoughtful as he ponders, "this primordial ache, an ache that precedes religion, is what makes us human and forgiveness is our attempt to be fully human."

But relationships consist of two people and often the other is not always so ready to participate. For Don Robeson, whose honor and pride were destroyed when he was fired from his job, forgiveness, whether for those who fired him or for himself has proven elusive and impossible, particularly as the other party has yet to acknowledge any wrongdoing. "Do I go to the person who fired me and tell him I'm sorry, you fired me and I'm very happy over the mess you put my life in? Do I get down on my knees to God and say I've had all the crap I can take?"

For Dan Glick, when his wife showed little remorse after leaving him to raise their two children alone, forgiveness appeared to lie somewhere in the future. "If I'm waiting for my wife to apologize, I actually think I would be waiting the rest of my life." But Dan found a measure of reconciliation by recognizing his own part in what happened, and by understanding that forgiveness is not an instant cure but something that grows over time. "I'm as flawed as the next person. Relationships don't happen in a vacuum, I had a role in this. I believe forgiveness is not something one achieves and then that's it, but is continually changing and unfolding."

Merle Long

Forgiveness or its absence is often most acutely felt in our very last hours. Then the need to be forgiven or to forgive urgently presses in on us and can be a source of either comfort or anguish. For over a year, Merle Long lived in a hospice, unwilling to die. He had a secret hidden from his family that tormented him and that he longed to reveal: At the end of an exemplary life, he felt unforgiven, but he believed that if people knew about this they would think he was a terrible person and would judge him harshly. Or, worse, they would find some dark truth hidden even from himself.

"I was in the Infantry during World War II," Merle finally admits. "I was an executive officer. At the time we were deep in Germany, close to a little town called Nordhausen. It was a concentration camp with hundreds of rotting bodies; I can still smell them. We had a bunch of German prisoners that we wanted to get back to our camp when someone came up to me and told me that one of the prisoners had killed my lieutenant with a pitchfork. The prisoner was unarmed but I was so outraged that I shot him. Everyday I ask God to forgive me. It hurts so much. It's not right to kill a fellow man, but I did. God forgive me, God forgive me..." Merle's torment is in his tortured voice and his expression, his face contorted with long-held pain.

Long's daughter-in-law, Deb, heard his confession. "He felt that what he did was so wrong that it was unforgiveable, for the man he killed was a person, he was somebody's son, somebody's father, he was a human being, despite having committed such atrocities." His son, David, realized Merle had kept the story secret for over sixty years. "He yearns to forgive himself, it has haunted him for so long, and yet he struggles against it. I can't help him through this. We've been over it so many times but he just keeps holding on. None of us need to forgive him for anything; he has to forgive himself."

There appear to be as many types and meanings of forgiveness as there are definitions of love. It can be experienced as disengagement, separating ourselves from the person who injured us; as empowerment, where we become the forgiver and no longer the victim; as reconciliation, when a broken relationship is finally repaired; or as turning the other cheek, when we seek to transform the offender through an act of love. And whether we believe forgiveness comes from God or man, whether it comes with conditions or is freely given, what is indisputable is that its power is real, and that it is sweeping and even immodest in its reach.

Forgiveness has also migrated into the political realm, ready to heal individuals, corporations, churches, even nations. It has spread to the Internet where websites hawk forgiveness in a cyberworld that promises freedom from guilt but little personal accountability. It has become almost a daily ritual on daytime television throughout America with our new TV-host priests offering public absolution. Admissions and detailed confessions of guilt and shame are followed by doses of well-meant but inevitably superficial forgiveness.

"These TV shows are the agents of forgiveness in a popular culture, but they highlight a certain amount of confusion about what forgiveness means," warns Lance Morrow, a professor of journalism. "Forgiveness is a profound transaction involving individuals and it really shouldn't be turned into some sort of pop culture trick, it shouldn't be blurred."

Law professor Thane Rosenbaum agrees. "We live in a much more compressed, globalized world where everything is instantaneously known, which means we have an absence of private life, there is nowhere to hide, our shame is much more evident. Sadly, there is a kind of public enjoyment and even voyeurism in this new ritual of forgiveness."

For Wilfred McClay, a cultural critic, this new therapeutic forgiveness is a troubling sign of the age we live in. He yearns for the time, "when forgiveness once again is concerned with the soul of the transgressor and the well-being of society, and not merely with the forgiver's good health or psychological revenge."

And so the questions persist: What is forgiveness? Why forgive? What are the roots of forgiveness? In the end, forgiveness knows no boundaries of time or place, and its origins appear to be embedded in our own psyches. Perhaps, at the deepest level, forgiveness is the memory of lost possibilities, the enormous presence of absence, an ache for what could have been but is no more.

FORGIVENESS IN THE PRIVATE SECTOR

AMISH GRACE: AS WE FORGIVE OUR DEBTORS

Amish Woman with Child - Nickel Mines

The Amish way of unconditional forgiveness out of obedience to God is awesome, amazing, of true mystery, of true and radial otherness, it has heroism and beauty to it, but in the end it may be dangerous. — Monsignor Lorenzo Albacete

On a cloudless morning in October 2006, a group of Amish children were gathered in their small one-room schoolhouse at West Nickel Mines, a peaceful village nestled in the lush rolling green hills of Pennsylvania. Amish schoolhouses are considered a safe haven for children, but on this particular day a man entered with an arsenal of guns and ammunition, two-by-sixes and two-by-fours embedded with metal bolts, containers of K-Y jelly, plastic cuffs, and a raging anger against God. He proceeded to shatter the serenity of this small community. That man was thirty-two-year old Charles Roberts, a local milk truck driver who, although not a part of the Amish community, occasionally made deliveries to Amish homes. He was married with three children. In a picture later released by the police, Roberts, dark haired and intense, smiles into the camera while surrounded by his family, all dressed in their Sunday best. Nine years earlier his first-born daughter had died minutes after birth. Roberts continued to brood over this loss, wanting to get his revenge against God.

Before barricading the doors, Roberts released the fifteen boys and few women who were in the schoolhouse. Two of them, a mother and her young son, ran to a nearby farmhouse where they called for help. Roberts told the remaining eleven girls to line up in front of the blackboard. It would appear from the items he brought with him that he intended to rape each of the girls, ages six to thirteen, before shooting them. Deputy Coroner Janice Ballenger believes he either ran out of time or changed his mind. "If there's any salvation at all, it is the fact that he did not carry out what he had planned," she says.

As police officers were nearing, Roberts was binding the girl's arms and legs with plastic ties. He warned the troopers to back off. They were planning to storm the building, but then the shooting began. According to one of the survivors, he told the girls to get down on the floor. One of the children suggested to the others that they say a prayer. Apparently Roberts said, 'I don't believe in prayer, but why don't you pray that I don't do what I'm about to do,' and the girl replied, 'if you are going to shoot us, then shoot me first.' Which is what he did. He then shot the other girls, killing five and critically wounding six, before he shot and killed himself.

Pennsylvania police believe that Roberts did not have any ill will towards the Amish people, simply that the schoolhouse provided easy access to young girls. Before the murders, he phoned his wife to confess that when he was about eleven he had molested two young girls, although neither ever acknowledged the abuse. In a suicide note, Roberts wrote that he had again started fantasizing about molesting girls. State Police Commissioner Jeffrey Miller reported that Roberts spoke with his wife before the killing, telling her that he was compelled to seek revenge for something that happened twenty years ago. This, compounded with the death of his infant daughter, appears to have mentally pushed him over the edge. A survivor said that Roberts told the children, "I'm angry at God and I need to punish some Christian girls to get even with him. I'm going to make you pay for my daughter."

"We knew the shooter was dead inside," says Ballenger, one of the first responders on the scene. "We entered the schoolhouse and the room was indescribable." A woman in her late thirties with a brisk, no-nonsense manner, she thought she had seen everything in her work, but she was not prepared for this. Her voice breaks as she describes the scene. "There was not one desk or chair in the whole schoolroom that was not splattered with blood or glass. I saw one dead girl lying on the right side and the perpetrator lying on the left. Both were engulfed in pools of their own blood. There were bullet holes everywhere. Blood everywhere. It wasn't just single shots to the head, later we discovered twenty bullet holes in just one child. But at that moment, while waiting for the medics, I tried to concentrate on anything but the bodies; I tried to find one square of linoleum that was not touched by blood. I saw a vase of fresh flowers on the teacher's desk and I kept my eyes on those flowers. Outside in the schoolyard it looked like somebody had taken several ambulances, turned them upside down, and then shook and dumped out all the medical supplies. For as many people that were there it was eerily quiet, other than the hum of the hovering helicopters waiting to take the wounded children to the hospital, and the sound of quiet sobbing coming from the Amish men, women, and children standing in groups together along the side of the road."

Despite this horrific event that changed so many lives, the Amish people did not judge or condemn. Instead, they immediately announced that they had forgiven the murderer. Forgiveness is a central theme of Amish beliefs and they genuinely try to live by this verse from the Lord's Prayer: "Forgive us our transgressions as we forgive those who transgressed against us." They are convinced that, "If you forgive, you will be forgiven; if you don't forgive, you won't be forgiven." That afternoon the father of one of the girl's who had been killed was heard to say, "He (Roberts) had a mother and a wife and a soul and now he's standing before a just God."

Hours after the killings, Amish members went to see Roberts' widow, Marie, and her family, including her parents and parents-in-law, to express their condolences and offer forgiveness. Among those who took food to the family was Gertrude Huntington, a midwife and specialist on Amish culture, who had helped birth several of the murdered girls. "They (the Amish) know the children are innocent and are going to heaven and that they will join the girls in death. The hurt is very great, but they don't balance the hurt with hate."

Local pastor Rev. Robert Schenck told CNN how he witnessed the grandfather of one of the murdered girls teaching younger relatives not to hate Roberts for killing his granddaughter: "We were standing next to the body of this 13-year-old girl as the grandfather was tutoring the young boys. He was saying to the children, 'We must not think evil of this man.' It was one of the most touching things I have seen in twenty-five years of Christian ministry."

On the television evening news, anchors Matt Lauer, Katie Couric, Brian Williams and others voiced their awe and respect for the Amish as the children were buried: "Dozens of horse-drawn buggies carried mourners to a simple hilltop ceremony, as four of the five children who were killed are laid to rest" … "Ironically the procession passed by the home of Charles Roberts, the truck driver who killed them and wounded six others" … "It was a lesson in dignity, forgiveness, incredible strength, and towering faith" … "Most of us feel anger and rage toward the shooter" … "An unimaginable crime, followed by an inconceivable response" … "The Amish are not calling for revenge, instead, they're preaching something very different: forgiveness."

The Amish mercy moved the nation. Within a week of the killing thousands of media stories were reporting on their ability to forgive, despite such awful carnage. The story traveled around the world—to Germany, Japan, England, France; it had enormous traction. "Instead of being one of those 'two-night' media circuses that we have on a regular basis, this story lasted for months," says Bill McClay, a long-time observer of the Amish. "It had national and international impact. People were fascinated, obsessed. But why? Perhaps because it brought to the fore our confusion about forgiveness in our culture, something we esteem greatly as being in almost every way a good thing. Here forgiveness was seen in its most selfless and sacrificial form, it seemed almost inhuman in its purity, and this deeply challenged our understanding of it."

Money poured in from all over the world to help the families. The Amish created the Nickel Mines Accountability Committee, which gave a portion of the funds to the Roberts family to ensure that they were looked after.

Roberts was buried a few days after the killing in a small cemetery a mile from the schoolhouse. Half of those who attended were Amish, including some who had just buried their daughters. Afterwards, they hugged Roberts' widow and parents. Marie Roberts later sent a letter to her Amish neighbors to thank them for their kindness. In it she wrote, "Your love for our family has helped to provide the healing we so desperately need. Gifts you've given have touched our hearts in a way no words can describe. Your compassion has reached beyond our family, beyond our community, and is changing our world, and for this we sincerely thank you."

As immediate as the forgiveness was, however, to forgive is not the same as to forget, and such actions did not soften the loss or mend hearts any faster. The community still had to deal with their grief and to find healing. "I've seen people stifle grief by trying to put it away and pretend it didn't happen, only to have to deal with it later," says Anne Beiler, who grew up in the Amish community. "I checked in with some of the women because we were concerned that the mothers might just sweep their feelings under the rug and act like it never happened. But they have a strong network of support where they are able to talk together about how they feel. One of them was having a bad day and exclaimed, 'I just want to pull him out of the grave and I want to shoot him again and again!' They're very real, very much in touch with how they feel, they talk about their anger and their frustrations and how they miss their children."

Family counselor Jonas Beiler agrees, "I'm glad when people express their need for revenge, as this is a necessary piece of the puzzle. God doesn't want us to act it out and get ourselves into deeper trouble, but there are times when that thought of revenge gives us a little wind in our sails to help us get through the pain."

Some members of the Amish community sought help from therapists. "I got a phone call asking if we could get in touch with Mr. Roberts' widow in order to help the families with their forgiveness," says Brad Aldrich, a local grief counselor. A shy man in his early thirties who speaks softly, he is protective of his neighbors and unwilling to invade their privacy. "We met in a fire hall about two weeks after the incident. All ten of the families were represented, and each was allowed to say what they wanted to Mrs. Roberts and her family. Frankly, we didn't know what to expect and I was on edge before the meeting began. Then one of the Amish fathers, who had lost his daughter just fourteen days earlier, stood up and said with total sincerity and tears in his eyes, 'I have not had the fortune of knowing you before today, but I would like this to start a friendship between our families. You're welcome in my house any day that you want.'"

The first responders also set up a meeting with the families and the state police. "I'm not sure how many attended, but it included all ten families who were involved, and then all the policemen who were part of that day, and the ambulance drivers and helicopter pilots, as many as could get in the hall." Among those who attended was Jonas Beiler, who was raised in a traditional Old Order Amish family but left because of his love of motorcycles and the openness of the sixties. He still retains his closeness to the community. "They shared with each other what they saw, heard, and experienced that day. All of them said that it was one of the most powerful meetings they had ever attended. If it had been in an atmosphere of anger or unforgiveness then some lawyer would have been saying you couldn't talk to this or that person. But there was nothing like that going on. No litigation, no lawsuits, and nobody blaming anyone for not doing their job. I also heard that Charles Roberts' mother went several times to hold the child that's still in a vegetative state. She just cradled this little girl in her arms and said how healing it was for her to be able to do that."

William McClay puts the Amish concept of forgiveness into this context: "It is completely dependent on their cosmological view of the world. The Amish at Nickel Mines immediately saw the massacre in terms of 'if we don't forgive, we don't get into heaven.' Forgiveness is moral protection for the afterlife and if they don't forgive others then their own sins aren't protected. Moreover, the Amish live with the expectation that the world doesn't make sense. In a sharp contrast, people responded to the shootings in Virginia Tech by asking: How can we change the gun laws, improve counseling in the university, or set up an alert system? There is nothing like this in the discourse of the Amish community. Their response was: These things happen, this is how the world is, and all that is required is to be faithful and to do the things we are instructed to do. I don't think they could have forgiven this massacre without such a metaphysical belief system. It is the warp and woof of their reality, it is as real to them as gravity is to us."

For Roman Catholic priest Monsignor Lorenzo Albacete, such forgiveness was astonishing. "The Amish way of unconditional forgiveness out of obedience to God is awesome, amazing, of a true mystery, of true and radical otherness. When the reality that one is trying to live by—God, Christ, the big lizard, whatever you call it —when it intersects with ordinary life it is an astounding thing. Something of another world enters this world. It is a sign of total grace in Christian terms. Such radical unconditional forgiveness is like this."

Many responded that the Amish forgiveness was extraordinary and potentially transformative. "When the Amish community forgave the murderer they did it in a considered way," says Susan Collin Marks, senior vice president of Search for Common Ground. "It cut through all the talk about when and how you forgive, it made everything else in our daily lives appear small in comparison. The story spread everywhere because it was so extraordinary. These people found in their hearts the ability to forgive in a way that most of us couldn't even imagine. They did something so counter-intuitive, so out of the ordinary, that it struck people with astonishment: If they can forgive the murder of their children, then what can we forgive in our own lives? It offered us all the possibility to create a more forgiving and loving world."

Such immediate and inclusive forgiveness, however, was also met with skepticism, leading some to question not only its authenticity but even its appropriateness. "You cannot imagine the horror, it's every horror that every parent, husband, lover, even every friend has," says Monsignor Albacete. "But the Amish forgiveness is not just words. They go at once to search out the man's wife and embrace her, to accompany her in this moment of loss and shock for her, because she didn't know. They don't sue her because she should have known. They embrace her. They become friends. And yet," he pauses, "in the end, to me, this could be dangerous. It is detached from the human context, the victim seems beside the point. Forgiveness doesn't occur because of a change in relationships with the victim but because they are obeying the will of a transcendent power. It is noble, it is awesome, but it scares me more than it encourages me for it is not mediated by the human experience. Forgiveness, if achieved, has to be real. It has to deal with not simply obeying a transcendent power but also with what was done. The Amish have their relationship with God but it isn't one that I would want to have—one of blind obedience."

After writing a *Boston Globe* article about the Nickel Mines shooting entitled "Undeserved Forgiveness," conservative commentator Jeff Jacoby was flooded with emails and letters from Christians, some of them very angry. "They wrote to say that I should understand that this is what a Christian is expected to do, that God is love and that we must love everyone. And I would write back to some of them and say, 'Are you trying to tell me that God loves Charles Roberts, the murderer in this case, as much as he loves the girl that he fired twenty bullets into? Do you really want me to believe that the God that you worship and the God who you say is love has equal love for both people?' And in many cases they would write back and say, 'Yes, that's exactly what I mean.'"

While quick to show his respect for the Amish commitment to their beliefs and values, and sympathetic to what he describes as "a horrible, pre-mediated, and bloody atrocity," Jacoby still is not convinced. An intense scholarly man in his thirties, he proceeds carefully. It is clear this is an important subject to him. "I admire the fact that they were trying as best they could to live up to their Christian ideals, even amidst such heartbreak. They take literally the admonitions in the New Testament to return good for evil, to pray for their enemies, and to turn the other cheek. At one level I admire that, but at a different level it really chilled me. I believe in God, but I don't believe in a God who can't distinguish between a murderer and the murder victim, between Hitler and the children dying in a gas chamber. God is with the victims. I wouldn't want to live in a world where nobody got angry when children were murdered. I don't think that makes the world a better place, and I'm very troubled by this idea that you just instantly forgive even the most horrific and evil act. How many of us would really want to live in a society in which no one gets angry when children are slaughtered? In which even the most horrific acts of cruelty were always and instantly forgiven? I believe that hatred is not always wrong, and forgiveness is not always deserved. And I firmly believe that there are times when you're not supposed to forgive, when you are supposed to retain your anger, which, on occasion, has been a great engine of progress in civilization.'"

Certainly, the Amish beliefs lie outside of most people's everyday experiences. To live and believe as they do demands a deep commitment and, as Rabbi Irwin Kula stresses, "practice." For Rabbi Kula, a religious leader known for his provoking questions, the Amish are the "great spiritual athletes of our time. They don't just wait until the tragedy arrives that will require their forgiveness skills, but they practice it daily, wrestling with everyday petty grievances and the forgiveness that follows. It is a thickly layered approach, for imagine the intense internal discipline it took to hold that stand at Nickel Mines. Does it come at significant psychic cost? As an outsider it seems so, but only they know for sure."

David Weaver-Zercher, chair of Biblical and Religious Studies at Messiah College in Grantham, Pennsylvania, believes that "surrender" is the defining word. "If you choose to become Amish you agree to give up a lot; individual desires and even individual feelings are frequently sacrificed to the community. You give up a car, you give up your right to wear what you want, you give up any possibility of higher education. And in the same way, forgiveness is also about giving up. It's about giving up one's right to revenge, and eventually giving up the anger that one naturally feels." He pauses. "However, I think this can be a danger in Amish life, or in any community that values forgiveness as highly as the Amish do, where people are compelled and coerced to feel something that they just don't know how to fully experience."

Ray Gingerich, a theology professor at Eastern Mennonite College, agrees. He has a personal insight into the world of the Amish as he grew up within their community before leaving to become a university professor. It took years for his Amish family to accept his decision to leave, and traces of the world Gingerich left behind still remain, such as his beard and a fierce concentration on moral issues. "Despite the fact that I've left the Amish and have many reservations about things in the Amish culture, my initial reaction to the horror that happened at Nickel Mines was one of great admiration that they were able to say 'I forgive.' It was particularly extraordinary to see this happen right at the time when the U.S. as a whole was at war and making threats about getting even with the people who flew into the Twin Towers. I looked at how we, as a country, responded to 9/11 and the anger that was felt by so many people; it seemed that we were just making more and more enemies. And then we contrast this with the Amish. Their illustration of forgiveness came without any negotiation, without even a lot of thought. It is as though there is something in the Amish character and community that has the power to just transcend, to rise above the death of their children, to rise above this immense tragedy and simply say, 'we forgive.' Instead of an eye for an eye, they gave good for evil, they absorbed the evil and offered forgiveness. And that has a religious or spiritual or even transcendent quality to it. Forgiveness in its deepest form is taking what society usually thinks of as weakness and passivity and saying no, this is the real power that transforms. They take the pain and suffering and transform it into something very positive. The negativity of woundedness and murder is actually taken up and reprocessed so that a positive component comes out of it.

"But I have to come back to the flipside of this." While deeply admiring the Amish ability to transcend horror, Gingerich also questions the personal authenticity of this versus obedience to religious doctrine. "Every time I hear the Amish saying, 'Forgive those who sinned against you for if you do not forgive them neither will your Father in heaven forgive you,' I feel impelled to ask, is this really life-giving if I do it just so I can find salvation? Maybe it is. I don't want to be too hard but it feels legalistic. It feels as though it is not coming from the depths but rather from the demands of religion."

Monsignor Albacete echoes this uncertainty about whether the Amish commitment to unconditional forgiveness comes from a genuine experience or from an unquestioned religious belief that could, in the long run, be damaging. "Forgiveness does not come immediately after the offense. It actually comes before, because it is based on a blind obedience, in this case to the words of Our Father, to the prayer of Jesus that makes your own experience of forgiveness dependent on how you forgive others. So already you are disposed to forgive. If nothing too bad is happening then such an attitude can be very inducing of peace, whatever it is you will just be able to forgive. But when something really awful happens—like when someone kills your child—then what? And when the Amish say that they have forgiven this man and express it in the best possible way by caring for his wife, it's not that I don't believe them. It's that I want to say: At what price? What happens to your feelings of anger?" Albacete struggles to comprehend. "What happens to your feelings of great loss? To your desire to reverse time? To regret … if only? What happens to the horror at the absence of someone you love? Your relationship with that person was a part of your life and now that part of you has been taken away. You are less. Can this radical obedience fulfill these needs? I don't think so. You can only deal with them by suppressing them in some way, and I think this is actually violence done to yourself."

Professor McClay's doubts are intensified by his experience as a parent. "I couldn't help but be moved by the moral grandeur of their willingness to forgiven the gunman who was dead and to reach out with love and compassion to his family with no desire for vengeance or punitive damages. But, at the same time, as a parent, I was appalled. There is a kind of ferocity that rises up when someone does something to children, an intensity with the parental bond that, were it to happen to me, I wonder whether I could even let the matter take its course through the courts of law.

I can't imagine letting go of those feelings, and I'm not sure that I would respect someone I knew who yielded their anger so completely. To renounce those feelings, to simply have that be a floor on which the elevator never stops on the way to the high ground of forgiveness, seems to me almost inhuman."

Far away in South Africa, a country that had gone through brutal years of apartheid, the event transfixed some of its citizens. Pumla Goboda-Madikizela, an eminent psychologist and one of the architects of South Africa's Truth and Reconciliation Commission, raised similar questions: "I worry that at a deep psychological level something has not been addressed. I am not judging the act of forgiveness as being improper or immoral, of course not. The TRC was created with the hope that reconciliation is possible even after horrific, seemingly unforgivable acts. But I am reflecting on this with my psychological mind. There is a great deal of pain that these parents are living with, but such pain appears silenced even before it has been felt. An important part of the journey towards forgiveness requires being in touch with that pain. Also—and I am speaking now as a believer—when the forgiveness is so quick, it almost borders on assuming the power of God, casting ourselves in God's image so that we do not allow the weakness of being human to overwhelm us. Instead, what we really need is the grace from God to empower us so that we can rise up from our pain and then reach out with forgiveness."

What is it that makes this "violence done to oneself" bearable or, as Ray Gingerich describes it, "this forgiving without really having allowed ourselves time to work through the pain?" For Ray, it is the value of community in Amish life. "The Amish can do it because they don't have to be alone when the tough days come and the company doesn't drop by anymore, or when friends don't tap on your door and say, 'how are you doing today?' The Amish would say they have their God. From my perspective, they have each other. They have the support of their family and their friends, and they always have the community around them." Ray concludes with a touch of sadness, perhaps even longing for the world he has left behind, "But what about people who don't have that kind of community? Where do those people go? Where do they find refuge? Where is forgiveness rooted among those who don't hold to a personal God?"

Each religion has its own insights and beliefs, many of which are radically different to the unqualified mercy extended by the Amish. "As I understand it, the Jewish response, for instance, isn't so quick to forgive, and it isn't so quick to spread love around." Jeff Jacoby believes that Judaism teaches there are times when it is appropriate to hang on to anger, and that forgiveness has to be earned. "There's no forgiveness unless it's preceded by repentance. And repentance isn't simply saying 'if I offended anyone I am sorry,' as politicians do so often when they are caught. It means you acknowledge that you did something wrong, you're precise about what it ˙as you did, you resolve never to do that wrongful deed again, you make restitution ˙e extent that you're able to, and you direct your apology, again as best you're ˙ the one whom you wronged. And for that reason I think that murder, by definition, is unforgivable, whether it's in Nickel Mines or in any other case where people's first reaction is to say, 'we forgive.' You have no right to forgive. You weren't the one who was murdered, and the one who was murdered is no longer here. So nobody has that right."

For Jacoby this remains one of the core differences between Judaism and Christianity. It can be a tender spot for Jews who have experienced criticism by Christians, as if their insistence on the necessary steps for justice is lesser than the glory of freely given forgiveness. He muses that perhaps, "this is the great divide between the Jewish view of the world and the Christian view. The terrible event at Nickel Mines actually goes to the heart of the tension between them over these tough knotty issues of forgiveness and evil. Please don't misunderstand me. I believe in forgiveness, but I question whether we can have a healthy or viable society that is based on this premise. Indeed, I found myself thinking how the Amish can only live this way because a few miles down the road there's a police department that isn't staffed by Amish people and they are not going to be so quick to forgive when somebody does something wrong. It is easier to survive like that when you are protected by a larger society that doesn't live that way."

There are also Amish members who have left the community and who remarked bitterly on the "unforgiving" treatment that they have received. Some have been shunned by their families and not seen them for years. They wondered why it was easier for the Amish to forgive a stranger who had murdered their children than to forgive their own children who had simply chosen to leave. Interestingly, there were reports that this apparent contradiction was not lost on the Amish. According to Janice Ballenger, "After the massacre some families did, in fact, reach out to their children, trying to repair the breach. It made them reevaluate the depth of the forgiveness they proclaim to have."

It does appear, however, that the Amish understanding of unconditional forgiveness reflects their ability to forgive the per petrator without having to forgive the act. A s one Amish woman notes, "When I saw the bodies of the little girls at the viewing it just made me real mad, but mad at the evil, not at the shooter." This attitude seems to immediately embrace the horror or revolt at what has been done, while also seeing the ignorance with which the perpetrator acted. In turn, this generates the capacity to forgive the ignorance.

"I knew that if there wasn't an Amish person in the Roberts home to extend forgiveness that first day, there would be before the next day was out," says Jonas Beiler. The Amish choose to handle such situations by immediately offering forgiveness. "Though it's difficult to comprehend how they can forgive so quickly, it's because it's woven deep into their culture. They believe that Charles Roberts didn't know what he was doing. Even if you bring overwhelming evidence to them showing how this man plotted and planned, it doesn't matter. They don't believe that the man knew what he was doing. And to some degree they're right, for a good and sane man wouldn't think or act in that way."

The Amish forgiveness suggests that without it we can become locked in a place of bitterness, emotionally trapped in the story that we have been wronged. Their approach, whether agreed with or not, appears to lead them to a place of inner peace, as some of the parents claim it has. Or it may stifle the healing process prematurely, as some psychologists believe. "But," as Professor McClay reminds us, "it is important to remember that the Amish understanding of forgiveness is at a far distance from the therapeutic approach dominating our era. It has nothing to do with feeling better in this life. It has nothing to do with asking for a better performance from the person being forgiven. If this occurs, they are wonderful benefits, grace notes. Rather, it's entirely about making yourself ready for the next life and to present yourself before God in purity, to a degree that makes concerns about justice seem trivial by comparison."

Late at night on October 12, almost two weeks after the shooting, the Amish community demolished the schoolhouse. By the time the sun rose, all traces of it had been removed. A new schoolhouse was built not far away, but this time closer to their homes.

"There was a group of three or four little Amish boys, maybe eight or nine years old, at the counseling session," remembers Ballenger. "It was a few days after the Amish had torn down the old schoolhouse. The children were whispering together and what they said, I believe, goes to the heart of the complexities and contradictions of forgiveness. I heard one boy say to the other, 'They can take down our school, they can take away our school, but they can't take away the things we remember.' And the other said, 'Hush, you're not supposed to say that. You know that we're supposed to forgive.'"

Judith Shaw-McKnight: THE THERAPY HOUR

Judith Shaw-McKnight

Forgiveness saved my life! If I hadn't forgiven then I'd still be out there, somewhere in the world, abusing myself. I would probably have died by now. I would be dead.
— Judith Shaw-McKnight

Most of us are hard-pressed to regard forgiveness as a determinant of life or death. Yet some scientists think it may be exactly that. Doctors and researchers who monitor HIV/AIDS patients at the University of Maryland believe that forgiveness might have tangible effects on the immune system and are devoting their lives and careers to investigating the intriguing and controversial question: Can forgiveness influence the progression of disease? Other scientists and psychoanalysts protest that this question could lead medicine down a risky path of misinterpretation. But if a complex web of emotional issues is present at the time of life-threatening infection with HIV/AIDS, as was the case with Judith Shaw-Knight, then some scientists maintain hope that forgiveness could be a vital, if unconventional treatment.

Diagnosed with HIV/AIDS in 1992, Judith had been raised in a predominately dysfunctional family of addicts and abusers. Her diagnosis was just one more in a long string of troubles. A woman in her late forties, her open face and confident manner belie her life on the street. "We were the picture of a perfect family. My five brothers, three sisters and myself were raised Baptist. My father was an usher and trustee of the church, my mother sang in the choir. But scratch below the surface and there was total chaos. Mom drank, Dad drank, all of us used abusive language— I got called bitch to the point that I thought it was my middle name—and most of us had some kind of addictive behavior, my brother was only twelve when he first got hooked on heroin."

Her voice is hesitant as she continues. "My uncle sexually assaulted me when I was seven up until I was nine years old. There was a field across from my grandmother's house, where we would gather for Sunday dinner. The grass was always high. He would take me by the hand out of the living room and I'm thinking we're going to the store." Judith pauses to take a deep breath. "We would get to this place in the field and he'd spread this newspaper that he kept in his back pocket and then he'd be all over me. When I tried to tell my parents they shut it out and made me feel that somehow it was my fault: 'You shouldn't be so hot in your ass!' Imagine telling that to a seven year old. I started wetting my bed then and would get my ass whipped for it. I realize now that it was because nobody would confront my uncle's abuse as they all had their own abusive issues they were dealing with. But from that point on I didn't feel like a child anymore as I had this secret that I couldn't tell anyone. Even today I carry it with me. You know that musky smell in summertime that comes off the trees? For a long time I used to wonder why, when I was walking down the street, I would gag on the smell and even vomit. My mind had blocked it out but my body still remembered."

Such a history of childhood abuse and neglect may lead to perpetuating negative behavior patterns by turning the abuse on ourselves as we grow older. Judith is a clear example. "I did a lot of self-abusing, drinking, smoking weed, dropping acid. I did some of everything, just so I could cope. I married at fifteen. Who in their right mind gets married so young? My mother had to sign for me to get married, so why did she do that? She said, 'You can get married, sure, then I don't have to deal with your bad ass anymore.' I was fifteen, but I felt like I was twenty-five, I was rebellious, I wasn't listening to anyone. It ended after five years. I was twenty-six when I got pregnant with my daughter, after I'd chosen Joe to be her father. He was an older man and he had a job so I knew he could support us, and I needed that. He was a strong man, very proud, and he was a good father. I loved him. We were together maybe seventeen years, so it was a long relationship. When Joe got sick he had to have one of his kidneys removed. We got through that but there was something else that wasn't right, and I couldn't put my finger on it." Her eyes wander over to her wedding picture. Joe, a tall man, stands behind her, his arms lightly draped around her. Unlike Judith, who looks directly at the camera, he is turning away from it, as if hiding something.

"One day he came to me and said, 'I need to talk to you.' We sat down and he said 'I just want you to know that I've got what Magic Johnson has.' And I'm like, 'What in hell does Magic Johnson have?' I honestly didn't know, I didn't understand what Joe was saying to me. At that time I worked with a wonderful team of women, and so I asked my supervisor what Magic Johnson had. She wanted to know why I was asking her. I said, 'Because Joe told me that he has the same as Magic Johnson.' She told me he has HIV/AIDS, and that I should probably get tested, which I did. That day was unforgettable, a day that won't ever go away. I can summon it up like that," she says, snapping her fingers. "The room was the darkest room I have ever entered in my life, the walls were yellow tile, the floor cement, cold folding chairs. The man who tested me was sitting on the windowsill, his arms crossed, looking down on me.

"'Are you an IV drug user?' he asks me. 'No.' 'Have you prostituted yourself for drugs?' 'No.' He didn't suggest any doctors I could see, just made the assumption that I was either a user or a whore. He never thought that I could be a woman in love with a man who loved me, unprotected. That was the longest damn day of my life.

"I was so, so angry. And I was so scared." Judith's voice breaks, tears fill her eyes, her words come slowly. "I wanted to die, but before I died I wanted to kill Joe. I wanted to blow his brains out. Then I wanted to shoot his peter off! I wanted to kill him, absolutely, no doubt. I made blueprints of how I was going to do it. I could have easily blown him away, gone home, washed my hands, fixed a tuna fish sandwich, called the police and waited for them to come get me. I actually went to his place with a gun behind my back. I rang his doorbell but when he opened the door I saw my daughter's face and I couldn't do it, even though I wanted to so badly."

At that time, Judith's way of dealing with her raging anger toward Joe for infecting her, and with the fear of what was going to happen to her, was to block it all out by getting high as often as she could. "I did that every day for a lot of years. To hell with taking HIV drugs. I could smoke some crack or some dope and I'd be fine. Have a drink and I'd be okay. At least, that's what I thought. I worked every day, I got high every night, and somehow I managed to raise my daughter, Jessica, to get her to school, to see that she ate right, and that she was taken care of."

Yet Judith became increasingly depressed. The disease, combined with the toxicity of so many drugs, was catching up with her. She needed help.

"Perhaps nothing in contemporary life has put us right in the middle of the drama of guilt and forgiveness more than has the AIDS epidemic," says Monsignor Lorenzo Albacete, who has counseled and listened to the confessions of thousands of people infected with the virus. "Everything is involved: how we help ourselves or can be helped, and who will help us to navigate this sea of ever conflicting feelings, emotions, and convictions. Think about it: from the very first moment of discovery that you have the illness, the drama of forgiveness begins." His weathered face is filled with kindness and caring. "Many seek forgiveness from God. Many ask me, 'Is God punishing me? Why can't I be forgiven? Why can't I be healed?' Then there is the question of who gave you this virus, for it doesn't just spontaneously show up. What about that person? Are they guilty? Can they be forgiven for either deliberately or carelessly infecting you? What will your relationship be with them? Then there is you. So many blame themselves: Maybe I wasn't cautious? Maybe I shouldn't have been doing this? God becomes the accused. How can a fair, not to mention a loving God, allow this to happen? What does forgiveness mean in this case? How angry can I be? And then suppose that you have given AIDS to your children—again and again, this questioning grows to almost an unbearable intensity."

Judith's doctor suggested she start seeing a therapist. By this time she was emaciated, her bones poking through her flesh, and she was listless and forgetful of her medicines. For most people starting out in therapy, their progress is incremental at best, but Judith was jolted instantaneously. "Thank God for therapy. It helped me to see where all this started from, how the root of it went back to my great grandmother who made her own liquor, and how addiction festered down through the generations. My mother was an alcoholic. My oldest sister died from alcohol at the age of forty-five. I got to realize that my mother was the way she was because she grew up with an abusive mother, that she just didn't knew any better when she called us every name under the sun, whipped us with an extension cord, hit us with a pot and pan or whatever she could get her hands on. The verbal abuse cut the most as you begin to believe that you're no good, that you'll never amount to anything in your life.

"I felt like no one could love me because of what my uncle did when I was a child, like it was my fault that all this had happened to me. I felt ugly and beat up and bad because of the drugs I'd put in my body. I felt like maybe if I hadn't been drinking, or if I hadn't been high when Joe came home, then I would have thought to tell him to put a condom on his ass or something. There was so much deep-seated stuff and I got to see how it went all the way back."

In particular, by showing Judith the bigger picture of her life, therapy enabled her to begin a process of deep forgiveness and to stop abusing herself. "I stopped doing drugs, I stopped drinking alcohol, I stopped smoking cigarettes. Therapy helped me want to take care of myself better, to take my medicines the way they're supposed to be taken. When I stopped hurting myself then the demons left, they had no power and I wasn't going to give them any." She pauses to wipe her tears away. It had been a long journey to reach this place. "I wanted to forgive myself for stealing my daughter's money and buying crack, for smoking it, for having her think she lost her money. We were never homeless—I always made sure that she had what she needed —but I took from her to feed my habit. I had to stop hurting myself, and when I did then I could stop other people from hurting me."

After three decades as a psychotherapist to patients suffering from trauma, Dr. Glen Gabbard knows that the process of forgiveness, far from being an easy experience, is one of undoing the past in order to heal the present. "In my years working as a psychotherapist and a psychoanalyst, I've learned that you can't simply say 'I forgive you' and the heavens open up. It's a slow and often painful process. To get to forgiveness, you have to first go through unforgiveness. It involves understanding the unconscious roots of a problem and the reasons you hold on to a grievance or to resentments, bitterness, and hatred. We see many people who are grievance collectors, who take pride in old wounds, old resentments: 'I have suffered more than anyone else. Don't try and take that away from me, I am special because of my suffering.' Not everyone is willing to give up that status. In some cases, those hurts are etched in the granite of their soul and so they fight the therapist who says, 'you can let go, you don't have to feel that bad.' I think we underestimate the pleasure some people have in hating, in saying I will never forgive you, or I will go to the grave hating you. There can be a feeling of moral superiority in that stance: I'm above you because you did something horrible, and I'll never let you off the hook.

"There's no cut and dry, one size fits all way that people walk out of this dark place. Sometimes it's an unexpected random experience that shocks them into feeling differently about that person. Other times they discover that they are leading lives of quiet desperation in order to pay someone back and that it's just not worth it, they want to live differently. Perhaps a new relationship adds the necessary changes. Above all there is no road map, contrary to what so many of the self-help books tell us." Dr. Gabbard's fervor at this point in our conversation suggests how much he wants to distance himself from this particular genre of literature. "For those who are willing to look at the darkest aspects of their inner world, they won't have to live their lives eaten up by hatred and betrayal that are often decades old. It can be life-changing to finally forgive not only themselves, but other people as well."

Which is what happened to Judith. "Once I could really and honestly forgive myself then I was free to forgive everyone else, even to forgive the molestation by my uncle, to forgive my mother and her abusive tongue, to forgive Joe for infecting me with HIV. It didn't happen either quickly or easily, it grew over time. Before he died, Joe got very sick as the disease took his mind; AIDS literally drove him crazy. He saw it happening so he pushed Jessica and me away, he wouldn't let us get close to him. I never got to ask him why he didn't tell me sooner, or how he could have done this to me. I was still angry and didn't cry when he died. I can't tell you when it happened that I was able to forgive him, I can't tell you if the sun was shining or not. But I can tell you that I woke up one day and I didn't hate Joe any more. And then I cried. I was tired of being angry with him. I had fed that beast for too long. The worst thing in the world was walking around with all that anger inside me. I remember telling Jessica, 'I'm not angry with your father any more. I want him to rest in peace. I want him to know that I'm okay.' I can say his name now and I don't feel that tightness in my chest. I don't feel that pounding in my head."

Forgiveness is a complex set of emotions and issues that affect every aspect of our lives. "When the cause of HIV was recognized—that it was transmitted through sexual relations, from a mother to her child, or through blood and shared needles—then the issues of forgiveness and unforgiveness became even more intense," explains Dr. Lydia Temoshok, director of the Behavioral Medicine Program, UMBI. "Because then it's about how you got infected by someone who had the virus. Can you forgive your partner for having sex with you? Or forgive yourself for wanting to have sex with your partner and exposing them to the possible transmission of HIV? You're unforgiven by the world for being a carrier of the disease. You can forgive or not forgive the community where you live, the community of hospital workers, of scientists who haven't discovered a cure for HIV yet, or the community of your religion. Can you forgive God? Can God forgive you? All of this makes the connections between forgiveness or lack of forgiveness and HIV/AIDS intimately and intricately interwoven."

Passionate about her work, Dr. Temoshok speaks from her own experience. A slight, attractive woman in her forties, she has a studied calm manner that hides her own difficult background. Her father suffered a family trauma as a child that haunted him in his adult life, permeating his identity and damaging his parenting abilities. As a boy, he had bought his sister a bicycle only to watch a car hit her as she was riding it. Wounded but still alive, he carried her to a store for help. But due to prejudice in their neighborhood, for they were a tiny minority of Ukrainians, the door was closed on them and no one helped. Lydia's father watched his sister die. The girl had been the most popular of twin sisters. Their emotionally abusive mother screamed her disbelief that the remaining sister couldn't have died instead. As a result, Lydia's father and aunt grew up with huge personal issues of unresolved pain, guilt, and unforgiveness that she witnessed manifesting in frozen communication and dysfunctional family dynamics.

As a professor of medicine, Dr. Temoshok believes that forgiveness has a beneficial impact on the physical body, and this impact is the subject of her ongoing research. "How does forgiveness or the lack of it affect the body? How does it affect the mind? How does it affect mental and physical disorders? As a scientist for twenty-five years I've been exploring issues of the mind and body connection, particularly how forgiveness is one of the quintessential paradigms affecting people who have HIV/AIDS, and how this plays a role in a person's well-being. It's hard to live with this disease, to deal with your family who are blaming you for it, with your partner who is worried about being infected, or with your feelings of bitterness towards the person who infected you. It puts you under a lot of emotional stress that can stimulate your physical systems—your blood pressure might go up, your heart rate increase, the stress hormone cortisol might be stimulated and the immune system activated. Any of these could cause HIV to start replicating faster. In this way we see that the systems of the body are not separate from our feelings. By understanding the link between unforgiveness and resentment, and how such negativity affects the body, then perhaps we could develop methods to enhance peoples' health by helping them to forgive. We can now see the beginning of a science of forgiveness that's trying to understand what forgiveness is, how it operates, and how it makes a difference in both mental and physical health."

Alfredo Garzino-Demo, research assistant professor at the Institute of Human Virology at UMBI, is exploring the correlation between forgiveness and the cellular production of specific proteins that block HIV replication and the possibility of their use as a viable therapy in AIDS treatment. "We are coming to understand how forgiveness affects the immune system," he explains. "We're looking at the correlation between forgiveness and having a better immune response, and whether cells are producing higher or lower levels of the protective factors called chemokines, which directly block HIV infection. Again and again we have seen that the people who seem to have more positive behavioral responses, such as forgiveness, also release higher levels of chemokines than people who are bitter and angry. There are two possibilities why this happens. One is that people who feel better are more likely to be forgiving, but it's also possible that forgiveness is making them feel better and that reflects on the production of these protective factors against HIV. I do believe there are definite links between behavior, the stress response, and the immune system; there is no question that they are constantly influencing each other. People who forgive take better care of themselves, they are more likely to take their medicine and have a healthier lifestyle. They also have a more balanced response to stress, they don't over-react so strongly and they recover more quickly."

Welcoming this new burgeoning field of research, Dr. Glen Gabbard believes that valid questions are being asked that could lead to "magnificent breakthroughs" in treatment. He reminds us that, "For years and years we had no research on forgiveness. It was primarily a theological term. Now we understand that traumas have permanent lasting effects that are measurable on the brain, the endocrine and hormone systems. In fact, with neuro-imaging we can actually see these changes. So it is eminently sensible that scientists ask questions about these psychological states and whether changes in our emotions might lead to alterations in the physical body and the brain, all with the hope that this could improve our physical and mental well being.

"But,"—he pauses for emphasis—"as a skeptical scientist I also urge caution. There are equally valid questions that these researchers must grapple with: How do we know in a complicated psychotherapeutic relationship what specifically affects the immune system? Is it forgiveness? How would we tease that out? There are so many subtle things that happen in such a relationship. Freud once said that 'the analyst pursues a course for which there is no model in real life.' No one listens to you in real life like a psychotherapist. Selflessly, without judgment, completely focused on your experience. In itself that has a very healing quality to it. Someone is validating you, saying your view is legitimate. There is also the phenomenon of someone not reacting punitively to you, not recoiling in horror but accepting who you are. These are all some of the qualities of good psychotherapy that may be just as healing as a specific focus on forgiveness.

"And then, how do we measure forgiveness? We can't even agree on what it is. Does it involve one person by himself saying, 'I forgive you?' Does it involve two people where someone on the receiving end of the forgiveness is also apologizing? Can you forgive someone who is deceased? And there is an even more complex question: Is forgiveness something on the surface, that acknowledges that I've been angry with you and I now release you, or does it go down from the conscious mind into the deepest ingrained layers of the unconscious?"

Recognizing the validity of these questions and the nascent quality of the research, Dr. Temoshok also acknowledges that, "We are only at the beginning of what I hope will be a science of forgiveness and we will have to address each of these questions and others. We will have to do longitudinal studies, controlled random-ized trials, publish in peer-reviewed journals, and always be mindful that we cannot confuse correlation and cause. A bias towards forgiveness has permeated our society for thousands of years through our religious traditions that exhort us to be for-giving. Popularizers of the research rush out to tell people that it is good to forgive, but this only contributes to the problem of inauthentic forgiveness that can be as damaging to our immune balance as hanging on to our anger."

A consistent critic of this rapidly growing field of forgiveness research, Dr. Richard Sloan, professor of Behavioral Medicine at Columbia University Medical Center, believes it is not sufficiently rigorous. "What you have is an interesting and important hypothesis, but at this stage there are no conclusions." He is also con-cerned that an emphasis on forgiveness could be heard as a subtle criticism, implying that if we are unable to forgive then we are in some way responsible for the progress of the disease itself. This can lead to shaming and humiliating. "I accept that these mind-body questions are important. Much of my work deals with how psychological factors contribute to disease, in particular heart disease. And I firmly believe it. In my field you want to understand how depression elevates the risk of heart disease, and how treating depression can be helpful. But that's different from saying to someone who is emotionally repressed that if they just forgive themselves they will feel better."

The many researchers across the country whom we have spoken to, including Dr Temoshok and her team at UMBI, are sensitive to these issues and agree that they must proceed with the utmost caution. At the same time they are excited about going forward. They see the science of forgiveness as a new frontier finally getting its due.

Through her work, Dr. Temoshok has identified some very specific steps that can lead to forgiveness, from recognizing and releasing the impact of childhood issues, to rebuilding relationships: "Helping people to recognize the problems in their lives, as well as the transgressions that occurred in their childhood that have been with them all this time, that's the first step. If they can come to terms with this and begin to change feelings of unforgiveness toward themselves, toward others, toward God, or toward the medical profession, then that will make a dramatic difference in terms of their health and well-being. The next step is to find a way to release their feelings. It's very helpful to act this out with someone else, such as a therapist, to talk to the person concerned if it is appropriate, or to write the person a letter. The third step is to build a new way of relating to oneself, and to any others where there was this unforgiving attitude. It's not enough just to let go. It's not enough just to say, 'I forgive myself, I was a different person then.' We also have to have compassion for ourselves, and even for the person who, for instance, infected us."

Judith has done just this, having experienced the direct affect of forgiveness in every aspect of her life. "I knew Joe was a whore but he was my whore, and I had to forgive myself for that," she admits. "It starts with forgiving yourself because you know what you did, and you know who you did it to, and you know who you did it with. There are other scenarios that are more difficult to forgive. You are a nice heterosexual lady, married to this wonderful man, this wonderful father, a nice wife waiting for your husband, thinking he's superman, and he comes in and infects you. You're not out selling your ass, you're not out shooting drugs, you're not out doing orgies with your friends. You're a wife, a mother, you go to PTA meetings, you make cookies, you go to softball games. But inside my home was a different story. Joe infected me with HIV, but when I hold on to unforgiveness it just makes me bitter. You take it with you everywhere. It's a ball and chain around your ankles and every day, wherever you go, you're dragging it along.

"Therapy helped me to learn acceptance," she continues. "Therapy said to me, it's okay, it's not you, it's not your fault. You didn't tell him to do those things to you. I was diagnosed in 1992, but it's only been the last eight years that I've found some physical, mental, and spiritual happiness. I spent years in therapy, long days by myself. No relationships, just me and my kid. As I got to understand more I was able to say to her, 'Don't you let anybody rent space up in your head. Nobody. Don't let people take you from being a nice person into saying things or doing things that are not who you are. Don't allow people that kind of power over you, or to bring that kind of energy into your space.' I have forgiven my uncle for molesting me as I know that he knew no better, but I wonder sometimes when I look at him, 'Does he think about it? Does he remember? Does he know?' Maybe he doesn't. I saw him recently. I walked up to him, embraced him, introduced him to my husband, and it's like he didn't have a clue. I forgive him because not to forgive him would mean I am giving him my power."

This reclaiming of power is an important part of the forgiveness process, Dr. Temoshok believes, for as long as we hold onto resentment and unforgiveness toward someone then we are letting that person continue to abuse us through our own negativity. She suggests that we have to emotionally separate ourselves from the abuser so they can no longer have any impact on our life.

"If I do not forgive the people that caused some of this grief in my life then it means that I'm giving them power, and I'm not going to do that anymore, not today, not tomorrow, not next week, not next year," Judith confirms, more forcibly. "The molestation with my uncle, my mother with her abusive tongue, Joe infecting me with HIV, I don't want to live with this kind of thing because I don't want to be a bitter old woman. I want to grow old gracefully. I want to enjoy my life. I used to have a problem sleeping at night; I couldn't get to sleep unless I had a TV on or a light or something. My mind never stopped, it was constantly thinking all the time. I would lie awake and think about things that had happened or things that could happen if I didn't stop doing what I was doing, to the point where I was concentrating so much on the stuff that was wrong that I wasn't concentrating on getting better. Now I don't take anything to help me sleep. I don't need the radio. I can actually hear the ants piss outside, that's how quiet it is for me. I don't know how it came but I cherish that peace. I love me today."

Dr. Temoshok reflects on Judith's remarkable progress. "There's no easy way to get through a situation like Judith experienced throughout her life. When she began this work she weighed 90 pounds, she wasn't taking her medicines, and she was on a trajectory to death. It speaks volumes for her character that there was a fragment of hope that pushed her to seek help. She had the courage to face her substance abuse, how much she hated herself, her massive unforgiveness. She had to grapple with such issues as a mother who told her that she was no good and would never amount to anything, and abusive relatives who took away her self-esteem and personal power. She had to face the pain and call it for what it was: This was horrible. Abusing a child is horrible. Not okay, not excusable. In this process she came to understand not only her own reactions but her abuser's reactions as well. Not to condone but to understand, to put it into context.

"Once she started to say 'I forgive myself, I deserve to live, I'm a good person, there's something that I can contribute to the world,' then she started taking her medication again because she felt worthy and wanted to live." Dr. Temoshok believes that as Judith was able to confront her anger and resentment, which was justified toward the person who infected her, then she could begin to rebuild her relationships and even begin new ones. "She saw that she could change, that she could let go of the toxic emotions of bitterness and resentment. I believe that it was through these questions of unforgiveness that she's been able to turn her life around. The therapy helped her to face a lot of her deeper abusive issues and it was forgiveness that freed her."

Judith is unequivocal when she reflects on what changed her life. "Forgiveness saved my life. If I hadn't forgiven then I'd still be out there, somewhere in the world, abusing myself. I would probably have died by now. It would be like a cancer inside of me left unattended. It took a lot of pain, a lot of sleepless nights, a lot of crack smoking, a lot of snorting, a lot of drinking, a whole lot of stuff to get to where I'm at now. I thank God for forgiveness, because it freed me inside. It's like a laxative. It purges you. It cleans out your heart, your mind, your arteries, you just get it out!"

But she also knows that such forgiveness is her life's work. "My process will probably be ongoing for as long as I live because I have some really deep-rooted demons, ancestral demons, generational curses that I have to deal with. I have a daughter that's going to be a mother some day. I have nieces that are going to be mothers some day. I have to let them see that they don't have to be cursed by this thing; they don't have to walk around with hate inside them. I'm healing me so they can be healed and it doesn't have to keep going."

Healing ourselves so that future generations do not have to suffer can finally bring the chain of abuse to an end. If we hold on to bad feelings then they get passed on and continue, but if we learn how to replace them with kind and caring feelings about ourselves then those are the feelings that get passed on. "It's so important to replace the angry, resentful, hostile feelings with understanding and compassion," Dr. Temoshok explains. Talking about forgiving ourselves is not enough, "We also have to have compassion for ourselves and everything we have been through. Then we can replace those feelings of 'I did something wrong, I'm bad, I'm ashamed,' with 'I understand why I did that, it was the best thing I could have done at the time. Now I see differently, I can let it go.'"

Now working as a receptionist at the Institute of Human Virology, at the University of Maryland, Judith helps process HIV/AIDS patients for a trial directed by Dr. Temoshok exploring the effects of forgiveness on the immune system. It is one of the very few federally funded scientific trials on forgiveness. She delights in doing a job that directly helps others. "I work at the Institute as the receptionist, so everybody that comes in to the clinical research unit has to come by me," she says, smiling. "I get to know the patients and I call each one by name. I see them when they first come in, when they are sick, tired, weary, beat up, worn from the floor up, and I hear the bitterness and the anger.

"I know what it feels like to hurt. I understand the confusion of being told that you have this virus that will be with you the rest of your life and you have to take this medication every day. I understand being so angry you don't want to take this damn medicine. I understand wanting to go and kill that man or woman who infected you. I know those feelings. But I also understand that you have to start the process of healing somewhere, and that place is within you. For those of us who are living with HIV and AIDS, when it comes to forgiveness, we have no choice but to start with forgiving ourselves. I've seen patients come in with a T cell count of 27. But even though the medicine was making them sick, I've seen their attitudes change and I've seen them keeping their appointments. When you keep your appointment that tells me you're loving you. You're taking care of you now. And I've seen their T cell count go from 27 up to 127.

"Forgiveness is a part of getting healthy." Judith firmly believes that for the T cell count to go up and the viral load to be undetected, then it's essential to forgive both ourselves and others. "You're not going to wake up one day and suddenly be able to forgive yourself or someone else. It's an ongoing process. Forgiving myself allowed me to go through thirty-three treatments of radiation for breast cancer; without it I wouldn't have cared about the tumor that they found in my breast. But I went through that radiation and it didn't matter that I was burnt and so sore I couldn't move my arm. Forgiveness allowed me to take care of myself." Judith leans forward, laughing, exuberant. "I love me today. I really do. I believe its attitude; it's not just about taking the meds. And sometimes I find it funny that all those people that did things to me, they're all dead and gone, but I'm still here, HIV positive and living well."

Deb Lyman and David Long: REDEEMING INFIDELITY

The word adultery sums up one half of human unhappiness.
— Denis de Rougemont, "Love in the Western World"

Throughout history, the subject of sexual betrayal and the unhappiness it brings has gripped our attention. According to professor of religion Peter Hawkins, Dante, the great Italian poet of the thirteenth century, accorded betrayal star billing in his 'hierarchy of sins' in the *Inferno*: "Lust is least offensive, murder midway on the way down, and counterfeiting money close to the bottom. But betrayal is the worst of the worst and Dante places it at the nadir of hell, locked in the ice surrounding the imprisoned figure of Satan. Betrayal, for Dante, involves premeditated malice, a deliberate severing of the ties that bind us together, undermining the trust that makes our deepest relationships possible, and depriving us of a world we can count on."

We all fear such betrayal and many of us may have experienced it, but what is it about marital infidelity that can sear more deeply than any other form of disloyalty? Why does something so commonplace wound so deeply and shake our foundations so profoundly? The author David Berlinski has pondered this question for many years. "Adultery is the most unfathomable of all normal human situations. What the adulterer feels is obvious: I saw something, I wanted it, I took it, or it took me, as the case may be. It is the *reaction* that adultery provokes that is so difficult to understand. How can one be overwhelmed with rage at betrayal when its source is precisely the ungovernable imperative of the human heart that created the betrayed relationship in the first place? The tissue of betrayal is the very tissue from which every affectionate relationship is made. So, the great philosophical problem of adultery is that if love is judged good, the magnitude of our injury has no appropriate target on which to attach itself."

Furthermore, Berlinski asks, "Who wishes to be the beneficiary of a false faithfulness? That is the tormenting thing about infidelity for the transgression is one of thought as much as action. I suspect that the injured never completely recover. Although it may cease to sting, it never disappears. It is perpetual; it covers every subsequent relationship; it undoes the sense of trust; it induces a world-wearing cynicism. In some deep sense, infidelity—far more than murder—represents something unforgivable. More than any other affliction, it prompts a sense of radical dissatisfaction with what it means to be a human being."

For some, however, such betrayal can be redeemed. After months or even years of struggle, some couples do find their way to forgiveness, though their relationship is changed irrevocably. Deb Lyman and David Long have been married for decades and have three grown sons. David began having affairs only months after the wedding and maintained a double life for much of his marriage. Deb chose to forgive him and they have recommitted to their marriage. But the wounds remain. Even now, eight years later, Deb's pain and humiliation remain fresh and her anger can flare up unprovoked, fierce and vengeful. David struggles to forgive himself for hurting his loved ones so grievously, and for having lied so consistently and successfully for such a long time, betraying not only his wife but also himself. There is now new life in their relationship, new generosity and understanding, but fragility too.

Their stories weave in and out of each other as they share the trials of their journey.

"We met in Sierra Leone, West Africa, in a small village without any electricity where we were both volunteer teachers in a school run by an Irish Catholic priest," says Deb, in her early fifties with an athlete's body honed by years of running. She enjoys telling this part of the story. "It wasn't until the second year that we really got together. We shared a sense of adventure and loved doing things together: hiking, running, climbing mountains. He enabled me to go beyond myself. An example of this was an extraordinary road trip we took. Within hours the motorcycle had broken down so we had to camp on the beach, but then we began to hear rumors of guns and boats nearby in the sea. We didn't have any fresh water and nothing to eat." She starts to laugh, "and even worse were all these crabs that ran around all night in the tent. Then Dave got sick and I had to hitch back for help." Yet throughout it all they still had fun. "I saw him as outgoing, outspoken, and very intelligent, but I was pretty guarded and I wasn't going to commit to him, even when we came home. I went back to Montreal, he went to Oregon, and for a while we had a long distance relationship."

David is also in his fifties, tall and with the tanned good looks of a dedicated athlete. Like his wife, he likes to remember the past and smiles as he recalls their first meeting. "I was teaching in the Peace Corps in Sierra Leone when this beautiful woman rode up on the back of a motorcycle with her arms wrapped around this guy who was another volunteer. He had taken her out to look at poisonous snakes in the brush. She was gorgeous. I was teaching math and she was teaching English and French. They needed some people to work in the library. We became the librarians so we spent a lot of time together cataloging books. We got close but were never sure where we were going with the relationship. It was like, okay, we're together and whatever happens we won't make plans. Once we got home we would meet up once every three or four months. Then we decided we wanted to take it further. We got married with the same amount of ambivalence and only told our parents. I think we expected our relationship to continue as if nothing had changed. We never talked about it. It would have made us far too uncomfortable to actually discuss what commitment and marriage meant, so it all went unsaid."

Deb agrees: "We never shared what we each thought about the actual meaning of marriage. We had a very basic ceremony with a justice of the peace. It was in French and in the middle of the ceremony the judge said to me, 'Does he understand what's going on?' I thought he did as he said 'oui' when he was supposed to, which means yes. But in retrospect it was an interesting question. I would have included monogamy as an expectation of being married, but I don't know that he would have done so. We were having a good time together; it was pretty smooth for the most part. He was in medical school and after he finished we went to work in Micronesia, where we adopted our oldest son, Chris."

Although happy in their relationship, they had little experience and no understanding of how to share their feelings with each other, let alone deal with difficulties. "About a week after the adoption I was assaulted. It was a hugely traumatic experience." Deb speaks slowly as she voices this painful memory. "But we had no way of talking about it, and no understanding of how to cope with or be prepared for the consequences. It was just put away. At the time, I couldn't connect with what was going on as I had a new baby, I was just trying to get through it. After that we wanted to go back to Oregon because Dave's family was there. We settled into married life: I was working, Dave was a successful doctor, we had two more children, we were both very busy, and everything appeared to be wonderful."

But the cracks were there, obscured by a limited knowledge of how to communicate more clearly. "I can see now how a lot of our marriage was very troubled but we just didn't have the ability to deal with it, we didn't know how to reach out to help or comfort each other." Deb fully acknowledges their emotional limitations. "We were really struggling with one of the kids and we had no idea what to do or how to handle trouble in a collaborative way. I was also feeling resentful that he was out being a doctor saving lives but too busy to come home to help our own. I was feeling pretty lonely."

David's relaxed manner disappears as he reluctantly starts talking about their problems. "Our oldest son was a difficult child. I don't remember how many times getting a phone call that he's not doing well at school, or he was doing drugs, or something," he says with wearied seriousness. "It seemed like every week there was another crisis, another call from school or from Deb. My personality is such that I think I have to fix things, I like the adrenaline rush from taking charge, but I really couldn't fix this situation and I felt so inadequate. I tried my best but I just couldn't do it."

The cracks widened. "I had a couple of short affairs while I was still in medical residency." David is well beyond evading the truth. "They were women I worked with. I chose ones who were safe, such as women who were married though not particularly happy in their relationships. I knew they weren't going to give up their partners and start pressuring me. Much later, I told Deb that initially my affairs were a kind of serial-monogamy, but once we settled down and had kids they got longer, some even went on for several years. They were totally hidden from Deb; I even thought they were hidden from the rest of the community. I believed I was doing a great job with juggling these multiple lives. In retrospect, I didn't do a good job of it at all.

"Hundreds of times I told myself that I was doing something wrong." Despite trying to stop, the infidelity continued unabated. "I'd be driving home, late, my heart racing, and I'd be saying, 'I am never going to ever do this again.' I knew my behavior was totally inappropriate but I would rationalize to myself that it was okay as long as I wasn't hurting Deb. There were a few women Deb thought she was friends with but she had no idea I was sleeping with them. I realize now how warped my thinking was, but at the time it allowed me to continue doing it. I knew something had to change but I didn't know how to change it. Even though I'm a health professional, I hadn't a clue who to talk to, who would understand, who wouldn't judge me, who wouldn't be horrified by what I'd done. The only people I could talk to were the women I was having affairs with."

Although both David and Deb knew that there were some significant issues in their relationship that were not being addressed, David chose to ignore the problems by finding comfort elsewhere. "We were struggling with the kids and it was hard to have an intimate relationship without problems intervening. It might sound like a weak excuse, but adultery was not only an escape but also a way of finding solace. I didn't have to be in charge all the time; it was like a short vacation with someone taking care of me and providing a kind of support that I wasn't getting at home. Some part of me said I could keep juggling these different lives forever and another part said, No, you can't, you're fooling yourself. You're going to trip and it's going to be all over. I was absolutely living on the edge."

Eventually the years of deception took their final toll. The truth emerged. David is brutally honest in his explanation. "Our marriage was not working. I was at the very bottom and I needed to come up for air, there couldn't be any more games, any more illusions, no more lies. We were in Hawaii on holiday and Deb and I were really cold to each other. She had no idea that every opportunity I got I would be e-mailing or calling this other woman. I was an unbelievably good liar. The night before we left I indicated to her that things had to change, I knew it had to all come out. When we got home I told her I had to leave, that I was having a relationship with another woman and I wanted to be with her. And I told her that I'd been unfaithful for most of our twenty-some years of marriage." His voice breaks. It is as real to him now as it was then. "It was the hardest moment in my life to tell Deb, to see the pain that she went through. I was in tears, I felt all the hurt, I knew it was devastating for her. Then to have our children come into the room and have to tell them, to feel their pain, that I wasn't who I wanted them to think I was, that I was a liar and a cheat and all the other judgments that I heaped on myself. And then I left. I fully expected that I would lose everything, and I mean everything. I thought I would lose my family, I'd be rejected by my siblings and my parents, I would lose my job. Everything."

Deb's memory of that time is a bitterly painful one. "We were in Hawaii at a family reunion. Dave was very distant so I knew something was wrong, but he didn't want to tell me. I stayed up all night asking questions but getting no answers. The next day, when we got home, he told me he hadn't been happy for years, that he was having an affair and wanted to leave. I was devastated, I felt myself freeze; I couldn't believe what I was hearing. It was like having a two-by-four hit me across my back. I went on autopilot, mostly terrified, and coming completely undone. I went through so many feelings: how angry I was, how unfair it felt, what a shock it was, what does love mean, how awful I felt, how scared I was. It wasn't easy to even feel angry because I had never experienced it before and I had no idea how to express it." She pauses for breath. As much as she has shared this before, each time is tough. "I felt so lost, I was collapsing so many times, utterly falling apart, crying and crying and crying and raging, I wanted it to all be over, I wanted to jump off a cliff, it felt that would be so much easier. I didn't know if I could get through it, I didn't know if I was going to be mad for the rest of my life. Adultery is a violation, that's the only word that feels true, it can't be undone and that's what makes it so hard to recover from."

Clinical psychologist and psychotherapist Dr. Janet Reibstein is an elegant woman in her late forties. Her intensity is a refreshing contrast to the impersonal professional manner of many of her colleagues. Leaning forward, gesturing, she focuses on the devastation adultery leaves in its wake. "In all my years as a psychologist I have probably seen most betrayals that humans do to each other. A betrayal by a father is a terrible thing, so is a betrayal by a mother, by parents, friends. But the one that is the most hurtful is that which happens between sexual partners.

"I think it is important to understand the pain of betrayal in the context of our first primary attachment. This attachment is to someone specifically attuned to us, such as our mother or father." Dr. Reibstein explains that this exquisite kind of attunement is also present later in life when we fall in love, but if the trust in that love relationship is broken it can leave us feeling like an abandoned infant. "Even though as adults in relationship we go back and forth between being the caregiver and taker, betrayal will render us as vulnerable as if the original primary person had betrayed and left us. It is a very primal and defenseless state. When partners are in my office discovering layers of deceit, I see them feeling like they are going to die."

Deb stands in profile by a window, remembering those times when she felt she wanted to die. "We have a walk here that goes out to the lighthouse, and I would go there to weep and scream relentlessly. Although he told me there had been several affairs he wouldn't tell me who they were, so at first I would go around town wondering if that was her or that was her or whether I was meeting them and not knowing it. That was so awful. Eventually I insisted that he tell me, I needed to know. But it didn't help; knowing and not knowing were both bad. When I later found out that of course other people knew it was devastating. I felt so naïve, so stupid. How could I have not known?

"There's an intimacy in a sexual relationship that is so profound and which makes betrayal so hard to deal with. For some people this wouldn't have been a big deal, but for me it was an unbearably big deal. I felt violated. The rug had been pulled from under my feet. It was a profound shaking, like an earthquake; I felt it could never be forgiven." Deb's anger and mistrust dominated her world. "At first I needed to be angry, I wanted to be unforgiving, I couldn't dismiss my feelings. I was freaked out for a long time about many things. I was as paranoid as it was possible to imagine."

The most obvious injury is to our self-esteem and no one, Dr. Reibstein insists, can escape it. "The self-doubt is corrosive. If this person whom I thought loved me for me, and honored me for me, and was honest to me because he valued me, then now it means I am not valuable. Which means other people probably don't like me as much as I thought they liked me. And maybe things don't matter as much as I thought they should matter, and what I thought was true isn't true anymore. The security that you need to stay in a long-term relationship means you don't have to keep questioning every day whether you're loved, whether the person's being honest, whether the person's being faithful. If that assumption is blown apart, then what else is not true? If he says that he bought a blue shirt, did he really buy a blue shirt? Maybe it's a yellow shirt. Everything is up for grabs. You don't know what to believe. There has to be learning of trust again so the two can rewrite their relationship."

"The person who now loves someone else first loved me, and if loving me was good, how could loving someone else be bad?" asks David Berlinski, highlighting the impasse betrayal brings us to. "The victim is left with a dilemma: If love is not good, then what is? It demands a reorganization of human passion, and we don't know how to do this, nor do we know whether it would be good to do it."

And yet, despite the damage, and with David away from the family home, the relationship was not over. "After I left I fully believed that our relationship was finished, that I was going to lose my family. I deserved it. I was absolutely accountable for what I had done, and I felt huge, unbelievable incredible shame. Deb called my sister who came out and kind of helped pull the whole household together and made sure the kids were eating. Deb was really, really scared. A lot of people told her never to talk to me again, but we had kids together so we had to communicate somehow." Within a few weeks David realized that it wasn't going to work with the other women, so he was on his own. "It was from that point on that we both began to acknowledge that although everything had to change, that it would never be the same as it was before, perhaps something else could come of it."

Through all the grief, anger, hurt, and shame, Deb and David never completely let go. In particular, Deb was willing to stay open to what could come out of the rubble. "Someone said to me that there are three different options here: you can split up, which is what most people do; you can go back to the way it was, which is the worst thing to do; or you can see what the possibilities are by proceeding with an idea of openness and without any idea of what the outcome will be. Given that we did love each other and had children that we needed to care for, to me that seemed to be the only path to take."

They were having coffee together in a small café when David shared how he was trying to make sense of his own behavior. "I told her how I was constantly asking myself why I'd chosen to have affairs. And that I had realized—and I know this sounds clichéd, but I feel it's true—it was because I had never known what intimacy meant. The only thing I knew was to make it sexual. That's where I thought I would find it." This made sense to Deb, even though it was excruciating for her to hear. "It was very hard for Dave to show any kind of vulnerability. He was always Mr. Fix-it, in charge of everything. That he was willing to look at what he had done, to look in the mirror so he could begin to understand what had motivated him, to me that indicated a huge moment of personal reckoning."

Dr. Janet Reibstein has interviewed more than a hundred happy, loving couples in order to discover just what makes a relationship work. "It would appear that the idea of marriage has changed radically over the last fifty years and has now become quite a feminized definition: your partner should be your best friend, be able to talk to you and support you emotionally. When people get married they have an expectation that the peak experience of friendship, sexuality, and emotional sustenance is going to be there forever. Unfortunately, this doesn't allow for the ebb and flow of most relationships, especially sexual frequency and satisfaction. And so it soon becomes a burdensome and even disappointing expectation. But as they don't know what to do with that disappointment they begin to turn it against the other person, even to believe the other person has shortchanged them in some way. And this is what I've seen as an essential reason why people become unfaithful.

"One of the things that's so terrible about sexual betrayal is that the aftermath is so self-destructive. When people are in deep pain from infidelity then anger overwhelms them, grief overwhelms them, guilt overwhelms them." Dr. Reibstein recognizes that infidelity is without a doubt one of the most difficult situations from which to recover. "So one of the first tasks of the therapist is to name these emotions and the things that happened, to name this is what you feel and this is why you feel it."

David's initial admissions of failure and inadequacy ultimately led him to an honest, if painful, self-reckoning. "I'm a guy who wouldn't even ask for directions but suddenly, for the first time in my life, I was lost at sea without a life ring. So I went to a therapist. It was really hard for me to accept that I had to talk to somebody, I felt so vulnerable and shameful. I'd been able to wall off my feelings for so many years and now I'd opened the floodgates and had to confront it all. I spent several hours with our minister, just talking. And I realized that he didn't have the same judgment about me that I had about myself. I was expecting the whole world to judge me. I called my medical partners in and said, 'I want to tell you what's happening. This is what I'm doing, and there are ramifications here for my medical practice. I don't know what's going to happen.' It was the first time I had ever been able to really talk about these things."

"There's juice in not forgiving. I wanted to be angry. I needed to be angry and unforgiving and I held on to it." As she moved though different emotions, so Deb was also confronting herself. "I didn't know about me, and I didn't know about him, there was so much I didn't know. I didn't know if I was going to stay mad for the rest of my life. Was forgiveness even possible? I didn't know if we could ever get there. I would feel some degree of it and then just fall right back into being so angry. How do you get through that? I needed to say what my feelings were as much as I needed to be heard." Deb's voice gets stronger as she finds a moment of humor amidst the pain. "I became pretty militant about telling the truth. I got to a place where there was no faking it; I was done with pretending about anything ever again!

"But I also needed to learn what had gone wrong, why Dave chose to have affairs, and what that meant about me." Confused and full of doubts, she was willing to ask herself some hard questions. "To what degree had I not been present, or had not been honest? What had I done that might have enabled this to happen? I asked myself how I could have been so stupid, so dumb that I didn't see this," admits Deb, shaking her head in disbelief. "People have asked me how I could not have known, so I had to ask myself how many blinkers and blinders was I wearing that I couldn't tell this was going on? Two people are involved in creating a relationship. So to what degree was I participating in this? I began to see how I was uncomfortable dealing with intimate issues, how I rarely looked any further than on the surface. I had to somehow find forgiveness for myself for not knowing that this wasn't the best way to deal with things. At first it seemed so unbearable; I couldn't imagine how we would heal. I didn't think it was possible to reconcile, not with a major hurt of this kind, it felt insurmountable. "

Throughout their ordeal, David's admission of betrayal, the confrontation and the separation, David knew that, ultimately, he wanted to remain with Deb. "I had loved Deb for so many years I never really questioned it; she was just always my best friend. For years we would run together every day on the beach, we would train for marathons together, it was a part of our marriage ritual and we continued to do that. Sometimes we'd run together and not talk to each other, but we would be together. I've always loved to be with her. And we had a ritual that every Thursday evening, whether I was on call or not, we'd get babysitters for the kids and we would go out to dinner. We maintained that throughout the time we were living apart. It gave us the opportunity to talk about how we could possibly reformulate our relationship, how we could try a different way of relating to each other. We both wanted the pain to go away, but we couldn't go back and live the way we had lived before, that was impossible. It had to be a different relationship."

But it wasn't easy to negotiate a life after such extreme betrayal. One was still the perpetrator, the other the victim. "I didn't want to be a victim and I realized that as long as I was unforgiving then I was maintaining being the wounded one. But trust had been obliterated, and it had to be completely rebuilt from the ground floor." Deb was struggling, sometimes successfully, sometimes not. "Dave would say that he didn't know if I would ever forgive him and that he didn't expect me to. He would say, 'I've done this, and it's really messed up my life. I'm really sorry this has happened, and I take full responsibility.' If I hadn't heard him take responsibility for his actions and for clearing things up, if he wasn't looking at himself to see what was underneath his behavior and why he'd told himself that it was okay as long as I didn't know about it, if he hadn't said he really wanted to understand himself then I wouldn't have been able to trust that it wouldn't happen again. But it took a long time to develop that trust."

"I'm sure there were many occasions when I asked Deb to forgive me." David did not hesitate to ask for forgiveness. "I thought that if she said, 'I forgive you' then in some way my pain and shame about what I'd done would just evaporate." Until he realized that even if she did say she had forgiven him it wouldn't necessarily be true, as forgiveness is something that grows over time: "There's no beginning or end to it, there's no state in which you're suddenly forgiven. We've worked so hard at understanding each other that at times I feel she has forgiven me and at other times she is angry as hell and is never going to forgive."

Deb's anger began to gradually diminish; there was a letting go and releasing, so it had less of a negative affect. "Part of this was finding ways to tell the story, whether in women's groups or in counseling; part of it was learning what was really going on; and part of it was seeing how I had contributed to the situation and taking accountability for that."

Such a movement toward forgiveness is essential if the couple is going to find solid ground again together, counsels Dr. Reibstein. "If a couple's going to recover from infidelity they have to reach a place of forgiveness. I use that word advisedly because it's an incredibly tricky business and, in truth, there is never complete forgiveness, there is always an awareness of what happened. When an affair is discovered, the partner who has been betrayed is in utter shock, utter devastation, while the betrayer is in a state of complete guilt. Once each is able to put aside his or her own pain and defensiveness and can feel what the other person is feeling, then recovery becomes possible. Then they can genuinely say things like 'I know what it must have felt like for him or her.' The couples who aren't going to make it are ones where the betrayer says, 'Why do you keep bringing that up? We've done this already!' They really can't hear their partner. Or they say, 'Yes, I feel bad that you feel bad,' with the emphasis on the 'I.' The ones who emphasize the 'you' rather than the 'I' are more likely to make it."

"Most important, we had to discover that it wasn't about fixing what was broken, rather it was about changing it into something else, something new, and then finding new ways of relating." For David, this understanding came at a crucial turning point. "About three months after we separated we were invited to participate in a relationship program. It was a watershed that enabled us to decide to come back together in a different format but with no idea what lay ahead. We did an intensive peers course with other couples, and we did the next course and the next and I don't know how many weekends driving out of town to do this work." He also had his own therapist he saw on a weekly basis and they had a couple's therapist they saw together. "We learned to communicate differently; I learned that I could be vulnerable, that it's okay to ask for help, even to ask for help from Deb. Through this whole time she became way more than a best friend."

Healing their marriage also involved confronting the pain their children suffered. David had joined a men's organization where he was able to talk openly about his feelings, but his middle son also needed the same support. "Our son Patrick had all this emotion bottled up inside him and so he was allowed to go through a weekend with the group. As I was on the staff I was there to witness it. He told the group how he knew that I was having affairs for at least for a year or two and how he hadn't been able to tell me or his mother or anybody else. And how painful it was for him to honor me and live with me while feeling really angry and despising what I was doing. When we came home he told Deb, and the three of us sat on the couch and cried for hours, tears of both anger and also relief because we were sharing all this together. Going through the process of forgiveness has resulted in our boys seeing that difficulties can happen and that repair is possible, which is a pretty important lesson. I think they respect how we faced ourselves; they're actually proud of us. How we responded to what happened has, I think, ultimately enhanced our family connectedness."

David's growing understanding has included a searing self-honesty, which ultimately came to include self-forgiveness. "Forgiving myself was really a separate process from Deb's forgiving me, and it was beyond just the affairs. To forgive myself I had to acknowledge every crazy thought I've had, everything I've done that only I know about. And I've done a lot; I've made a lot of mistakes. At times I can fall right back into this hole of self-judgment and shame, feeling that I'm somehow intrinsically bad. But I've learned to keep that in front of me so that the guilt can't control me from behind. I've asked my kids and my family to accept my humanness, to accept me for who I am as opposed to what I thought I was. It doesn't mean that I'm not accountable for what I did, I'll be the first to admit that it was wrong and hurtful, but I don't think my family looks at me as a bad person, they love me in spite of what I did. And if that's forgiveness, then I can't ask for anything more."

"I've learned that both partners have to acknowledge there's been a breach and that it's of the highest order of injury." For over thirty years Dr. Reibstein has watched and worked with couples struggling with infidelity. "Many adulterers feel that they too have been injured in some way, let down by an unfulfilling marriage, so it is one of the hardest things to get them to say, 'Yeah that's true, but this is of a higher order.' Once they can do that, you're in business. When a couple begins to reconnect after an infidelity, they open up and listen to each other and they start to ask: Why did this happen? How did we end up in this place? When both feel they have been understood then they can move on: We are more than we were when we started, we are rejoined and understanding and loving each other. And that's an ecstatic place."

"Dave had to come off the pedestal. I had to see how he has all these different qualities, both light and dark, and that a relationship can't work if we idealize only one and don't see the bigger picture. It was critical to have empathy for his weaknesses and vulnerabilities so I could see him as a whole person, complete with both flaws and goodness; I had to have some empathy for what it was like to walk in his shoes before I could forgive him."

"There was no 'aha' type experience saying it's over, it's done, I'm forgiven," David acknowledges. "But every time we talk about it, it gets easier, there's less of our own judgment. It's about reconnecting, feeling better about each other, falling into those deep holes less often. It's about Deb being able to express her anger and not walk out, and her being present for my shame and still feeling connected."

Perhaps the biggest difference is in their ability to fearlessly share their feelings. "We were recently walking together on the beach, and I said something about how I felt I'd released much of my self-judgment and that I now had a lot more compassion for myself. Deb immediately laid into me: 'You know, it really pisses me off when you can say you've forgiven yourself, because I want you to suffer as badly as I do. And for you to be able to forgive yourself is like a huge cop-out.' I know that that's not what she feels all the time, but there are moments that we fall back into the holes and we feel the pain. The difference is that we can talk about it now."

Deb remembers that moment well and starts to laugh, recalling how "pissed off" she really was. "I wanted to clobber him. But those moments are rare. I never thought much about forgiveness before I was so enormously betrayed and it was a painful and overwhelming struggle to go through. But forgiveness has profoundly changed my relationship with myself, with Dave, and with my children. It means I don't have to carry around this huge weight, this concrete ball of stuck, painful, awful, suffering and rage. Forgiveness has meant that I've been able to let go of all those really difficult emotions that were just so unbearable."

David and Deb know they will be working with forgiveness for years to come. "It's not a linear course, it has its ups and downs, but I know in my heart, I know in my soul, I know in the being of who I am that there's a lot more forgiveness in our relationship than there was a year ago, then there was five years ago, then there was eight years ago, and ten years ago we didn't even know who we were and what it was all about." Deb is grateful for the openness they now have. "There's no 'there' that you get to. But there's feeling better, feeling more alive, feeling more happiness, more peace, there's feeling more acceptance. The world crashing down on me didn't mean the end of the world. It was actually about opening doors. There may be many more fires to walk though, but we'll keep walking."

Terri Jentz: THE POWER OF RIGHTEOUS ANGER

Terri Jentz

I think that we can only talk about forgiveness and the appropriateness of forgiveness, if we also talk about the existence of evil. Because if there is evil—utter and radical evil—then some acts are unforgivable. I have come to understand this in a very personal way, for the crime perpetrated against me and my roommate was an act of radical evil. — Terri Jentz

Terri Jentz provides startling counterpoint to the predominant ideas about forgiveness in our culture. Her story complicates the all too easy psychological and ethical assumptions that it is always best to forgive, and that those who embrace anger are the lesser for it. According to this thinking, such people lead diminished lives; they are obsessed, narrowly focused on their injuries and slaves to the past. With marked irony, Terri refers to them as our culture's designated "spiritual underachievers." Instead, she believes that forgiveness is not always possible or appropriate and that the anger used to energize and seek justice can be as transformative and liberating to the human spirit as is forgiveness.

Late one night in a deserted picnic area outside of Portland, Terri and her roommate were the victims of a savage attack by an unknown man wielding an axe. The ferocity of the attack left her and an entire community devastated. Now, some thirty years later, Terri, a tall, striking woman in her fifties, has returned to the campsite to remember this horrific event. She has told the story before but being back provokes new memories and gives her voice urgency and freshness: "My roommate Avra and I were sophomores at Yale. In the winter of 1977 we got this idea to cycle the Bikecentennial trail 4,200 miles coast to coast. Everything was possible at that time, it was the era of, 'do your own thing, go your own way.' So we decided to do it alone, even though most people went in groups, as it was physically a very challenging expedition.

"When June came we got on the Greyhound bus and headed out to the West Coast. It was absolutely spectacular. The mountains were huge. The trees were huge. Everything was oversized. We rode our bikes up to the top of the Cascade Mountains where the tundra was black lava. We were two girls on bicycles, open and vulnerable to the elements, and it was exhilarating. Coming down off the mountain we found ourselves on a high desert plateau, a reddish landscape of dirt and Ponderosa Pines stretching all the way to the Midwest. We headed to Cline Falls State Park, a picnic area listed in our guidebook as a place where we could stay overnight. When we arrived we realized that it wasn't an overnight place at all, it was only for picnicking. There was something extremely spooky about being there but I made the decision that we needed to stop, even though Avra wanted to go on. We had this feeling that we were being watched and looked all around us but couldn't see anything."

Despite their reservations they pitched their small two-person tent, ate dinner, and went to bed around 11 o'clock. "Not long after I had been asleep I was awakened by a very loud sound and then I felt this terrific weight on my chest, so heavy I could barely breathe." Terri talks slowly as she puts her memories in order. "I thought that one of the kids that had been cruising the park road had gotten drunk and accidentally run over our campsite. My first impulse was to think: 'You dumb asses, get the hell off this tent.' Then I heard Avra screaming, 'Leave us alone! Leave us alone!' I heard several more blows and she was silent. Then I was being hit and I was thrashing from side to side to avoid the onslaught. I struggled to open my eyes and when I did I saw this young man standing over me with an axe in his hand. His head was hidden in darkness but I remember he had a very lean and neat torso, his shirt tucked into his pants so that not a crease of fabric showed, and I thought he was such an attractive cowboy. How could this man be murdering me? He stood with an axe in his hand, poised over my heart. Strangely, he brought the axe down very slowly so I was able to catch the blade in my hand, just above my chest." She stretches out her arms, demonstrating, completely caught up in the memory. "I knew intuitively that I had to somehow humanize myself, to speak to him as a human being. I looked up at this meticulously dressed cowboy torso and said, 'Please leave us alone. Take anything, but leave us alone.' And seemingly it worked because he pulled the axe out of my hand, stepped over me, got back into his truck and drove off."

In a state of delayed shock and trauma, Terri's consciousness was ebbing away. "I felt a rush of warmth filling my body, taking me away from the pain, the horror and the fear. I could hear the murmuring of the white water. I could hear the crickets chirping. I looked up into the trees above me and saw the outline of the leaves and I thought how this could be any ordinary cool summer night except for the fact that I was lying there completely mutilated. And I remember thinking I am too young to die; it is a waste to die here. I crawled over to Avra and heard this awful moaning, a kind of wailing like the sound of a wounded animal. I put my hand under the back of her head and it went right into her, through her skull and into her brain. Her head had been crushed. I knew that I had to move quickly, and even considered riding my bike into town, until I realized that the bones in my upper body were all broken. Somehow I rallied an extraordinary will to try and get help. I rummaged through the tent, which was now just bloody fabric on the ground, to find my contact lenses. I put them on with blood from my hair as lubrication. As I blinked away the blood the ravaged campsite was clear under a dim moon. Then I saw a pair of headlights coming slowly around the park road. I knew it could be that same cowboy coming back to finish us off, but it could also be help. I struggled to wave our flashlight with my broken bloodied arm to get their attention. Thankfully, they stopped. I somehow staggered up to the window and there was the face of a teenage girl staring back at me, horrified."

Darlene 'Boo' Isaak and her boyfriend Bill were on their way home from a night out. Their memories are vivid and precise. "As we approached the turnaround we saw a light waving back and forth. We stopped and saw this bloody, bloody woman; she looked like she'd been swimming in a pool of blood, dripping everywhere. It was utterly horrendous. She cried out to us, 'I've been attacked, my friend is dying, can you help us?'" The two teenagers immediately jumped out of their truck. "We searched through the campsite, which looked more like a bomb had been dropped: there were supplies strewn all over the park, a ripped up tent and mangled bikes. Then we found her friend lying partially in the water. She was moaning and moving a little so we picked her up and put her in the truck. Terri was trying to help us even though she didn't even have a shoulder. We drove straight to the local hospital and on the way we heard Terri's friend making animal noises, moaning. It was a night I will never forget." Boo pauses, shaking her head. "It changed me completely. My innocent understanding of mankind was demolished."

The girls were both near death and needed several blood transfusions before they were flown to a larger hospital. Three nurses at the hospital in Bend became their main caregivers. Nurse Kathy Devlin was horrified: "The call came in that two young women had been axed. Not a head injury or a trauma, but they had been axed. That word was so descriptive; it was so palpable." The first thing nurse Jane Krause noticed coming into Terri's room was, "this arm up against the blue drapes with all these hatchet marks and skin peeled back." Avra spent a long night in the operating room. Where her head had been smashed had caused one of the major arteries to be severed and a vein had to be grafted from another part of her body. Operating room nurse Marcy Riley felt a wave of anger at the mutilation: "These were innocent girls who had ridden their bikes over the mountain to come to our beautiful area and this happens to them. I was so, so angry. I felt so strongly that somebody needs to get this sonofabitch. Such violence opened my eyes to the fact that there is true evil in the world. It had just come out of the darkness and it touched all of us that night."

Meanwhile, Terri was in extraordinary pain, both physically and emotionally. "The truck had run over my body from my waist up so I had a contused lung, a crushed right arm that actually bore the tracks of the tire, and broken ribs. My left arm had been virtually severed. And I had a very severe head injury, which was causing a fixed and dilated left eye. But I was also deeply tormented about Avra, whom I thought could die. It was a night of sheer anguish. In the morning I awoke to the face of my mother who came with the news that Avra was out of surgery; she had lost part of her sight but she was alive.

"I felt this tremendous burden of guilt and responsibility, as I had been the one who wanted to stay in the park that night. If the perpetrator had been hauled out of wherever he came from then we would be blaming him, but instead there was just me. And this was the seventies, when two women biking and camping alone were somehow seen as 'asking for it.' It was implicit in the news accounts: What were they doing in that campground? Why were two girls traveling alone? This just added to my remorse."

The police failed to make an arrest. "Every day when we went into work, we asked, 'Who did this?' expecting an answer. And we didn't get an answer, and we didn't get an answer, and we didn't get an answer." For Kathy Devlin, it was as if some evil force had been present and everyone was just happy it was gone. "But we knew that someone out there had caused this. When someone takes an axe to another human being for no apparent reason, no revenge involved, no score to settle, it cannot help but rock your world. The bottom falls out. It is beyond evil. I know it happened, but my heart just didn't want to think that one human being could do this to another human being."

For the next twenty years, although physically healed, Terri lived a half-life of denial and fear. "Immediately after the attack I felt immortal. I had survived the un-survivable. For years I felt that I had a special destiny, that I was somehow invin-cible. I would take unnecessary risks, jogging late at night through the park, I chose an apartment in an unsafe area." Until she realized that she was no longer the same person she had been before the attack occurred. "Rather, I had a feeling of stuckness, of paralysis, there was a loss of concentration, and a seizure of my ordinary, unflap-pable will. With each passing year it got worse."

With subdued melancholy, Terri begins this part of the story about the lost years. "I was in my early twenties living in New York and I began to fear everything. I felt like I was split between a kind of wildly overreacting, intensely emotive, even manic self, and then I would switch into this completely numbed out, deadened version of myself that was asleep, narcoleptic. Some invisible, hampering paralysis had set in. It was as though my ability to take my own destiny in hand had been wrested away from me. I have a photograph that was taken in 1982." Terri takes her old passport picture out of her folder; the anger and fearfulness in her young face is startling. "Looking at it now, I see the rage that was evident in my forehead, in my peaked eyebrows. But at the time I was unaware of the anger I was carrying. I would say, 'I'm not angry. I'm above all of that.' And people would affirm, 'Oh, as you're not angry you must be very evolved.' I believed it. But there were a few people who would just shake their heads and say, 'Oh, boy, do you have some lessons to learn.'

"My body held the trauma." Terri started trying to deal with the inner torment through therapy and various forms of bodywork. "But I knew that if I started crying I would just cry forever, I would be washed away by the tears. I had no way to contain the amount of emotion that was inside me; it was so deep, so cellular. The minute that truck hit my chest some part of me had flown away and has not come back."

Writer and film director Julie Talon got to know Terri after the attack and over the years they became close friends. A tall, angular woman with chiseled features and waves of chestnut hair pulled back in a simple knot, Julie is guarded at first, both of her privacy and Terri's. But she has strong opinions and unanswered questions. "When I first got to know Terri in New York City, it seemed that she was unhappy and kind of bogged down. She had a gloomy apartment; the walls were painted a dark color and covered with books. I'd come to see her and she'd just be lying on the couch. She had a very tough time connecting to people and her relationships were with such gloomy marginal people that I would shudder when they came into the room, or I'd bring her to a party and she'd just sit in the corner. Terri would tell me how she used to be this incredibly productive, intense young person, so different from the melancholy person lying around, unable to get out into the world. It was clear that she was struggling with depression and confusion; she was trying to stay afloat when she was really under water." Julie pauses, gripped by a specific memory. "Terri had a compulsion to tell the story of her attack, even to people whom she had barely met, and she would describe it in the oddest, most detached way."

"Right after the attack people would want to hear what happened to me but I'd launch into my tale in a way that really disturbed them." Terri would use as many details as she could, however gory they were. "At the end I would giggle and laugh inappropriately. In retrospect I can see how I had frozen this traumatic tale into a calcified memory as a defense against the blood and misery of what had really happened. But then my stunned audience would ask, 'Well, what happened to the guy? Who attacked you? Was the crime solved?' and I'd have to say no, they never caught him." At the time she didn't think that much about him, at least not consciously. "I had some idea that I should be like Gandhi in the face of this attack, that I was somehow humming on this higher spiritual plane by not being concerned with my attacker. Looking back on it, I had granted him a kind of easy forgiveness and cheap grace. I didn't believe I was angry, yet it was simmering right under the surface."

As her previous roommate was uninterested in discussing or exploring the incident further, Terri was very alone with the memory of that night. Initially hurt and confused by Avra's rejection, she has now come to understand her reluctance. "For Avra, the loss of her memory was a gift; she was determined that the trauma would not limit her and she's led a very successful life." But, for Terri, her memories continued to press in on her until she eventually realized that if she was to move forward with her life she had to go back, she had to reclaim the past so she could have a future. She leans forward and gestures emphatically, for this is the heart of what is important to her. "I knew I had to confront the trauma in myself in order to be free. I had to go back to that incident in 1977 and find out as much as I could about what had happened and who had participated, so I could find myself again. What was the larger story? Who was this person that attacked me? What was the nature of this crime? And as the crime was still unsolved, I had a huge, unfinished mystery to unravel."

She told Julie that she was thinking of going back to Oregon and trying to find the man who had attacked her. Julie was thrilled: "I felt instantly that this was absolutely what she had to do. It was what she had needed to do for a very long time so she could become free of the mire she was in. This was her life's journey; she had to do it in order to save her life."

It took fifteen years before Terri was ready and it was clear that the time had come. By then she was living in California so it was easy for her to go back and forth to Oregon. "In the fall of 1992 I set out to retrieve the crime investigation files from the state police in Salem, Oregon. I began with great trepidation. I was afraid. My attacker was unknown. He didn't have even a face; to me he was just a headless torso. Over the years he had grown into a force of wickedness and violence that could erupt at any time. The more I didn't deal with a specific man who had tried to kill me and was still at large, the greater my fears became. So it was vital for me; I had to find him."

As she passed the "Welcome to Oregon" sign Terri felt an involuntary clenching in her body. The smell of the desert, the black lava rocks, was bringing it all back, but this time she was looking at this extraordinary landscape through a scrim of sadness and fear. It seemed malevolent and its beauty obscured. She stopped to retrieve the crime report from the Oregon state police in Salem. "What I found out was that the statute of limitations on the case had expired in 1980. That meant the case was open and I was free to pick up the papers, but there could be no prosecution. Wait a minute. Immediately, the first piece of repressed anger started to come up. I hadn't really thought about a prosecution but now I found myself exclaiming, there's never going to be any justice?" Terri becomes even more animated. "There was still a man out there who had not been held accountable. There had been no reckoning for this. And there couldn't be, ever? I was appalled.

"That afternoon I decided to retrace my steps and drive to the campsite. It was an extraordinary experience to have the events come back into focus outside the car windows. In a bizarre way it was deeply nourishing to repeat what now seems like a mythic journey up to the tundra, through the black lava fields and down into the desert. The smell of the junipers and the sight of the volcanoes evoked the same feeling of foreboding that had overtaken me years before. I was reconnecting to my lost feelings, to the wounded, injured self that I had abandoned that night. The anguish I felt for my dying friend. The feeling of wet, viscous blood and the cool, dry desert air."

When Terri got to Cline Falls State Park, she walked straight to the spot, dropped to her knees and lay on the ground. Today, she struggles to explain this dramatic act, still confused by the powerful emotions that impelled her to do it. "Perhaps there was some part of my being, some part of my nineteen-year-old self or my blood that had been left behind in that soil, that I wanted to soak in and reclaim. After I visited the campsite I was able to leave by my own will, not mutilated, not in someone's pickup, and that simple act was vital.

"I would drive road after road just for the sake of driving, because it was about mastering my own destiny. It was about taking back the power that had been taken from me. It was about rebuilding a new destiny, one in which I could ride my bike wherever I wanted to, drive my car down any road I chose. It was a profound ritual and it worked. I began to feel a wave of righteous anger about getting to the truth of what had happened. The anger woke me up and brought me back to life."

The nature of trauma is that it cannot be hidden. "You can never silence trauma, it rises up, constantly," says South African psychologist Pumla Gobodo-Madikizela, a soft-spoken woman in her fifties whose rich insights come from years of working with trauma victims. "This story really captured how trauma continues to live on in the victims' life, and how anger becomes the vehicle through which the voice of trauma speaks. Some people find the journey of healing through the words of forgiveness, but Terri's healing was through the language of anger."

Victims advocate Dee Dee Kouns, who suffered her own deep trauma when her daughter was murdered years earlier, had an immediate affinity for Terri's longing for truth. "I have dealt with many victims and I could see that Terri really needed to understand what had happened, even though it was so many years later." Having known this painful journey so intimately herself, Dee Dee understood how not knowing the details of such a traumatic event can create the lack of self-control that Terri was feeling. "Terri talked about her 'skeleton self', that she had been left with this partial self because the perpetrator had taken away everything that had made her the strong, intelligent woman she had been. She felt that she had lost her life and was desperate to find it again."

Both Dee Dee and her husband Bob provided essential help to Terri during the years she spent commuting back and forth from California to Oregon, investigating her assailant. They had conducted their own investigation into the murder of their daughter and had solved the case, though without the satisfaction of having the killers held accountable. They taught Terri how to look through voluminous court records. They emphasized the diplomacy required to enlist the help of local officials and coached her in making cold calls and arriving unannounced, no matter how terrifying the dark alleys or the growling dogs.

Terri began driving up gravel driveways to meet the people who had been a part of the drama, trying to get whatever clues she could as to what had happened that night of June 22, 1977. She particularly wanted to talk with the people who had seen the mutilation: the nurses, doctors, Boo and her boyfriend. It was a drawn-out way of putting the pieces back together and, in the process of reconnecting with herself. "I realized that I was so shut down to my own pain, so unable to have tenderness for myself, that my sympathy towards other's suffering was limited." Although able to feel concern and sympathy for her roommate and what she had suffered, Terri was unable to find any for her own pain. "When I first met with Boo, who had rescued us from the park, she was able to describe what I had looked like: 'Your arm had a piece cut out of it, cut like a slice of pie, chopped like a branch.' She described what she had seen in the window of the pickup: 'a bloody vision of hair just dripping in blood.' These details of my injury were vital for my psyche because they enabled me to turn the light back on myself and, finally, to actually have some feeling, even compassion for my own injuries."

Her friend Julie saw an immediate difference: "You could see it in the way she held herself. The light was back in her face, suddenly she was organized, she had focus, she could get things done, she was vital and animated. She had gone to this little town and become friends with the people. The questions she asked, and the circle of people that answered them, grew and grew. It was the opposite of what had been happening in Manhattan, where she'd just closed in on herself and gotten smaller and smaller and darker and darker."

At the same time Terri was aware that certain townspeople were avoiding her, refusing to answer any questions. One woman warned her to watch her back. "You don't know who this man is related to." For a moment she felt as if she were in enemy territory. Soon after she discovered that the community actually knew her assailant. He lived in their midst yet he had never been reported. It was stunning news.

"It was very early in my pursuit, in 1994, when I met a woman who told me that she believed she knew who had committed the Cline Falls Attack." Terri was shocked at this information. "She said it was a local boy, seventeen years old at the time, who was well known in town as a bully. He was a good-looking young cowboy with a hot temper and a reputation for beating his girlfriend. And she told me that a lot of people in the town had suspected it was him. I found the first piece of real evidence that connected him to my crime when I spoke to his ex-girlfriend, Jeannie Fraley. He'd tried to kill her the very next day after the attack on us. He had brutally beaten her and then, when she jumped into the lake to escape, he swam after her to drown her. When neighbors tried to take her to the hospital, he hung on the side of the car, pounding on the window and screaming at her cowering in the back seat."

Jeanie had heard about the attack on the two girls the night before, and she had wondered if it was him?" A middle-aged woman whose small town prom queen beauty had endured, Jeanie knew he always kept an axe in the back of his truck. "But that wasn't enough. I actually went down to the park, walked past the orange tape outlining the crime scene and identified the tire tracks as coming from his truck. They were unmistakable as he'd had a flat tire and he'd put the spare on the front, so the truck had mismatched tires. The following Monday my mother and I went to the police and reported what I'd found. I told them, 'Yes, I think it's my boyfriend. He beats me up, he has a violent temper, I think he's the one who did it.' They probably thought I was an irate girlfriend trying to get revenge because they didn't do anything about it and somehow those records completely disappeared."

Once Terri had identified the axe man she began her own investigation. "I drove a lot of dirt-gravel roads for a number of years. I followed him so closely I even got the police to take a look at him. He has consistently denied attacking us and he was never charged with the crime. I got to know his malevolence as I learned from a string of other women about the torture he inflicted, but nothing prepared me for the escalation of his malice that I discovered when I interviewed his ex-wife." Her voice gets stronger, more outraged. "He made her dig her own grave! Night after night, he'd send her out with a shovel to dig her own grave. He taunted her that he was going to kill her slowly and leave her there. He once broke her arm and took her to the doctor to get her pain pills. When they returned home, he swallowed the pills in front of her, letting her suffer. He suffocated her son's kitten in front of her son. The list never ends of the tortures he inflicted on her and other women in his life." As Terri goes through the list she shakes her head in anger and disbelief.

Long-time resident Robyn Edy, an outspoken woman in her late forties who lives in the rougher area of Redmond, knew him: "He was an evil man. Every scene with him was violent. You look into his eyes and all you see is cold hard hate. He's probably the meanest person, with the exception of my first husband, that I have ever met in my life."

Robyn knew why Terri had returned to Redmond and she had some answers for her. But she decided to wait for Terri to show up. Robyn laughs, remembering their first meeting: "I live in a little trailer out in the desert and Terri somehow found me. She's a very determined woman without being obnoxious. Nonetheless, she looked a bit nervous, not knowing whether I'd throw her out of the house. I'm sure that she was warned that I'm a bit nuts and she had every right to be scared." She laughs, clearly relishing her reputation. "She won me over by not digging aggressively for the information but by taking her time, making me her friend first. So I decided to give her the final piece of the puzzle."

Terri was riveted when Robyn described in detail her last meeting with the suspect who, at that time, lived next door. "He came out of the garage with a hatchet and came up to me saying, 'I hurt someone with this and I have to get rid of it.' Then he smiled and added, 'That's why they call me the Hatchet Man.'" More afraid than curious, Robyn slowly followed him inside his cabin. There, in front of her: "He threw the hatchet into his woodstove burning full blast in the middle of summer, collected the ashes and the metal hatchet head, put them in a plastic bag and dropped them in the dumpster outside." For Terri it was as close to direct evidence as she would get for a long time.

The fact that many people in the town suspected it was this man and yet said nothing was deeply disturbing. As the only person who went to the police, Jeanie Fraley was baffled by the silence after the attack. "It was like a dark cloud that hung over the town. The whole community was wounded but in denial. A lot of people felt the same way I did, they knew he did it, but they never did anything. I will never understand it."

Terri searched for some sort of reasoning so she could alleviate the hostility she felt towards the community. "There were moments when I felt terrific anger toward members of the town. How could they not have done anything about him? For all the good intentions of these decent people, none of it compared to stepping up to the evil in their midst. Why did this happen? I really think there was a culture of not wanting to say anything bad about anybody, not wanting to stick their neck out and be the one who caused trouble, as well as not wanting to risk his anger turned on them. No one called in clues because they assumed the police had a handle on it, so there was a massive disconnect. I think also that people just don't want to believe bad news about human nature."

As she continued with her investigation, however, the community soon began to feel not just Terri's but also their own pain, especially people who had lied to protect themselves, or others who felt guilty for not acting on the information they had. Robyn knew that Terri's feelings needed to be recognized: "What she really needed to hear from us was that we were sorry. We're sorry it happened. We're sorry we bred such an animal in our midst and did nothing about it. The people who needed to tell her they were sorry were those who looked her in the face and lied to her. I didn't lie to her but I'm sorry. And she should know that this community punished him for he was as ostracized as a person can get. We didn't open our arms to him. He had no golden key to our town."

Greg Robeson, formerly a classmate of the suspect and now a radio announcer in Portland, remembers an eerie moment soon after the attack. "We were all hanging out at the 86 Coral, the only watering hole in town. There was a country western band playing and this guy, now known as the axe man, got out on the floor with his girlfriend. And it just cleared. One by one each couple left, until the two of them were dancing alone on an empty dance floor."

As Terri came to know the community and to understand what they had also been through, so the picture of her attack began to widen: it had not just affected her but so many of the town's residents as well. Each had their own shame, inner fears, and self-doubts to reconcile. Remarkably, this stirred understanding and not blame in Terri. "I felt a profound feeling of forgiveness for this community because they were struggling, just as I had struggled, to come to terms with what had happened. We were growing alongside one another as we tried to figure out how this egregious attack could have taken place and how it had gone so unanswered."

Julie Talon watched Terri go through a powerful and deep personal transformation. "She was going back and back and back to the worst thing that ever happened to her. She forced herself to revisit this axe attack over and over, pushing her memory for every detail. I didn't realize how often she was going to go there, but it was over a period of six, seven, eight years. When she began this research Terri was still bitter, she was mistrustful. She was angry at the town, resentful that no one had helped, that they dropped the case so quickly. But what happened over the years, as she got to know the people, led her to completely forgive their failings. It was like she had gone from black and white to color."

Terri began befriending battered women in the town and in shelters throughout the state. She worked with grieving parents who had lost their children to psychopaths. She talked to people with trauma—from car accidents or war injuries—stressing the importance of going back to the incident, putting the scene in a larger narrative, giving it shape, a beginning, middle and end. She met with local officials to change the law for attempted murder. She testified at hearings and, ultimately, Oregon's bill 641 was passed, abolishing a three-year statute of limitations.

But even more important, she was able—retroactively—to forgive herself for her fateful decision to stay in the park that night. And also, as Julie describes it: "To forgive herself for all those years of not being able to work, of not being that dazzling girl who entered Yale when there were so few women, of squandering opportunities, and of taking so long to get to the place where she is now."

The other participants from that night also needed healing. "By pushing hard to find answers and put the puzzle together, Terri found her peace. Her justice came through being able to tell her story from beginning to end. But," nurse Kathy Devlin adds, "it healed us too, because a wound had been with us since the day it happened. It was almost as if the incision had been open for thirty years and at long last it was closed."

Finally, in 1997, the axe man got caught for a crime he committed against his hunting partner. For Terri, this was a moment of reckoning. Despite reservations, she wanted to see him in person. "I was in the courtroom and I was able to actually lock eyes with him. He was a striking figure, handsome, with flowing long hair reminiscent of both Charles Manson and one of the Renaissance pictures of a blue eyed Christ. I never allowed myself to be intimidated, as I knew I had the upper hand. I had an unspoken confrontation: 'I know you did this,' was what I was silently saying to him. 'And I am still here, I am strong, and I want to see you pay for your crimes not only against me, but against all the people in the community.' He went down for four years. As the sheriffs took him away past us, chained and manacled, walking with a swaggering carriage, my body erupted involuntarily. My scalp was soaking and my eyes wet. It was a kind of justice, not just for me but for all of his other victims, which had started to become more important than my own personal justice."

For Terri this was not, however, the end of the story. There was still an issue of forgiveness for her assailant. "Forgiveness had rendered me inactive for many years, because this tremendously detrimental cheap grace I had granted him had left me powerlessness, with an inability to acknowledge my anger and allowing injustice to continue. That was the mode I had gone into by default because that was my training, and what I thought I should be doing. During those days when I was seemingly on this spiritually high plane, I was ineffectual, depressed. If I'd remained in that place of easy forgiveness the truth would never have emerged. I also needed to come to terms with a more meaningful forgiveness toward myself for taking on so much of the responsibility for what happened, and forgiveness for Avra who wanted nothing to do with this journey of recovery. Finally, I had to ask myself if I could ever, under any circumstances, forgive this man. I wonder if life is long enough to atone for the crimes that he has done? In this case I would say no. A single lifetime, the years he has left on the planet, would not be enough."

"Our society has a kind of compulsion about forgiving," says Dee Dee Kouns. She has seen it with many, many victims. "They feel that it is their duty to forgive but this just adds another layer of pain and stress. Sometimes they hear this drumbeat of forgiveness in their places of worship. I think that it is very sad that, as a society, we expect the person who has been victimized to forgive the victimizer, or that somehow it is our duty to reform them when it is their duty to reform themselves."

Watching admiringly as Terri took her power back, stopped being a victim, and became the poised, articulate accomplished woman she is today, Julie Talen still has concerns. "There is this piece of rage that Terri has not let go of and, while I am not at all critical, I have wondered over the years whether she hasn't paid too high a price. It's almost like a possession of her soul. Perhaps she'd be better able to heal if this man actually confessed and apologized. The anger and hurt of not being acknowledged is a very deep one. When the person who did this terrible thing to you withholds admittance then you are forced to live in a world where a lie is allowed to flourish, if only in this man's own mind. And I think that this still causes Terri pain." Julie pauses, almost speaking to herself. "It is almost an eradication of self to forgive that level of evil."

While admiring Terri, Robyn Edy also expresses a similar concern. "As much as Terri has been appropriately angry at the town and at the axe man, she also needs to recognize the difference between what's her anger and what's his. He took his anger and laid it on her that day. So, as long as she carries this, she's carrying a part of his anger. For her own mental well-being she has to look at her heart and say, 'Okay, am I going to keep carrying this anger, let it weigh me down and make me feel confined and oppressed, or am I going to let it go because it's his anger, it's not mine?'"

Jeannie Fraley disagrees, believing that the lack of forgiveness has been immensely strengthening for Terri. "Forgiveness means that you have to let go of something that happened to you, but it doesn't mean that you have to forget what happened to you. You don't have to put a big old target on your butt and bend over and let him get you again, but you can move on. Terri refuses to forgive this man for what he did to her. That unforgiveness is her strength, and she's found peace with it." She pauses, remembering how Terri was when they first met. "She didn't really stand straight, she was sort of hunched over. Later, I saw a different person, I saw this fantastic, dynamic, beautiful woman. She was very proud and secure with herself. I believe that through her searching for truth she rediscovered who she was."

Where the Amish are unconditional and inclusive in their forgiveness, for Terri forgiveness is inseparable from the reality of evil. "I know we can only talk about forgiveness and the appropriateness of forgiveness if we also talk about the existence of evil," she says. "Because if there is evil, utter and radical evil, then some acts are unforgivable, and I believe in the existence of such evil. I believe that the crime perpetrated against me and my roommate was an act of radical evil. It was a radical transgression. I think people commit evil deeds sometimes for the sheer joy of doing it or because they like to do it, and I think that this man was looking for an experience of absolute control over another human being that night. His choice of an axe revealed his desire to evoke the maximum terror. He enjoyed our blood, our life force ebbing away, he felt omnipotent, never again would he be an ordinary boy. One of the reasons the trauma remained for so many years in the memory of the community was because it was so out of bounds that people couldn't even tell the story, it exploded the usual constructs of storytelling. This event traumatized these people as deeply as it traumatized me; it was an act that defied all comprehension. How can you forgive an act like that? It's unforgivable."

Her unforgiveness, however, is not a cold, detached state, for it also includes compassion. "This man has committed so many crimes against people, none of which he has ever admitted. He has done nothing to deserve the softening of our condemnation of him. But I have felt compassion for him. I don't forgive him, his act was utterly unforgivable, but I also don't feel any bitterness toward him. It no longer weighs me down; I'm not carrying his anger. I do believe, however, that to forgive a man who hasn't confessed the crime, who has never atoned for the crime, who continues in his malevolent behavior toward other people, to forgive him under those circumstances would actually be creating another act of violence against myself.

"People still ask me what could he do, what would it look like if he went down that path of trying to earn forgiveness." Terri pauses, for the question is a provocative one. Then, as she describes the necessary steps towards forgiveness, her voice rises, impassioned. "It would mean admitting every crime that he had ever committed, and certainly in detail what he had done to Avra and to me. It would mean changing his behavior so that he never committed another crime. It would mean atoning by teaching men not to batter women. And he would have to do that every day of his life. And maybe at the end of his days, if I saw his record and was certain that it was true and real, maybe then I could say, 'I forgive you.' But I don't think his life would be long enough."

And then she adds smiling, "The fact that I can sit in this place, in the crime scene, and feel the beauty of the sky, the trees, soothed by the rustling water, and not be catapulted through the years to these awful memories ... to just feel utterly at peace, I guess that is a kind of forgiveness."

In 1997 Terri decided to go public. She gave press conferences in three cities in Oregon where she announced: This is what happened, I believe this is who did it, and I want you to know that, I want the public to know that. "It was very scary for me but it was critically important that I did it. In some ways I was setting up my own little truth and reconciliation commission. It's not enough just to tell our friends, but if possible we also need stand up in the public sphere and name our perpetrator. It carries huge rewards."

As she spoke his name into the microphone she was overcome by an irrational dread. "There was no reason to be afraid. I lived in another state, I was stronger, I had an authorial voice, and yet I was haunted by a scary image: I was living alone, stark naked in a house with all glass walls and I knew his eyes were upon me, watching my every move, invisibly powerful over me." Even today, while these fears are rare, they are never completely gone. They are part of the internal scars she carries with her.

"Public acknowledgement came in a grander form when my book came out. Then I was telling the whole world that I was a victim of this crime. In a way, by giving this crime to the public, it released me from holding it all in myself." Terri's book was accompanied with glowing reviews—most notably on the front page of the *New York TimesBook Review*—and continues to inspire conversation and reflection.

And then, in December 2010, thirty-three years after the attack, Terri received a surprise phone call from an investigator for the district attorney's office in Deschutes County, Oregon. A local man, Owen, had voluntarily come forward to testify that on the night the girls were attacked, a young man he knew had arrived at his home covered in blood and crying out that he had killed two girls in Cline Falls State Park. He said he had run over them, repeatedly, trying to kill them. Owen didn't call the police because he didn't want to be involved. The reason he was speaking up now, so many years later, was because he had been baptized and wanted to come clean. The investigator also interviewed Owen's wife. Although in bed at the time, she had overheard her husband's friend say he had driven over a tent in

Cline Falls and axed two girls. She didn't have an answer for why she never spoke to the police or anyone else, other than she didn't like to think about bad things. This news came after Terri had finished years of hard investigative work. She had repeatedly heard that her attacker had confessed the crime to one or more people the night he committed it, but this final piece of confirming evidence had eluded her. "When I heard this I felt calm and powerful. Validated. It was as though, through the force of my own will, the whole story, including its darkest secrets, had finally revealed itself."

While this story is unusually violent, certainly out of the range of ordinary experience, people still identify and wrestle with it, as if they sense that it taps into some of the great existential themes and questions that preoccupy us all. Perhaps Terri's journey touches so many lives because it has a mythic quality to it. She went into the shadow world, into the underworld, and became her own Orpheus on a mission to rescue the poor, sad, lost, and wounded girl she had left behind in the campground so many years ago. Mysterious strangers opened doors for her at critical moments that guided her to her next discovery. She had encountered evil and looked at it closely but did not, as those poor souls did in Medusa's myth, turn to stone. She instinctively knew that she had to go into the darkness but she did not to let the darkness come into her.

Don Robeson: THE DANGER OF RIGHTEOUS ANGER

Don Robeson

Suppression of anger is harmful. Enslavement to anger is equally harmful. What is the way? — Monsignor Lorenzo Albacete

For many, their sense of honor defines them. If it is sullied in some way and there is no redress, or if they are isolated and shunned as a result of having taken a stand, then how do they go on? What role does forgiveness play when there is no possibility of redeeming one's honor and reclaiming what has been taken? If the truth becomes irrelevant and justice impossible, is forgiveness warranted? What does forgiveness mean when there is no one to forgive, or no one thinks a wrong has even been committed? Is forgiveness relevant? And more importantly, is it even possible?

While Terri Jentz used her anger successfully and creatively to liberate herself from her past, Don Robeson's anger has consumed his life. He discovered financial improprieties at the hospital where he worked, but when he brought them to the attention of the director, he was immediately fired. In a single day his life was irrevocably changed. Suddenly, trusted colleagues and old friends no longer spoke to him. Security was told not to let him into the hospital where he had worked happily for so long. He was treated as a pariah in the community.

"For a number of years I was the supervisor at a clinical laboratory of the hospital, and then I stepped into a semi-management position and was director of materials management." Don is now in his seventies, his face showing both the weathered lines from working outdoors and the lines of burden from many years of anguish. "I served on the budget board of the school district for years. I was elected to the board of directors. I served as chairman of the board and we built a new high school. I was active in my church. I raised three successful boys, who didn't cause any trouble. I gladly contributed to my community. We also had a farm of forty acres. At one time we had fifty-six mother sows that were producing piglets year-round, and my wife and I were so happy. Bonnie was the best OB nursery person I ever saw as she took care of baby pigs night and day. Then we would take them to market. We were paying for our kids' education with this farm."

"I would sit with those babies even if it was in the middle of the night," says Bonnie. "I'd wait for them to be born and make sure that they got where they should go, up to their mom. It was a wonderful freedom to dig in the dirt and have a big garden, or to have animals. We loved those pigs." A small, compact woman in her seventies, she looks strikingly similar to her tomboyish younger self in a picture on the mantel in which she is feeding a baby pig with a small bottle of milk.

But then it all came to an end. "'Clear your desk out and you're gone.' No time, no explanation." says Don in a voice that retains his initial shock. "I later heard that a note had been put up in the nurses' station that said to the effect if I were to appear on the premises that they were to call the police and have me evicted from the building. I was fired from my hospital position and nobody except my wife stood by my side. No one came forward. It seemed like I was just out there all by myself, trying to defend my honor."

Bonnie, Don's wife, worked at the same hospital and was stunned: "He picked me up after work that day and there was a box on the seat of the truck so I asked him what it was. He said, 'I was just fired.' I was as dumbfounded as you can imagine. I worked in the laboratory at one end of the building and he was in the purchasing department at the other end, so I had no idea that the administrator had come in and told him to clear out all his things. It was so sudden, I was so shocked." Her voice reflects those initial moments of distress. "The man who fired him was doing things that he shouldn't have with hospital funds and he knew that Don knew so he wanted to get him out of there as quickly as he could. What a sorry and pathetic man it is who has to do something like this to cover up his own misdeeds. Don met with the board one time but they wouldn't let him talk much. It was a closed door."

One of Don's three sons, Greg, was equally shocked. "My father suspected that the administrator was using funds from the public hospital to build his own private company. He took it to the authorities who basically ignored it. When the administrator found out my father was fired. He immediately hired a lawyer, sent copies of his superb job ratings to everyone on the board, but no one seemed interested. He was never able to find conclusive proof of the administrator's misdeeds, nor reasons for his own firing. It was a crushing blow for him. He believed that he had lost his identity and it drove him to a place inside that made it really hard for him to have relationships or to trust anyone. He's a very proud man so to lose his job in this way was mortifying. It was the sort of thing that, in his mind, identified him for the rest of his life."

Don lost more than his pride and honor. Forced to sell his beloved pig farm, he still weeps at the memory decades later. "When I lost my job we lost the farm because we hadn't reached the point where it was self-supporting, so I needed an outside income to keep it going." His voice trails off into lost memories; tears fill his eyes. "We went into debt to the bank for operating expenses. I found this to be very embarrassing, like a mark on my character, as I'd given my word that I would repay the loan and now I wasn't able. We had to have a dispersal sale. I contacted a live-stock buyer and he came with a couple of semi-trucks and took our animals. The money went to the bank but it only partially paid the bills. The mortgage holder on the farm came shortly after that. We lost everything we'd worked for, everything, with nothing left to help the kids who were in college. That farm meant the world to us. I'd be there today if this hadn't happened, but once they'd foreclosed and taken everything we left the area. They took my life at the same time. I was fifty-two years old without a job or a home."

They moved to a university town where Don got a well paying job and achieved professional success. But the humiliation and injustice of his past continued to haunt him. "Those words still get to me: 'You're being fired.' That means you're incompetent, you're incapable, you're disliked, you're a thorn in the side of manage-ment." Bonnie agrees: "To be called incompetent and to have those words printed in the town's newspaper, it was a massive blow to his pride, which was probably the worst thing of all for him."

Don's reputation had been tarnished and even though few in his community, if any, still remember the event, in his own mind the taint remains. Never having been given a chance to challenge the firing or reclaim his honor, he and his family have been very nearly destroyed by the anger and pain that has obsessed him. No one ever asked for forgiveness, no one seems to care that his reputation and life were ruined. There never was nor will be justice. But Don is shackled to his past humilia-tion as surely as if he were in jail.

Can such righteous yet unrelenting anger be a path to healing? "Yes, of course it can, because it's an expression of the need for justice, and of the awareness of the radical injustice that can accompany life," believes Monsignor Albacete. Years of helping those in need have given him a clear perspective on this most human trait. "Anger is as human as the thirst for forgiveness and the need to forgive, to reestab-lish relationships. The longing for justice is just as desired." But, he warns, "If your anger keeps you focused only on this need for justice, then in the end it will limit and harm you. It has to be pursued with great caution. Suppression of anger is harmful. Enslavement to anger is equally harmful. So what is the best way?"

Don knows full well how that one moment in time irrevocably scarred the years that followed: "The effects of that time have rippled out to the rest of our lives, including taking its toll on our marriage," he admits. "I've been unable to forgive and forget what happened. The anger that I've shown towards my wife, who sometimes pushes this anger button I have in me, has made her suffer unnecessarily. I know I'm like a volcano, how all of a sudden I can erupt. The smallest things can set me off. Maybe I'm reading the newspaper or listening to television or just talking about something and I get angry. I'm constantly saying to Bonnie how sorry I am, because it shouldn't be happening. On many occasions she will cook a wonderful meal and I'll be thinking about losing the farm, losing my job, anger over this, anger over that, and then I can't even eat. My guts are just in turmoil. And that's unfair. We had to rent a house for twelve years before I could even think about buying one. That was another big embarrassment."

"It can be like walking on eggshells, you never know how he's going to react," Bonnie says, with a hint of her own anger. Don's anger has, at times, made their marriage untenable. "After the firing he locked his feelings up, he pulled himself in and just kept everything to himself. If this hadn't happened I'm sure we would have had a happier relationship. I've suggested several times over the years to please find somebody to help him handle these feelings. I don't think anyone will put him down for them or say they are bad feelings, but he has to learn how to handle them. The longer he stays miserable, the more those people are winning, the ones that were involved in his firing."

Greg Robeson watched his father become entrapped in his anger and emotionally unavailable. Both father and son share a wiry, athletic body, but Don's face is taut and guarded while Greg's is more open and relaxed. "What happened to my father took a huge toll on so many levels. More than anything it took away his ability to live in the moment. Instead, he started to live with this script in his head that kept repeating itself, over and over, and absolutely didn't allow him to live with what's happening here and now." Greg is objective in his evaluation, without skirting around his father's behavior. "I know there's been a huge chasm in my parent's marriage, mainly because he's so shut down. There was an equally big impact on his relationship with his sons, as he just wasn't able to be there for us. We always knew there was this gnawing anger in him, like a cancer that's been untreated, and it's devastating to watch. He's been stuck in the past for nearly thirty years now."

Don struggles with forgiveness daily. "On many occasions my wife has said, 'Why don't you just put that aside and forgive and forget?' And I've said to her, 'Forgive what? I didn't do anything.'" He appears to be at a loss and has no idea how to change his attitude. "I'd very much like to get rid of this hot coal of anger that exists in me. But I don't know where I should go or who I should turn to. Do I go to the person who fired me and tell him I'm sorry you fired me and I'm very happy over the mess you put my life in? Do I seek out the individual members of the board of directors and tell them I forgive them for being so incompetent? Do I get down on my knees to God and say I've had all the crap I can take? I don't know what to do. I go to church, I go to communion, I ask for forgiveness, and I do all of these things I'm meant to do, but that event in my life just doesn't want to go away. So, if I were to forgive someone for that, then who in the world would I forgive? I really don't know. I haven't forgiven myself because all my energy has been directed towards somebody saying, 'I'm sorry for what we did to you,' and not toward what I have done to somebody else.

Don may not know who to forgive but he freely admits that if a board member from the hospital were to approach and apologize or even acknowledge that a wrong had occurred, he could move on. "If I were to hear from one or two of the members who were on the board of directors at the time that this happened, if just one were to say to me, 'Don, I'm sorry for what happened and I ask you to forgive me,' then I would accept it. They'd have to really reach down inside of themselves to come forth with a message like that, and I'd respect that. It wouldn't be a surface thing coming from them, so it would be meaningful to me."

But such an apology has not been forthcoming and so Don's anger has gone unabated. "I've felt like shaking him 'til his teeth rattle to make him understand that he's wasting so much time when he could be happy, and how much I resent it," says Bonnie. "I think of how my husband's gone through more than twenty-five years of being in misery," she pauses, and the control she has maintained throughout the conversation gives way to quiet tears. "I think of all the time that's gone by when we didn't have a happy marriage, and all the happiness that he's lost, things that he'll never be able to recover."

Despite his father's inability to make peace with the past, Greg has come to recognize his own emotional limitations. "I work at finding a way to be understanding and empathetic with what caused his inability to connect with me and instead to retreat inside himself. I spent many years feeling angry and isolated from my family. I never really took ownership of my own part in this, by which I mean I didn't make any attempt to recognize or absorb the impact the past had on my father. I just wanted him to get over it, get rid of it." Greg is striving to overcome his resentment in the hope that this may, in turn, also help liberate Don. "The more I've looked back and seen what it did to him has made me a lot more compassionate, because I can feel what happened to his feelings. I believe that part of the process of getting my father to forgive himself is for me to forgive him, to forgive the moments that were taken by his anger. I'll never be able to feel it completely, but now I have a young son so I can finally see what it means to have a father. That has changed my understanding of forgiveness, which I now see as being able to just live in the moment. And I'm confronted by it every day. As I didn't really grow up in an emotional world it can be hard to get to that place, but to forgive I have to be able to feel what I'm forgiving. I can intellectualize forgiveness, but feeling it in my heart, in my soul, continues to be a challenge. I have to work at it. I'd love to get to the place where forgiveness is as natural as breathing. And I do hope that by forgiving him he might be able to forgive himself."

Bonnie feels that maybe forgiveness is the wrong word. "A better word might be acceptance. I think for Don to just let go, to say that 'it's over and I've been miserable long enough,' that would be wonderful. I don't think he'll ever be able to say that he forgives the man who fired him, or the board of directors. But I think he may reach a point where he can't handle it anymore. If he were able to say, 'Dear Lord, take this from me because I can't take it anymore,' then things could start to change and maybe heal."

Don's own struggles with forgiveness have made him even more aware of others for whom forgiveness comes with greater ease. He was moved by the story of a local Mennonite woman who lost her entire family of children in a car crash, yet was able to immediately forgive the driver. Don was unable to put it out of his mind and read everything he could about it. "There had been an automobile accident," he says. "The kids were riding in the back of the pickup. They were hit by another car and the children were all killed. The father, who had been driving the pickup, and the fellow who caused the accident were both taken to hospital. This brave, young mother, who was pregnant at the time, went to the hospital to comfort her husband, then immediately went to the bedside of the pickup driver who had killed her children and she forgave him. That is probably the bravest act that I can recall hearing about in my lifetime. What strength and courage and belief in God that young lady must have had. I'm drawn to the forgiveness that she experienced in this tragedy, which is far more devastating than what I experienced, but still she was able to forgive." He takes a deep breath and lets it out slowly. "I'm just not there. I can't seem to do it."

The loss of Don's job and farm is not the only difficulty he and Bonnie have experienced, but it is the one that devastated his pride so completely that it stopped him from being able to fully enter into life again. "We've gone through my son's divorce, and practically losing a couple of grand-kids because their mother didn't want us to be part of their lives, and we weathered that storm," Don quietly lists a lifetime of experiences. "My wife had cancer and a hysterectomy, and we weathered that. She had a knee replacement, which put her out of commission for a while, and we got through that. But this bundle of crap that I carry around inside me just stays there. It doesn't want to go away and I don't know how to make it go. I know that the greatest gift I could give Bonnie would be for me to forget and forgive the past and to move on. We don't have too many years left. I'm seventy-seven and she's just turned seventy-five, so we're getting up there. She's lived with this for twenty-six years now and I don't think she cares to live with much more of it. This is probably hard to understand for anybody who hasn't experienced such a disaster in his or her life and let it grab hold of them like it has me."

Bonnie has tried to help Don understand what it means to forgive, but with little success. "To me, forgiveness means that you forgive the act but that doesn't mean that you're going to forget. But Don feels that if you forgive somebody then you're forgetting it. I think no, you forgive it and that way you don't let it bother you so much anymore, but you don't forget. Don talked to our pastor, he counseled with him several times. And the pastor told him that he had to forgive, that forgiveness was part of being a Christian. But Don just never bought it."

"Forgive?" exclaims Don. "Everyone says I should forgive. But it hasn't happened and I don't know what should be said or done now. If I think of anything that sets me off it's all directed back to what happened then, which was so long ago but I haven't been able to forget. It's not that I can't forgive, but I can't forget what happened."

Greg is keenly aware of how the limitations in Don's upbringing hamper him emotionally. "I come from a family whose dynamic is not one of closeness, is not one where you share, is not one where emotional connection is recognized or even supported. That's because my parents both came from backgrounds where they didn't share, they didn't talk about hurt, about anger or fear, they didn't talk about emotions or feelings. I think my mom is recognizing this as she looks back on her life, she sees what this has caused, not only between the two of them but to her whole family, and I think she yearns to find a way to change it. Intellectually my father appears to understand forgiveness, but somewhere in his gut he just can't do it; there's a place in his soul that absolutely yearns to let go, to be free, to be present, he just doesn't know how. I talk far more with my mom about the need for forgiveness and the need for my father to move on than I do with him. I pray that at some point, something or someone comes into my father's life and enables him to wake up so he doesn't have to end his days still eaten up by his anger."

"But then again," Bonnie adds, "it's been so much a part of his life and if he gives it up then what does he have?"

Which raises the question of the role anger plays in a thwarted life. We can explore its negative aspects but as an intensely felt emotion, anger is also about passion. "For someone who feels dogged by emotional pain or humiliation, anger makes them feel alive," explains author Lesley Karsten DiNicola. "If they feel unable to influence the course of their own destiny, anger can often create the illusion of control. The paradox confounds everyone. Although Don appears to others as victimized by his anger, he may experience it as a way of reclaiming the power he lost: 'I will never surrender what is left of my pride, my sense of what is right and wrong. You have taken everything else away from me, I won't give you the satisfaction.' Don is shadow boxing with the past but it's *his* past, *his* dreams and *his* battle to win or lose. As long as he is engaged in the fight, there is still a chance he might win. If he abandons his anger and the mighty space it has occupied in his life, it'll create a vacuum to be filled, but with what? Fear, shame, grief are all options. But in this uncharted terrain, Don might also find a semblance of peace knowing that he did the right thing that life-changing afternoon."

The wounds of hurt pride run deeper than most of us may realize. "The loss of a job may not be comparable to the Holocaust, or a great tragedy, or the massacre of your family, but it is equally fundamental. In fact nothing is more fundamentally human than the idea of work," says Monsignor Albacete. "Work is where we prove our worth by contributing and bearing fruit. Look at the Biblical story of Adam and Eve: she was created as a companion in work, so even sex was secondary. The question here is what defines the value of a life. Don defined the value of his life in terms of a job that would allow him to care for his family and live a happy life. And no matter that he believes it's not his fault that he was fired, it makes him question the value of his life. And the wound can be so deep that we can get hooked in that question for years. Unless we can find something else that affirms the value of our life, the past events will always haunt us. Don says that he would be moved to accept an apology, as this would affirm the value of his life. We need to be embraced and gazed upon in such a way that it raises us from the dead, because the loss of a sense of value is like death. We are dead while we are alive and no amount of prayers, words, or reasoning can bring us back to life. A life-affirming embrace is the path to healing."

"I hope one day there will be a visible or a physical event in my life that will indicate it has gone, like a ball of fire or a l ightning strike, and I'm saying, 'Hey, you did it, it's all over.'" Don yearns for such redemption. "It would be a wonderful, wonderful experience if something like that were to happen. I'm just not there yet."

Liesbeth Gerritsen and Dan Glick: THE LAST TABOO

Dan Glick

The elation of suddenly being seen as other than a mother is hard to talk about, certainly to my children. Because it's like, how can I feel elated at all, given that I have just left my kids? How is it even possible? What kind of monster am I?
— Liesbeth Gerritsen

A mother's love, considered the one inviolable love, presumes sacrifice at all costs. "But what if that love has been violated? What if a mother betrays and abandons her children? It's considered unconscionable, a whisper behind the hand, a nightmare that can startle you awake," reflects novelist Michele Zackheim. "To be more precise, such a psychologically rebellious act by the mother has the power to kill the hearts of her children. As a result, she will be considered an assassin to be both shunned and shackled to an unforgiving world. But this does not hold true for men. Even though men betray and abandon children far more often, they are more readily forgiven. Why? Is it because men lack a fundamental ingredient of the natural world? Or is it because women have been taught not to expect it from them? Whatever the reason, the children are the ones who suffer. Is this forgivable?"

It is now fairly commonplace to wrestle with once taboo subjects such as incest or clergy abuse, but the ultimate taboo yet to be confronted may well be the abandonment of children by their mother. Few things are less comprehensible or elicit greater contempt. Liesbeth Gerritsen, suffocating in a marriage for reasons she didn't—and still doesn't—fully understand, left not only her husband but also her two young children aged seven and eleven, moved out of state and created a new life. Zoe, her daughter, begged to go with her but Liesbeth refused. Angry, defiant, and heartbroken, the children turned to their father for love and stability. Encouraged by him to forgive their mother, neither child has yet been fully able to. How do they forgive what for them is incomprehensible? How do they negotiate the pain of abandonment and loss? How can they accept her after experiencing such rejection? Yet, years later, Liesbeth now yearns for their forgiveness and acceptance.

She remembers the early years of their courtship and their family life with pleasure but also with an underlying sense of its fragility. "We met at a modern dance class at Berkeley. He was standing behind me but I could see him in the mirror and I was captivated by his intensely blue eyes. For the first few years of our marriage we were traveling: we had one-way tickets and our bicycles. After three years of going around the world we returned home and Dan went to journalism school in Berkeley. I didn't have the drive to be a lawyer or doctor or to follow up on my degree in architecture; I wanted to have a baby." Tall and slender with a cap of blond hair framing her face, Liesbeth's pain is etched in her eyes. "I chose to stay home while Kolya and Zoe were little. On cold winter mornings I'd hear people getting into their cars to go to work and I would lie cozy in bed with my little guys and it was lovely. There was no part of me that would have traded places with anyone, I loved being a mom."

When a relationship falls apart, for whatever reason, it is rarely a sudden occurrence. Liesbeth searches for the right words. "For a long time things on the surface looked good. We looked like a pretty perfect family. But in a very subtle way I didn't feel quite as witty, as quick, or as bright as Dan. That dynamic of feeling less than, those seeds were there from the beginning and became one of the most damaging things in our relationship."

She speaks slowly, struggling to be precise about a period in her life still shrouded in confusion. "I'm not sure when I started to feel lost. I had surrounded myself with very interesting people, women who were working part-time, or simply taking a break from their well-established careers, and I started to get to know myself in ways other than just being a mother. By this time Dan's job at *Newsweek* had become all-consuming and he was on the road a lot, so I was often alone with the kids. I began to feel an overwhelming sense of loneliness, and then I started to get sick. I had several bouts of bronchitis, two of pneumonia, bladder and other kinds of infections. I had panic attacks that made me feel like I was going to die; I once thought I was having a heart attack. I would be in emergency rooms but it was all completely stress related. I felt so hemmed in, as if I was locked in my own invisible box. My body was saying: 'I need space, I need air, open the door, give me a window, let me look out.' I would scream and cry but then not saying anything to anyone." Her eyes tear up. "It was as close to suicidal as I've ever been."

Dan remembers these anxiety attacks but it is evidently painful for him to revisit them. We sit in silence in his back yard in Denver, Colorado, the Rocky Mountains towering behind us. He is a strikingly handsome man in his late forties, his physique honed by years of hiking. Dan is a gifted writer rarely at loss for words, but he is now. Finally, he says quietly, "I do remember one time when we were leaving for Maine for a vacation and Liesbeth said she felt like she was having a heart attack. So we stopped in an emergency room on the way and it turned out to be a panic attack. Neither of us could talk about it at the time. I was frustrated, I didn't know what was going on, and she didn't know how to express herself."

The communication between them was clearly lacking, as Dan readily admits. "I think one of the things that we didn't do very well was take care of our relationship and give ourselves time together. Liesbeth couldn't say what was going on. She got sick and it seemed she was somatizing some kind of deep conflict or problem, whether in our relationship or something else was never clear. But I didn't pay enough attention to it, and we didn't stop to look for words to describe it. Instead, we walked around it. This began a time of concern, doubt, and wondering what on earth was going on."

"It takes two and I acknowledge that I was never able to say: this isn't working for me, or I'm feeling bad about this, I need change. Rather than having a panic attack, it was more like a shriek attack!" Liesbeth was being tormented by her own sense of failure. "Other women had part-time jobs and seemed to do fine with their kids. Other women stayed at home all the time and didn't have panic attacks. Some women even went to work full-time and managed that. So how come I couldn't?"

In a longing to expand beyond her life, Liesbeth's searching for answers led her to take several classes and seminars. They lived in Colorado but some of the classes were at a process-oriented psychology school in Oregon. This started to put an increased strain and pressure on the family dynamics. "It wasn't clear yet where it was going, I just knew something was pulling me in that direction," she explains. "It was like a door opened and there was no way I could close it. I started doing therapy and working more on myself. As I began to change, the family system got stressed, because all of a sudden things weren't the same. I was expressing my own needs, my own wants, my own interests, all of which led to huge tension. Dan and I started to fight about it: 'I want to go to a week-long seminar in Oregon,' followed by, 'What do you mean you want to go away? Where is this going? Where is this leading?' To me, at the time, it felt like he was putting up roadblocks, and I didn't want to be stopped.

"The door that opened felt like a magical door, like in those C. S. Lewis books where all of a sudden you're in Narnia, you're in this other land. There was no way I could go back. It was a very difficult time for several years, until I reached a point when I could no longer compromise. I realized it meant taking this huge step of leaving and I remember thinking, 'I don't know if dying is any better than this because I can't make the choice. How on earth can I do this?'" Liesbeth's face expresses some of the horror she felt at finally making this enormous decision.

"When I told Dan I was leaving him, to his credit he fought it all the way. He never said okay, fine, until the very end. Our conversation was so extreme that night, I felt so hemmed in, and at the same time I knew that I was leaving an essentially good home. I wasn't abused; I had these lovely children and husband. We argued and I ended up on the bathroom floor, which was cold linoleum. I must have looked mad huddled there, terrified of the next step, of leaving, most especially of leaving my kids.

"I said that I was moving a thousand miles away and Dan immediately replied, 'You can't take the kids with you.' I said, 'I know, I'm not going to take them.' It was a huge moment for us both." Liesbeth looks away, out of the window. "We gathered the kids to tell them. I remember the profound shock on their faces. I'm sure they had heard us argue but there had been no indication I would actually leave. For the first six months I lived next door but then I moved to Portland, and it was a long way away. I had to disavow some of my feelings because if I'd let them in I don't know if I could have gone on. That's still true today. I have to let things in slowly, in doses, or else the devastation is too great. People get divorced and one partner moves three miles away or ten miles away. I moved twelve thousand miles away, partly because of the fear of staying. I couldn't have broken out, I couldn't have done it without this huge distance between us."

Her decision to move so far left Dan in pieces, baffled and confused. "By the time we told the kids the unraveling had been going on for the better part of a year. No doubt they had figured out we were going to couple's therapy. But even after therapy, even after a lot of really rough times, it wasn't until she said she was actually leaving that I realized it was really going to happen. There was a transition period where she lived close by and the kids were going back and forth every week to our respective houses. That gave us a little bit of time to get used to the idea that we were getting divorced. But I still couldn't quite grasp that she was actually moving a thousand miles away and was leaving me to raise the kids by myself." Very few fathers have to become both parents when a mother leaves the family. Dan struggled to pull it together. "I didn't choose it, Kolya didn't choose it, Zoe didn't choose it. Liesbeth called all the shots. I was floored. I was floored for the kids and I was floored for myself. I was just a puddle. I never anticipated that the marriage was going to fail and the idea that she was leaving the kids was unfathomable. I don't think they knew anybody else whose mom had moved away. As a parent the first thing you would do is to lie down on the train tracks to save your kid from pain. To be as powerless to help them as I was and to see how crushed they were was awful."

Liesbeth's decision to leave her family reverberated throughout their lives, affecting each one of them profoundly.

Kolya, at eleven years old, was on the brink of becoming a rebellious teenager but with an understanding that went beyond his years. "The image of mom and dad being together got ripped apart and it shattered everything. The fear was huge." Nine years later, he is a tall, lanky and handsome young man, trying to reconcile his past. "The divorce devastated my world, my foundation, what my life had been built on up to that point. I was angry more than anything else. When I knew that it was my mom leaving, that my mom was causing this, I felt a huge amount of animosity towards her."

Liesbeth Gerritsen

Zoe, just seven at the time, was completely distraught. Now seventeen she has long dark hair and soulful eyes. "I would call her seventeen times a day and leave seventeen messages. I missed her so much. I didn't understand why I couldn't move with her. She said she needed to think about it. I can distinctly remember her calling me back and saying, 'A child doesn't fit in my schedule.' That was followed by months when I was just so angry I never wanted her in my life."

Dan had to stand by and watch helplessly as Zoe suffered. "Zoe really needed to hear her mom say that she still loved her, but Liesbath was always clear that she didn't want Zoe to come and live with her, that it wasn't part of the plan." He is distraught remembering this time. "It was agony to watch Zoe longing for this affirmation from her mom. Night after night she'd come to my bed in tears. She couldn't sleep, she was afraid of the googly-monsters. Her mom had left her and all her childhood fears piled up on these other fears of being unwanted and being left behind. Eventually I had to be straight with her: 'Zoe, it's not going to happen. You've got me, and you've got your brother, and we love you to death, and we're moving on.

This is our life now. Mommy lives far away. You'll have a relationship with her because she's your mom, but you guys are not going to live under the same roof again.'"

As her big brother, Kolya was especially angered by their mother's attitude toward his sister. "Zoe was definitely hit harder by the divorce than I was. She was devastated. She'd cry nightly after that, she just longed for her mother so bad. When she wanted to live with mom it made me angry that she wouldn't let her. It's one thing to move away but it's another thing to so entirely reject the life that you had before. Once mom left, I was done. It was like okay, you can leave, but don't try to be my mother. Don't tell me what I need to do; don't tell me how to live my life. You forfeited that right."

"It got really unhealthy for me." Zoe's voice is laden with unresolved rage and hurt. "I got so angry I started cussing mom out, 'You're such a bitch,' and then she would be mad at me and say, 'Hey! You are not allowed to talk to me that way.' That's when this boiling fire of hatred started. I'd use the power of my hate to make her mad." She stops and takes a deep breath. "I visited her a couple times a year and every time I came home I would be so miserable. I loved being with her but I hated her more than anyone in the world. I wanted to forgive her and then I didn't want to and then I hated her and never wanted to talk to her again and then I wanted to live with her. It was a real roller-coaster of emotions. I wasn't enough to make her stay; we weren't enough. I'm begging with all my might, please don't go, and she still left. It's been hard for me to accept that I wasn't enough, that her feelings for us weren't enough for her to want to stay with her kids. When she said, 'No, a career is more important to me right now,' it was an intense thing to deal with. Your mom chose work and another life instead of you. She chose it! That was her decision and her choice, not mine. I'd stay up all night crying. I would cry in school. I'd come home and I'd cry. I'd visit her and I'd come back and I'd cry. I would call her and I'd cry. And she'd call me and I'd cry. It was so draining to hate her that much, yelling at each other for hours on end. It was exhausting and I got so tired of it."

Liesbeth found this period excruciatingly painful as well. She was aware of how upset Zoe was, but knew she had to steel her heart, that there was no way back. "Zoe wrote these really dire poems, suicidal, just terrible. I couldn't let it in and still stay away. I would've had to go back. Someone in the community who helped take care of the children if Dan had to go on a trip, called me and said, 'You are working with people who have mental illness. But you're creating a mental illness in your own daughter.' I can't tell you…" she searches for the right word "…the devastation." She is full of tears as she shares this. "I was studying psychology, studying the patterns of how we learn to love or not love, I was becoming aware of all these things, yet here I was creating these gaping wounds in my own kids. Kolya withdrew the most; he didn't really let me in. Zoe was the opposite. She begged for me. She screamed for me. She'd cry herself to sleep. And that lasted for many years. I do profoundly regret when she asked me, 'can I live with you?' that I didn't move heaven and earth to make it happen. I felt I had to say no in order to preserve that other piece of myself that felt like a baby, that hadn't yet blossomed, but I wished I could have somehow managed to say yes, for this was the second injury. The first one was leaving, and then here's the second no. It wasn't just a double injury, it was exponentially more."

Dan decided he had to do something drastic to help the children and to create a new family out of the wreckage. "Not too long after she left, I got this harebrained idea to travel around the world with the kids, just take an open-ended journey to give us the space to forge a new family of three using adventure as the crucible." They left on a fine day in July and began what became a five-month journey circum-navigating the planet. "I didn't have too much money so we had to live pretty low to the ground wherever we went. We spent four days in Borneo on a houseboat with mosquitoes, giant pythons and pit vipers in the water, and we went to the jungles of Vietnam where we were looking for the last Javan rhinos and Zoe got covered in leeches. The kids began to realize that we were doing something really life-affirming. Not only did we take this big trip around the world but since then we have traveled many other times. We lived in North Africa together when I had a fellowship in Algeria. They said, 'Sure, let's go together.' Zoe and I have been around South America, we've traveled the Middle East, we've had these extraordinary experiences and they all brought us so much closer."

"The trip with dad was about the three of us coming together and it worked, it really did." Kolya remembers the first journey as making a huge difference. "We spent every day and night together for five and a half months so we got really tight. We got to know each other. At home we all have our own schedules, but traveling like this meant we had to spend all our time together and we were all doing the same thing. Of course we would lose it with each other, but we would have to get over it quickly so we could keep going. It was brilliant."

While the three of them were recreating the family, Liesbeth was struggling. "During those first few years I was emotionally checked-out. I called the kids regularly. I went back to visit. I did all the things I was supposed to do to be a good care-taker by physically being there as much as I could. But I think I was emotionally numb to their intense emotions of what it was like for them. I felt a huge and deep shame, which is different from guilt; the shame of not being able to step up to fulfill one's responsibility is huge."

Liesbeth was also finding it difficult to talk, either to those friends who hadn't deserted her or even to new friends. "The pain is something that people can under-stand and is easier to talk about. But the elation of all of a sudden not being in the role of a mother is so much harder to understand. How can you feel elated at all, given that you just left your kids? How is it even possible? What kind of monster are you that you feel anything other than pain? And yet, along with the pain, there was this incredible freedom of my time being my own that I could barely express. I went back to school; I got a PHD. My brain was like a sponge. I went to every study group, every seminar, every class, I never missed a day."

Forgiveness in such circumstances is not easy but somehow, through it all, Dan realized it was actually essential. "I never thought that forgiveness would have as much importance for me as it has over the last nine years. I've tried to find a way to understand Liesbeth, to have some compassion for her and ultimately to forgive her, so that the kids and I can move on without being burdened all the time by this burning anger. First it was a search for understanding, and then it was somehow reconciling myself with what had happened. Unforgiveness is like a knot in your heart, in your spirit. Unraveling that knot doesn't happen all at once and then it's gone, pshew! It's ongoing in every moment. It actually felt like a cancer, and it was going to start spreading if I didn't do something to exorcise my feelings. I had to keep coming back to unravel it a bit more by asking, 'What's this doing for me?' It was really important to remind myself that it was not serving me to be unforgiving.

"Given that the world does not in general look kindly on women who leave their children, she knew the impact of what she was doing." Dan is generous in his ability to go beyond his own feelings in order to understand Liesbeth's. "This helped me appreciate that she really didn't have a choice, that even though I saw it as a choice, she didn't. The fact that she left knowing what she was doing showed me that she was seeking something so strong and powerful that not to go was not an option. In that realization I felt a little glimmer of forgiveness."

The possibility of forgiveness has meant something different for each of the children. Zoe is not so sure that forgiveness is the appropriate word, as it seems so loaded. "I want to be careful about how I go about this forgiveness business because this has been the most hurtful and damaging thing that's ever happened to me. I want to make sure it's not just, 'I forgive you. We're even. Let's start over.' It seems to be about acceptance and I've begun to gradually accept what happened, to the point of realizing that it was probably the best decision she could've made." Zoe sounds older than her years, having matured through her experiences. "She was so unhappy. I really believe that if you're not happy with who and where you are, then it doesn't matter how many great people are around you, you'd still feel dead inside like she did. Unless you love yourself and you love who you are, then you really can't love anyone else. I remember her apologizing and saying she was sorry. I said, 'Sorry for what?' There was never really a clear answer. She was sorry for the pain it caused me, but she wasn't sorry for what she did, and now I'm glad she wasn't. I know that she feels remorse that she missed all those years with her kids but that's the price she paid."

Dan Glick with daughter Zoe

With a wisdom informed by grief and loss, Zoe reflects on what all this might mean for her in the future. "When I look ahead at relationships with friends or lovers, I suppose what scares me most is the fear of being left, of not being enough, of wondering, are you happy with me? I am always afraid that people will leave me. No matter how many times people tell you they love you, I'll never leave you … Well, my mother said she'd never leave me, and she did. It's given me a skewed idea of what love really is."

Kolya began to make sense of his past many years after Liesbeth left. "The really big moment for me was when I was about seventeen and mom explained to me that she had been very depressed at the time, even suicidal. Hearing your mother say this is incredible. I had no idea that she was in such personal turmoil. It was like the first time I saw my dad cry, which was intense. It's hard for a kid to take because you see your parents as this strong and stable foundation for you to lean on. I realized that she's a person and not just a mother, and that if I was unhappy I might do the same thing. She needed to change things and so she did a complete flip-around. I could get that. Last year she asked me, 'When is this going to be over? When is this going to stop being over my head?' I think she feels like she's done her penance, done her time, that maybe she deserves to be forgiven, and she wants to hear me say it. But I don't know if she's forgiven herself. Perhaps that's one of the reasons she is looking for forgiveness from us, because she hasn't forgiven herself. It's never going to be entirely put behind us. It's always going to be looming, because it formed how our relationship is now."

Another big turning point for Kolya was when his mother accepted—although not without intense arguing—that she had lost the right of parental control. "She still felt she had a right to be my mother, to tell me what to do, how to live my life, but she wanted that power while living in another state. I didn't even start to think about forgiving her until she gave that up, until she made a sacrifice."

"I've been thinking a lot about forgiveness and the question, do I have something to forgive myself for?" Forgiving herself is as important to Liesbeth as is asking her children to forgive her. She pauses before she attempts to answer her own question. "I need to forgive myself for intentionally being the agent of such pain in people whom I love, like my kids and Dan. I need to forgive myself for making choices and performing actions that knowingly would hurt them." Such self-honesty does not always have easy answers, as Liesbeth knows. "I've been afraid to ask because I don't want to hear the answer. Fear has stopped me, and maybe not yet feeling I really deserve it. I think the moment when I can completely forgive myself is probably when I can truly ask for forgiveness. I'm not there yet. I know that up until then I'll always have some excuse: I had to do it, I was going to die, I was this, I was that. But I know they need to hear from me: 'I did this thing, it had a profound effect on you, it caused you a lot of pain, and I'm sorry, and I want to be held accountable, I want to make amends if you'll let me.' She looks into the far distance as if talking to her daughter. To Zoe I'd say, 'Will you trust me again? Will you allow yourself to love me and to let me in? To allow that vulnerability?' There's always going to be that fear of abandonment in the background, so I need to say, 'Please know that I won't abandon you ever again. I won't.'" She takes a few minutes to collect herself. "I'd say the same thing to Kolya, but as he's an adult it feels different to say that I won't leave him again. I once asked Kolya as we were driving, he was probably fourteen at the time. I said, 'I know that I wasn't the mom that you probably hoped you'd have, and I know I made decisions that profoundly hurt you, and I just hope some day that you'll forgive me for those.'"

"There was an important shift for me when I realized that forgiveness could happen even without me totally understanding why she did what she did." Dan has continued to grow in his understanding of forgiveness. "I could actually find forgiveness without having to have all the answers." He has also begun to see his own part in the conflicts with Liesbeth. "Another shift was when I took on some of the blame for what had happened. I realized that I'd love to think of myself as this wonderful partner, good husband, and great father, but I'm as flawed as the next person. Relationships don't happen in a vacuum, there were things I did and didn't do along the way that must have contributed to this. I had a role in it; I was keeping her down. I look back on those days in Washington where she had the first panic attack and I was flying around on Air Force One being a boy reporter in the big leagues, and I was totally unable to respond to her needs. I just wanted everything to be okay, please don't rock the boat. She was trying to say, 'Hey, things aren't as beautiful as they seem and I'm having some problems here,' but I didn't have a lot of sympathy, I didn't stop to ask what was going on for her. I finally got this wasn't just about her doing something to me, but it was about a relationship unraveling, and I was a part of that. This was a huge step to forgiving both her and myself and moving on."

But Dan's growing clarity confused his son even more. "The only part of it I still don't understand is my dad's relationship to my mom. It still baffles me to this day. How could he have forgiven her, or at least appear to have done, only a few years after? They have even stayed friends. It just doesn't make any sense to me. I know a part of him is hiding it, pushing it under the surface but still, having your wife of eighteen years just get up and leave… I wanted him to be angry. I was angry for him. I was angry for myself. If my wife had left me I would be raging furious. But actually, in the long run, seeing my dad forgive her did help me to forge a new relationship with my mom."

Forgiveness is intimately involved with Dan's ability to pick up where Liesbeth left off and to be an active and involved father. In the process he has come to deeply appreciate the beauty of parenting. "It's kind of a small thing, but I remember going to Zoe's elementary school to drop off her lunch or something that she had forgotten. I wandered in and got talking to the school janitor. I knew who he was because I had been around the school enough, but I realized that I'd never have known his name if Liesbeth hadn't left. It was especially poignant as I had been so angry at Zoe that I had to leave my office and go take her lunch because she had forgotten it and how tough it was being a single parent and having to do all this on my own. But the fact that I knew when her classes began and when lunchtime was and I knew her schedule was a really touching moment for me; I liked knowing those details and I couldn't have had such moments without the loss. We can travel around the world together. We can play soccer in the living room if we want to. We can have pancakes for dinner or eat hamburgers for breakfast. The kids have had some brilliant experiences and insights as a result of what happened, and that can't be bad. And if it's not all bad, then why be so pissed off about it?"

Dan still worries and wonders about what lies ahead for his children and for himself. "I don't know how they'll forgive her, or even if they ever will completely. They'll need to come to that place themselves where they say, 'I want to figure this out.' I need to figure it out too; I've got my own trust issues. I put all my eggs in one basket and she stepped on it so it's been devastating to pick up the pieces and even harder to find relationships that work for me. The anger doesn't just disappear. When I'm starting a new relationship and I'm fumbling through the difficulties I get so pissed off that I have to do this." He starts to laugh, "And even worse when I'm asking how many brothers and sisters do you have. I want to shoot myself and then shoot her; actually I'd have to shoot her first!

"I think the kids have that 'but' hanging in there. Pain doesn't just go away, anger doesn't just disappear. It comes up in different ways, at different times. Maybe there's a temporary forgiveness or temporary understanding that we come to, and then it flitters away and we have to chase after it again. But it's a pretty good place to get to when you can say, 'I do understand. I have compassion for what you did. I honor and respect the decisions that you made because you wouldn't have made them if there was another way for you.'"

Kolya has appreciated getting to know his mother now that he is becoming an adult, but is not yet willing to forgive wholeheartedly. "I went out and visited her. I saw her new life; I could hear how excited she was. When she graduated and got her PhD, I was excited for her. All these new things piece her life together and show me that she's recreating herself, which is really important for me. It's made me understand how she'd had these very real conflicts in her old life. Sometimes people need to recreate and redefine themselves. That's something I can appreciate and it really helped me start forgiving her. I feel like I'll continue to forgive her as I spend more time with her and get to know her better. I know she'd really appreciate an acceptance of her decisions."

Zoe is not so reconciled. "Forgiving her for leaving, that's hard, because there's part of me that may never understand how she could cause us that much pain. But, totally contradicting myself, I think forgiveness needs to happen in order to move on, in order to be at peace with this, in order to establish a relationship with her that won't be as parent and child. When that day comes it's not going to be like, 'Hey mom, I forgot to tell you, I forgive you for leaving us.' It's going to be something more like her knowing that I respect her decision. I think I am about ready to have that conversation with her."

Liesbeth's journey is inevitably full of regrets while knowing she cannot go backwards, cannot undo what has been done. She can only amend where she is now and ask the children to join her there. "Do I regret the things that I missed? Of course I do." She pauses before starting to list all the missed moments, and then starts to speak rapidly as if lingering on any one of them is too painful. "Some of Zoe's plays that she was in that I didn't fly back for, some of their birthdays, Kolya's soccer games, watching them interact with their friends, the whole development of their social being, what they do and what they're into, the music they listen to, and the kind of banter that you can only have if you're with somebody every day. Knowing what I know now, who I am now, the knowledge I have now, I would do it very differently. I would have Zoe come to live with me. I would send that same invitation to Kolya, even if he didn't want to. I hung on to trying to parent from afar because I didn't want to give up as a parent; I resisted this picture of me no longer being a mother.

"I wanted my cake and to eat it too. I wanted to move a thousand miles away but I still wanted a role in their lives. I left my marriage, I left my kids, and now I'm trying to reestablish those relationships that I broke. It's been about nine years and I long to be a part of their lives again. In order for that to happen I know there has to be forgiveness for some of the things that I've done, for the ways that I've wounded them. I need their forgiveness and I need to forgive myself. My therapist said to me, 'You have to own that you left your kids, and you need to tell them that you failed them as a mother. And that at some point you would like to be forgiven.' It's so simple and yet so simply difficult to do. If I can't forgive or atone for the things I've done that have been wrong, then how can I expect anybody else in the world do that for me?"

Kathy Power: **PERPETRATOR TURNED PENITENT**

Kathy Power

I wanted forgiveness. I wanted to receive forgiveness. I wanted to earn forgiveness. And the hardest work was to keep peeling back the layers of defensiveness, the fearfulness that I was a monster, that I would be unforgivable. — Kathy Power

Not forgiving is a choice. It can be an honorable one and may provoke the deepest questions. But atonement is another choice altogether and it can last a lifetime. It too can bring clarity, but not necessarily forgiveness. Kathy Power, a fierce opponent of the Vietnam War, participated in a violent act of protest in which a policeman was killed. After twenty-three years on the lam with an unsettled conscience, she turned herself in, only to discover that an arduous penitence awaited her: that she had to forgive those she had fought so hard against before she could begin to forgive herself. Ultimately, this proved to be even more important than gaining forgiveness from the family of the murder victim. Her penitential journey is filled with a drama, pathos, and sacrifice that are unusual for our time.

In the fall of 1967 Katherine Ann Power, the eldest girl in a strict Catholic family of seven, arrived at Brandeis University in Massachusetts. With a small frame, shoulder-length brown hair, big glasses and a wide smile, she did not fit the image we have of someone who would soon become a violent activist. She was an exceptionally intelligent, bright, and high-achieving student, and Brandeis awarded her a full scholarship. Kathy had grown up in Denver, Colorado, where she was the class valedictorian, won the state history contest, the Betty Crocker Award, and was a National Merit scholarship finalist.

Looking back today, Kathy struggles to understand her fateful choices as a young student. She reflects on her early Catholic upbringing as a critically important influence. "Worship was really an important part of my inner life from when I was very young. There was something about the formation of conscience that is established in the liturgy that made me want to be good, to do the right thing. My uncle was the chaplain at St. Joseph's and I had my first experience of spiritual ecstasy during the May crowning as I was lifted up to put this crown of flowers on the head of a statue of Mary. And of course I grew up on stories of the saints who got their heads chopped off for the greater good. One of the key ideas of the Catholic culture is that you should be willing to suffer and even die for your faith or for what is right. I always imagined how glorious that kind of sacrifice might be."

But there were also darker aspects of her childhood Catholicism that cast a long shadow. This is difficult terrain and Kathy speaks hesitantly. "Because of my neat handwriting, I was chosen to go to the rectory after school to help the priest record the results of the collection. He abused me from around the time I was nine till when I was eleven. I have memories of being suffocated in the starched and ironed folds of his floor-length black Cossack and also of a penis being shoved down my throat. I never spoke about it to my parents for the priest was our confessor and a favorite in the family. That level of betrayal by a sacred authority figure held a tornado's worth of destructive energy. It meant that I couldn't trust God or anyone in authority, which, by extension, meant I couldn't trust the police, the government, or anyone legitimately trying to guide me to true and right behavior."

Years later and already in prison, she heard that the priest has been deported back to Switzerland because of accusations by young girls, some of whom she had known. Finally she was able to tell "her secret" to her family. But even today it is difficult for her to discuss, and when she does she carefully emphasizes: "I do not want it to be thought that being abused by a priest in my childhood is in any way an excuse for my own crime."

Kathy's entrance into the world of Brandeis is as vivid to her as if it were yesterday. "It was truly another world, thrilling in many ways, scary too. I was a naïve young woman from a Catholic family; I literally had two dresses that I had made myself. I wanted to put as much distance between college and home as possible and I succeeded beyond my wildest dreams." Free love, contraception, drugs, all of these were hot topics on the campus. It was not only a different world, but it also offered a new sexual and political vocabulary.

This was the time of deep divisions in the country over the Vietnam War and Brandeis was the headquarters of the National Student Strike Force, which organized protests against the war across the country. Some of these demonstrations had turned ugly. As a result, more than four hundred colleges and universities that had erupted in protest were being closed down. David Harris, a respected anti-war activist and one of the few who went to jail rather than be drafted, remembers those times as profoundly destabilizing. "The turbulence was extraordinary. There were demonstrations on the street, sit-ins, and riots involving both faculty and students, and confrontations with the police. People were screaming and sometimes clubbing each other. Buildings were being burned and on occasion bombs were set off. There was a pervading sense that this outbreak of rage was taking over the country."

"In the late sixties we almost split this country apart over this war," agrees Rev. Donald Shriver, formerly the president of the Union Theological Seminary. A distinguished gray-haired man with chiseled Gary Cooper features, he has more than a line or two from his impressive resume as a civil rights activist and mediator in Ireland and South Africa. "We had guns that were trained against our own young people who were protesting. In the Kent State incident, for example, four of them were actually killed. We were at a point when it was almost as though our government was at war with a large part of our own citizenry."

The war was widening. The news came that President Reagan had been secretly bombing Cambodia. No one knew how far it would go or what other countries might be included. There was a kind of panic in the air. Professor of law Garrett Epps remembers the urgency of that time. "Society appeared to be trembling. It seemed to be just shivering, as if it was about to fall to pieces." Professor Epps, then a student at Harvard, reminds us that it is hard today to understand the menace of that time because we know the end of the story. "We know that America didn't collapse but back then it seemed to be on the brink. There was this panicky sense that things were getting worse by the day. Every day we waited was a day that was wasted."

Like many of the Brandeis students, Kathy Power found herself at demonstrations that started peacefully but often turned ugly. "In my freshman year I was tear gassed and watched terrified as a line of policemen in helmets moved toward us, swinging their batons. My friend Stewart got hit and couldn't walk so we had to carry him to safety. It felt as if the moral order of the universe was being turned upside down."

These uncertainties and fears were not only causing panic, but also a deep and upwelling anger. "We were horrified about what was happening in Vietnam." Psychotherapist Jim Hannon was there, watching it unfold. "There was no end to the war in sight, it was simply the forever war. We were dealing with an atrocity and we were enraged. It is what we were going to do with that enragement, and what we actually did do, that became problematic."

Kathy was appalled at what was happening and longed to play a part in stopping the war: "The world was on fire. Literally, Vietnam was on fire. I had to do something with my life about this war, I had to figure out what it was and have the courage to do it."

At this time some leaders in the anti-war movement invited her to go to Cuba with them and meet with the Vietnamese. She was being groomed for a leadership position, as their plan was that she would return and lecture around the country. In a fateful move, she turned down their offer and to this day looks back on her decision with regret and bafflement. "I looked at David Dellinger and all the other big name activists in front of crowds and saw it as a powerful temptation to become a star. To be the person that everyone is looking at, to fly around and give press conferences. Instead I mistrusted myself and saw the offer as potentially corrupting. So, rather than become a leader I became a foot soldier in a clandestine army."

Brandeis was one of a group of universities in the Boston area that sponsored an experimental parole program allowing convicts a chance to leave prison and receive a college education. It was through this program that Kathy met Stanley Bond and two other ex-convicts: Robert Valeri and William Gilday. Bond was twenty-five years old, a former Vietnam veteran with brooding charisma and a history of crime.

Kathy was immediately attracted to him: "Stanley approached me on the campus and said 'I've heard that you want to do something more active against the war. And I said, 'Yes, I do.' He said, 'Well, I'm trying to put together a group of people who will be a revolutionary cadre.' I immediately stepped into that because I felt that this was my chance to be connected to someone who could teach me the low levels of sabotage that I thought were needed to make the war stop."

This meeting turned her life around. She saw Bond as a leader who could act, not simply theorize, and by the time she was twenty-one Kathy was deeply committed to radical change. She became a bastion of the Brandeis Strike Information Center, established to monitor information about student and campus resistance across the U.S., and was regarded as an authority that others would look to for guidance. In 1970, between Bond, Gilday, Valeri, and Kathy's roommate Susan Saxe, a plan was formed to engage in a series of violent actions in order to get the funds necessary to continue resisting the war.

Looking back on this now, Kathy says sadly, "I want to emphasize the danger of stepping into a closed group, because you don't think critically anymore; you don't subject your ideas to the test of an open discussion. I surrendered my critical thinking." When pushed about the likelihood of someone dying, she returns to her culpability, "I didn't think straight. I was running around with people with guns. I was robbing an armory, and I couldn't connect that with the inevitable outcome that someone was going to get shot. Instead, I kept thinking if anyone's going to get shot, it'll be me. And if I die, I will be a martyr."

During that summer the group traveled across the country robbing banks, stealing cars, and transporting guns. While Kathy denies having taken part in these actions, she acknowledges that she did join the group to break into the Newport Guard Armory where they stole military equipment and ammunition, storing it in a rented apartment in Boston. Then they decided to rob the State Street Bank in Brighton. She did not anticipate that anything might go wrong. "The plan was that three of the group members were going to rob the bank and then leave in a stolen car, and they were going to rendezvous with me in another car about a half mile away."

In fact, the bank robbery went tragically wrong. A few minutes after Saxe, Valeri, and Bond had robbed the bank and driven off to meet Kathy, officer Walter Schroeder and his partner arrived at the scene. At that moment William Gilday, who was sitting in his car across the street, inexplicably sprayed thirty rounds from a submachine gun. Walter Schroeder was hit in the back as he ran for cover.

Following the shooting, Schroeder was rushed to hospital and into surgery. The shot had entered his heart and destroyed the aorta. Two hundred and twenty people lined up in the hallways to donate blood but it was to no avail. He died the next day.

That time is etched forever in the memory of his daughter, Clare Schroeder, then a high school senior. Clare, tall and lean with short salt and pepper hair, has a commanding presence and she speaks dispassionately. "I was called out of class into the principal's office. Earlier we had heard ambulances and sirens and of course I hadn't made the connection. But when they paged me, I walked to the office with dread. I can still see my uncle standing against the window, his back to me, and the principal just looking at me. He didn't have to speak, I knew what Uncle Jack was there for and I knew that all the sirens we had heard were involved in what he had to tell me. Reluctantly, he said that my father had been shot and we needed to leave for the hospital.

"On the day that my father died, my mother had nine children from the age of eighteen months to seventeen years. My siblings were all with different relatives so my mother could be at the hospital. I walked to each one of my uncles and aunts homes so I could tell my brothers and sisters. Every time that I had to do it I cried all over again. It took me the entire afternoon." At this point, Clare's voice breaks. "I haven't thought about this in a long time, but it felt important that the news come from me.

"The funeral lasted for hours," Clare continues, not without a touch of pride. "They extended the time because of the volume of people. Police officers came in from all over the country, even Canada. The governor and the mayor came. On the way to the church the street was lined with people, and as we got closer the entire length of the street was a sea of blue, as far as you could see in all directions, lined with all the officers in their blue uniforms who had come to say goodbye. I remember the bagpipes playing and people coming up to me sharing stories about my father, how he had saved their life, how he did this, he did that. I remember a woman telling me that he had saved her drowning son. I felt so proud but also so hollow that my father was unable to enjoy their praise.

"The day after my father died, I remember sitting down with my mother and asking where do we go from here? Did I need to leave school? Should we start packing the house to sell it? She had nine children, and my father had been the sole provider, so there was a lot of concern."

Meanwhile, reactions to this event ranged from anger to incredulity. In the Boston area, Walter Schroeder was a well-known, beloved figure who had been publicly commended for unusual valor. One of his brothers had recently been killed in the line of duty. So the response in Boston was one of disbelief and fury, while whatever sympathy there was in the radical community was muted. Many people in the movement struggled to understand how Kathy Power had crossed the line into violence. For psychologist Jim Hannon, it was "the bad thinking" of the radicals that shocked him: the idea of a bank robbery to get money to end the revolution. Incredulous, he adds, "And to give funds to the Black Panthers? This is where a lot of people slipped off into romanticism. It wasn't just stopping the war; they wanted to overthrow the United States government. That was crazy. That just wasn't going to happen."

Activist David Harris reacted to the violent turn with anger. He was a respected student leader with a long activist history; he had been in the South signing up voters when it was exceedingly dangerous; he tutored disadvantaged kids, worked in soup kitchens, marched and demonstrated. So he was furious when he heard about the botched robbery and the murder of the policeman, and even so many years later his voice rises. "I devoted ten years of my life trying to stop the Vietnam War, including two years in prison refusing to serve in it. And I looked at this group of two dozen people—Kathy Power and her little band of followers and the slightly larger group of Weathermen who had self-proclaimed revolution on their minds—as a slander against what the rest of us were trying to do.

"Yes," David continues, trying to be measured in his criticism, "all of us were angry, it was impossible not to be angry about the war. The mistake was assuming that anger gave you license to go out and rob banks, steal guns from armories, blow up public restrooms, or place bombs under police cars. It was a travesty. And it cast a shadow on what we were trying to do. America was filled with decent people who had accepted the war because they had no good information to the contrary. It was our job in the anti-war movement to reach out to them and help them understand. And we were doing a pretty good job until these self-proclaimed revolutionaries arrived. My heart literally sank when I heard about the robbery and the shooting."

The Boston police swarmed over the crime scene, setting up a statewide dragnet. Within twenty-four hours they had discovered the apartment rented under Kathy's name that was filled with rifles, ammunition boxes, and blasting caps, most of them stolen from the local National Guard armory, as well as a field telephone switchboard. In the next week the three men were caught but the women, Susan Saxe and Kathy Power, escaped. Among other states, Massachusetts rule determines that if someone is killed during the enactment of a crime then all those who partook in that crime are equally culpable of murder. Although they had escaped, the women were now wanted killers. They went on the run. Susan was caught in 1975 and spent seven years in jail, but Kathy remained at large.

"Running away meant driving the car out of town, getting on an airplane, getting on a train, cutting off my hair, coloring my hair, buying different pairs of glasses, and living in terror, terror, terror." Memories of her fugitive life tumble out as her voice quickens. "I got an apartment, I got a job. I didn't see my family, although I'd go to libraries and check the phone books to see if they were still listed. But none of what I told anyone was true. When someone recognized me because he'd seen my face on a poster I'd immediately be on the next bus to somewhere else. My bag was always packed. I think the survival part of me just pushed aside what had happened into a place where I wouldn't look at it. I ignored it for a really long time. When I finally looked at it, I didn't know how I could continue to think of myself as a human being. I spent the next twenty-three years of my life with a divided awareness, that on the one hand I was a monster and on the other hand I was going to live."

Kathy lived underground for nine years before she moved to Oregon and changed her name to Alice Metzinger, taken from a baby that had died the same year she was born. She made her home and got a job in a small-town community in the Willamette Valley and she had a child, Jamie. She formed relationships, started a successful restaurant, and won a culinary prize as the chef of the year. Later she married her long-term partner Ron Duncan. She became a known and liked figure in the community.

Meanwhile, back in Boston, the Schroeder family tried to put thoughts of the murder to the side and to get on with their lives. As the anniversaries of the killing came and went they would hear news of sightings, rumors of Kathy's whereabouts. For Claire, "It was like living with the open wound of Kathy's unresolved crime, like having a cut and scratching at it and then having it bleed. It meant the pain was constantly revisited." With her characteristic precision, she adds, "We needed closure and what we got was the periodic 'whatever happened to...' or 'where do you think she is?' The fact that she was in hiding for so many years indicated very clearly to me that she felt guilty. If Kathy really believed all those things she espoused and the rightness of what she was doing, why was she hiding?"

Despite being free, Kathy was also in pain, albeit of a different kind. She had begun to suffer terrible bouts of depression intensified by the shame and guilt of what she had done, the endless fear of being caught, and the loneliness coming from the separation from her parents and siblings whom she had not seen in over twenty years. She was contemplating suicide when she finally sought therapeutic help. The lie had been going on for too long and she needed to relieve her conscience and find some peace. She ached for the truth to be told so she could have her life back.

Linda Carroll, a family therapist, was giving a lecture about depression at a local hospital in Oregon and remembers a young woman sobbing openly in the back of the room whom she later discovered was Kathy. Over the next fifteen months, Kathy started seeing Carroll at her office and grew to trust her enough to tell her story. Sometimes she would sit in silence, other times she would be crying or trying to make sense of her past. Linda Carroll describes Kathy as, "traumatized and not unlike a burn victim who has miraculously survived. She was massively depressed. The forced hiding, the running, the ongoing vigilance, the isolation, and the terror were precisely the qualities she needed to survive, but at the same time they were the conditions for depression. They fed each other."

"The life that I was living wasn't sustainable, although to everyone else I looked pretty ordinary and even successful." It is difficult for Kathy to put this time of her life into words. "The shame of what I had done was dragging me down, it made me feel like I didn't deserve to live, that I didn't deserve the good things that came from working at my restaurant, or from building a family. I felt that I deserved nothing. I had longer and longer bouts of depression, until finally it was so bad that I couldn't go out of the house. I had always thought that prayer and contrition would be enough. I remember the Catholic prayers preceding confession when I vowed to change myself so that I would never do wrong again. But it became clear that just trying to live a good life, to be a good person, was inadequate. Deep inside I knew that I had to surrender."

"I know that she struggled with how could she possibly leave her son and her partner, just because of her own needs," says Jim Hannon, who met Kathy in jail during one of his classes at the prison. They established a strong bond that endures today. "But this was not an 'I need this' situation, which is at a shallow level. This was at the deepest possible level. I think Kathy knew that she had to do this repentance work and public confession not just to do the right thing, but because otherwise she wasn't going to survive emotionally."

Kathy had been on the Ten Most Wanted Fugitives list for fourteen years, longer than any other woman in history, and she was the cause of the largest woman hunt the FBI ever conducted, fanning out across the country and pursuing every lead. It had been unrelenting. They had showed up at a small feminist commune where Kathy and Susan had briefly stayed, and interrogated the women. Some cooperated, most didn't, and three of the women who refused to reveal any information went to jail, one for twelve months. Ultimately, the leads dried up. Kathy disappeared from sight and was largely forgotten. Until now. Finally, after twenty-three years of living a lie and being on the run, she was ready. In 1993 her lawyers initiated negotiations with the authorities and, after a year of tense discussion, they agreed on the terms of her surrender. She left Oregon and gave herself up in Boston.

"I put my hands behind my back to be cuffed and one of the officers said, 'I arrest you for the murder of Walter Schroeder.' It was like being hit in the face. Murder is a very hard word to hear about yourself. I didn't want to hear it, but I knew I had to; it was the opening up of that place of shame. I was taken for finger printing and booking, and then to the courthouse for the arraignment, but in some fundamental sense I was still not surrendering. I had so much defiance, a burning anger that wanted to say, 'Okay, so when are the generals and the politicians going to pay their dues? Robert McNamara is responsible for hundreds of thousands of deaths so when is he going to be held accountable?' There was a lot made of why I was smiling while I was at the courthouse. My friends said I was seeing my family, that's why I was smiling. And my critics said, look at her, she is unregenerate and triumphal, that's why she is smiling. And my therapist said she is in shock, which is probably the most true. But I think it was because I was carrying myself in a way that said I had surrendered in body but not in spirit."

Talking about her motivations, Kathy is rigorous and precise. "I didn't surrender because I knew that I had to go and answer for the death of Walter Schroeder. Of course, that was there at the deepest level," she acknowledges. "But I was so defended that I couldn't even get close to that. No, I had to surrender because the life I was living was wrong for my son. He was growing up without a family and I couldn't be a good parent to him if I couldn't tell him the story of my life. And it was wrong for my mother, father, and my siblings. I had to surrender so that my life wouldn't be divided anymore, and so that I would stop feeling so terrible."

Despite her anger, she was repentant and longed for forgiveness. "I tore something that can never be untorn. Walter Schroeder died young and that doesn't go away, no matter what I do. It lives with me. I really wanted forgiveness. I wanted to do what had to be done so that forgiveness would be offered and I could receive it."

However, Kathy's surrender was not as welcomed as she might have wished. Clare Schroeder wanted a moral and judicial reckoning. "I think it's important for people to realize that sometimes the results of what we do have a lifelong impact," she emphasizes. "Very simply, my father never got to live out his days with his family and grandchildren. My mother never married again, she pretty much stayed alone with her small circle of family and friends. Each person in the family—his children, parents, aunts, and uncles—was affected differently by his absence. We may have led productive lives but we have been forever marked by the loss."

It is the anniversary of her father's death, late afternoon in a Boston cemetery, the time when Clare visits her father's grave. We speak nearby under a massive maple tree; the light is dapped and the setting serene. The gravesite seems to unlock memories and melancholic reflections. "There are times when I especially wanted my father to be present, such as my graduation from college. It would have been a momentous occasion for him as I believe that I was the first in his family and in my mother's to go to college. It would have been a milestone in terms of his being a parent and his ability to raise his children and to afford them opportunities. For both of us it would have been a shared moment of accomplishment." Momentarily overcome, she pauses, and then quietly adds, "There is always that 'Gee, I wish that Dad could have seen this'… But he didn't."

Not only were the Schroeders unrelenting in their dismissal of the idea of forgiveness, but they were horrified as they watched Kathy became the center of a media blitz that stirred up long-lost memories of the sixties, hippies, and the often violent protests against the Vietnam War. "I was stunned at the national media attention. I was horrified to see her smiling face on the cover of *Newsweek* magazine." Clare Schroeder was amazed, as if the hero of the anti-war movement had come forward to claim her throne. "Then I read this article about Katherine Power and a nameless, faceless police officer who was killed. My father. The *New York Times*, the *Washington Post*—the story was everywhere. I was blown away at what I felt was such an inappropriate response. All I heard in the courtroom was, 'Yes I was there, yes I did this, and no I never thought anyone was going to get hurt, and my life's been really difficult since then.' I was totally blown away!"

At the time, Peter Gelzinis was working as a city desk columnist for the *Boston Herald and* was particularly struck at how the limelight had shifted. "This strange thing happened when Kathy emerged from the mists of time. All of the attention was focused on the return of this famous former radical. But when I was in the courtroom the thing that caught my attention most was that she was no longer a radical, she was a homemaker. She was a wife and a mother. I wasn't prepared for her husband and her child, for this very ordinary family person." Dressed in suits and ties, Kathy's husband Ron and son Jamie sat in the courtroom throughout the trial: a man and his teenage son, looking no different than any other family.

During the proceedings Kathy made a statement about the killing of William Schroeder, but it was not a statement of deep regret, apology, or remorse: "His death was shocking to me, and I have had to examine my conscience and accept any responsibility I have for the event that led to it... the illegal acts I committed arose not from any desire for personal gain but from a deep philosophical and spiritual commitment that if a wrong exists, one must take active steps to stop it, regardless of the consequences to oneself in comfort or security."

She later admits that this statement was inadequate. At that time, she was still very self-protective and not focused on the depth of the damage. "What the family who had been wronged saw was a really incomplete statement that didn't express genuine remorse, because I hadn't fully recognized the harm that I had caused." She is fully aware of how limited her awareness was at that time. "The statement I prepared for my surrender was defensive, it contextualized my acts in the violence of the Vietnam War, it took credit for my intention, which was not to harm anyone. All this, rather than acknowledge the fact that someone was killed. I took limited responsibility for what I'd done because I couldn't even look at it. I hadn't done the far deeper work of a penitent, which was to keep peeling back these layers of protection, and the fear that I would be unforgivable."

At the sentencing, Clare Schroeder read a victim impact statement that confirmed the family's abhorrence of Kathy's arrogance. Clare remembers walking to the microphone "with a visceral powerful anger." In the courtroom footage she speaks with barely controlled fury. "I wish I could take at least some comfort in knowing that Katherine Power feels genuine remorse for her crime. But over and over again I have read the statement she made when she surrendered to the Boston police and there is not a single shred of apology for the murder of my father. She does not even mention my mother, or any of us.

"My family is not vengeful. Nothing could be farther from the truth. We struggle everyday to understand and forgive as much as our hearts are able. And I do acknowledge that Katherine surrendered voluntarily, knowing that at some point she was going to have to stand up in a public forum and accept responsibility. Many other people in her circumstance would not have done this. So I do have a small measure of respect. But we have been waiting twenty-three years for justice. She is attempting to explain and to justify her acts without so much as an apology to us. The woman I saw that day in court was an arrogant woman."

Kathy was sentenced to eight to ten years. She had done what she had so longed for by coming clean and receiving due punishment.

Janet Landman, a professor of psychology, studied and wrote extensively about Kathy's life and attitudes. "I'm a scholar of regret and I had just written a book about it when Kathy surrendered. So I wrote to her in prison." In her mid-forties, her thick gray hair catches the light as she tilts her head, remembering. "At one point I asked her how she felt when she found out that someone had been killed as a part of the robbery, and almost immediately the tears started flowing down her face. She responded slowly, 'I was terribly shocked. This was not supposed to be about killing. It was supposed to be about stopping the killing.'" Professor Landman pauses, recalling the impact of that moment. "I assumed that this very powerful act of giving herself up, waiving her right to a trial, pleading guilty, and accepting prison, that this was the result of a lot of inner work that had been done, and I wanted to know about it retroactively. What I discovered was that Kathy actually had a long way to go. She described herself as 'painfully peeling off layer after layer of defensiveness."

One of the layers she had to peel off was her anger. And here Janet, a woman with a soft sympathetic voice, assumes a tougher tone: "Kathy first arrived in prison an angry woman. She had been given the understanding that she'd be serving her prison sentence in Oregon, where her husband and son could visit her. She believed that the state had reneged on that promise when they told her she would serve her sentence in Massachusetts, the state where she committed the crime."

In fact, what Lucinda Franks remembers during her interview with Kathy for *The New Yorker*, was rage: "During those first few months in prison I didn't see much humility, but I saw fury at the government for violating their agreement. She was sorry about Walter Schroeder—she had never wanted to kill him or anyone—but the family's pain was not on her mind. When I first met her she was afraid of what she might say and of the anger that would roar out of her. So she was hidden, opaque, and difficult to talk to."

A year or so later, Janet Landman saw something change. "I will never forget the day we were sitting at the orange Formica table in the prison visiting room, when Kathy said to me, 'Janet, you know, serving my time in Massachusetts is the best thing that's ever happened to me. If I'd been in Oregon, my friends would have visited me and said things like, 'this is insane, Robert MacNamara belongs in prison, not you.' And I would've agreed. But here in Massachusetts I come face to face with my history, and that's the work I have to do as a penitent. Here there are guards who call me cop killer, and there are local newscasters who describe the pain of the Schroeder family day after day. Because I've had to serve my time here I can't escape what I'm in for. I can't escape the scrutiny of people who won't put the history aside until it's time to do that, who can't say, okay, it's time to live in the present, all is forgiven, until justice has somehow clearly been served. And I know that part of that justice is that I have to be seen to suffer.'"

Another hurdle for Kathy was giving up the idea of herself as a righteous national warrior against all that was violent, brutal, and unjust. "I had to let go of that glamorized idea of myself as a noble outlaw; I had to acknowledge that the politics of rage that was informing my behavior was actually very destructive and self-indulgent. Even more difficult was letting go of my shame. I hid it for a long time, was immersed in it and paralyzed by it, until I finally came to realize this shame was an indulgence. It allowed me to hide; it was about my comfort and not about the Schroeder's legitimate needs. And while the shame was horrible to experience, it was still about me and not about them. I had to get out of my story and focus on theirs."

As she began to deepen her self-reckoning, Kathy had to step beyond her own limitations. "She had to get past the 'yes, but' which is the way I heard her describe it." Jim Hannon saw how Kathy was making excuses for her behavior. "Yes, I did a terrible thing but look at what Kissinger and McNamara and the others did. Yes, I made a bad decision but it was in the context of this atrocity. In the language of the twelve-step program, and particularly the fourth step, while she made a searching and fearless moral inventory of herself she also got to see the reality of what the leaders did about Vietnam. But it was irrelevant." Hannon carefully refines this provocative thought. "In the process of repentance it doesn't matter what other people in our lives do or did. It is the same in a marital relationship. If you want to do such a moral inventory it's not about yes, but he's a jerk or she's a jerk. Rather it's about keeping the focus on the bigger picture and your own involvement and that's hard, it takes time and courage. The 'yes, but' doesn't mean we are ignorant of the other person's stuff, it's just not relevant to this process."

Kathy was willing to do that work. But being so brutally honest with herself was more difficult than she had expected. "I wanted forgiveness. I wanted to receive forgiveness. I wanted to earn forgiveness. But it was so hard. And the hardest parts were my defensiveness, the fearfulness that I was a monster, that I would be unforgivable, and the comfort of not looking at what I'd done," she confesses with sadness in her voice. "And I did that. I really, really laid myself bare. I was utterly connected with the harm and suffering that my actions had caused, the holes in lives they had left, the fears they had created. But there was this one place where I was blocked, the last of the 'yes buts', which was the generals and the whole war machinery. It was: How come Robert MacNamara, who's responsible for all these deaths doesn't have to be held accountable but I do? I was so aware of this unjust order where some people get away with bad things and other people are made to pay. I was in prison with prostitutes but the johns didn't get prosecuted. So the johns and the generals, and all the people who are responsible for all kinds of suffering, why didn't they have to answer for it? I was really stuck there and I knew it. And it wasn't getting me anywhere."

A powerful breakthrough led Kathy to a deeper understanding of the forgiveness she so wanted. What she came to realize was that she had to forgive those very people she was so angry at. "One day I was sitting in my cell writing about 'why don't they have to,' muttering to myself, and suddenly these words came to me from the 'Our Father' prayer: 'Forgive us our trespasses as we forgive those who trespass against us.' And that was it, that was it! I forgave the generals for being who they were, doing what they did. I forgave the johns. I saw a world of forgiveness where we are all in the embrace of that forgiveness—of that forgivableness. And I saw how I could never get there unless I also got those people I hadn't forgiven there. And I was through."

In 1998 Kathy was up for parole.

Fred Bayles, a reporter at the *Associated Press*, remembers the effect this news had, "A buzz came that Katherine Power was up for parole, and it became emblematic for the whole Vietnam-era issues. Not just who was for and against the war, but who served in the war, who got out of serving in the war, and the idea of privilege. Everyone was asking, do you seek retribution or do you forgive? And as the hearing approached the volume grew in intensity."

The outcome of the parole board meeting surprised everyone. Kathy had done more work with herself than even she had realized. "I walked in with my hands shackled and I sat in a chair facing the parole board. I was alone without an attorney. Five people from the board were there, as well as many members of the Schroeder family and some other people in the back of the room. I was asked really probing questions. Then Clare Schroeder talked about when I had been sentenced and how the family had agreed to it even though it didn't feel long enough. Clare said, 'We like what we are now hearing, but anybody with a brain would know that you need to show remorse at a parole hearing, so it's in her self-interest to do that. But we don't hear that she really feels it.' Then it was my turn to speak and in that moment I knew what I had to do. I told them all that as long as my statement of remorse and accepting responsibility for what I had done was attached to my asking to get out of prison at this time, that my remorse couldn't be seen or heard, so I would withdraw my request for parole."

Bayles was shocked. "It was really a holy shit moment. It stopped everybody in their tracks. What was there to say? She had done more than anybody had expected. Very few people say they were wrong in such a public way, very few are willing to face their p unishment, certainly by today's standards. And then Power said, 'I was wrong, I was slow to admit it, but I admit it now, and I apologize and I will serve out whatever I need to serve out.' I think it was a remarkable moment for society. It certainly just flummoxed those of us in the room. I've seldom seen anything like it in my life."

But it came with a cost. Once back in jail, Kathy had to think about the impact her actions had on her son. "I didn't want to feel disappointed. I didn't feel it was right, because I was so aware that my son really needed me. I was worried about him and that I couldn't go and be with him. I tried to explain this to the parole board, that it wasn't about getting away from the hardship of prison but that my son needed me." Still, today, this memory of her son's pain cuts through her measured delivery. "It was very hard to know that it was going to be another year and a half before I could be with him."

Clare Schroeder

Kathy's acknowledgment of arrogance and her willingness to atone further moved the Schroeder family but it did not change their view that she should serve out her time. Nor did it change their views about the appropriateness of forgiveness. Erin Schroeder-Withington, the youngest Schroeder daughter, said at the time, "I respect her for the fact that she withdrew her request and that in essence she did that for my family. Do I support parole at a later date? No, not at all."

Clare Schroeder agrees that Kathy had shown some remorse. "The fact that she was doing something beneficial for us said something in regards to the growth that had occurred, that she was able to acknowledge on a greater level than in the past what she had done and the harm that it had caused. Certainly, I did admire the fact that she requested to withdraw her request for parole and to stay longer, because it goes against the grain of what a person would want to do," she says thoughtfully. "Katherine is not a monster, in some respects she is a good person who had a need to atone for what she did and redeem herself. She did not get up that day and say, 'Today we are going to kill Walter Schroeder.' It was not an intentional thought. But I have to look at her not as who she is but as what she did. When you are directly responsible for the death of a human being, when you entered into activities and actions that you knew or absolutely should have known would result in that, it's not forgivable. Because what she did is not something that I have the authority or the power to excuse or forgive. I am not the dead person, my father is. He's not here to say what she did was okay and he never will be. In my eyes what she did was not okay; it will never be okay. Very simply, I do not see that it is forgivable."

Curious, Janet Landman asked Kathy what she had hoped for with respect to the Schroeder family. "Kathy said—and I'll never forget this—'I have no right to expect anything from them, I have no right to ask anything of them. It feels to me like a violation of them as victims to say that they have some further work to do.' And that seemed so right to me," Landman is visibly moved. "It's at variance with some of the thinking in our culture today that suggests that if we've hurt someone we should make an inventory of how we've hurt them, make it explicit, go to them, confess, apologize, and then ask for forgiveness. But to me, that point in her thinking seemed more right. It would have been adding insult to injury to expect or even to ask for forgiveness."

By this time, Kathy had realized that atonement and forgiveness were considerably more complicated than she had once thought, and that while repentance was essential it must be undertaken without any expectation that forgiveness automatically follows. Moreover, forgiveness wasn't something that was to be given to her. Rather, it was something she needed to give herself.

Political consultant Sally Castleman, a friend who visited her regularly in jail, watched Kathy reach a place within herself where she no longer needed to be forgiven by anyone else other than herself. "It was a very interesting journey to take with Katherine, to follow her growth and her different iterations from, 'I need to tell the story of the war' to 'I need forgiveness from this woman' to the realization that she could let go of needing to be forgiven by Clare and the Schroeder family. She really got that she'd probably never get it, and that was okay, it wasn't even important anymore. Once she had the realization that she had to take responsibility for her role in what had happened and the depth of the damage, then she knew that she was the person who needed to forgive herself. It wasn't about anything out there or anyone else; there was no one who could get her off the hook. The forgiveness she was looking for was essentially from herself."

In 1999, after serving six years, Kathy was released from prison. "When I finished my sentence a certain set of obligations was satisfied. I had done what had to be done. It's not as if I got to a place that said okay, the past didn't happen. No, the past did happen. And the suffering and the harm that came into people's lives, it will always live on in them. I am aware of that. It's just that I was no longer solely defined by it. I think that this is what we mean when we say that someone has paid their debt. It means that we are no longer defining them by one moment in their life and its consequences."

Clare Schroeder disagrees, although without any anger or bitterness. "I understand her desire not to be defined by a moment or by a single act. But sadly, it's like the bell that's rung and can't be unrung. It is a moment that is fixed in time and it can't be changed. Regrettably, my life and her life intersect at that moment." Clare shakes her head, sadly. "And the same is true of my family and of so many others for whom her name and the death of my father are synonymous. So, in my mind, it's inevitable, this will always define her. But it doesn't mean she can't go on to be the person that she hopes to become. That's a great goal and I wish her well with it."

Shortly after her release, Kathy presented at a public forum on peace, where she spoke strongly against the use of violence in the quest for the end of war. "The consequences in other people's lives of acting out my rage will always be a story that I know. That is why I feel obligated to talk to people about the politics of rage. It is a cautionary tale. I was so wrong in my thinking, so caught up in what mattered to me that I acted in a way that destroyed a life and left its mark of loss on a whole community of people. That doesn't go away."

For Jim Hannon, Kathy's deep engagement with repentance went well beyond what society normally expects from its wayward citizens and disgraced politicians. "Kathy is the gold standard, a model for a nation that has so often confused cheap grace with the real thing. I think it is a very powerful invitation for us to engage in this process, and she offers us a kind of road-map. When I think of Kathy I'm reminded of Flannery O'Connor's line, 'reality is something that we must be returned to at considerable cost.' The process is slow because if it wasn't we would all disintegrate were we able to see ourselves fully in a moment of clarity. Never mind looking at the face of God, simply looking at ourselves would be too much. I think that Kathy's journey is one that is shared by all of us; it's a very human journey and that is what's so compelling about it."

Having watched Kathy find her peace, Janet Landman agrees, "I sometimes see it as a Dark Pilgrimage. It is dark because much of it is done alone in the secret grotto of mind and heart. It's dark because it hurts. It is painful. Peeling layers of defensiveness away is not easy. To be able to admit, as she did, that she carried this blind rebelliousness in herself up to the age of fifty, to admit that is painful. And yet I do see it as a pilgrimage with light at the end, and the possibility of redemption."

Kathy's story resonates on yet another level: the political. It raises questions about our own unfinished moral business as a nation that has yet to come to terms with the war that changed our lives. Her personal drama of atonement and forgiveness mirrors the larger political drama of the Vietnam Era. She went to war against war and became an accessory to a crime. She took a private journey of intense self-examination and made a public confession and expiation. On a far larger scale there are some—and Donald Shriver is one of them—who feel that our country has not yet understood nor publicly taken responsibility for the dimensions of our actions.

Rev. Shriver believes that the Vietnam War Memorial in Washington D.C. is the beginning of a long deferred journey of introspection. He describes it "a symbolic offering of grief, a place where veterans and their families come, putting their hands and their tears on lost friends and relatives." But, as he reminds us, "With the exception of Robert MacNamara there has not yet been a single confession of error by our leaders, nor an acknowledgment to our veterans that they were sent to fight a war of questionable purpose, one that many officials at the time knew was unwinnable."

FORGIVENESS IN THE PUBLIC REALM

THE LANGUAGE OF PUBLIC APOLOGY

Willy Brandt

Forgiveness is that human capacity to allow the past to be past, to release yourself from it, to feel that you are not going to constantly repeat it. And this opens the possibility of a new life, of a new beginning. It was the urgent hope of many people after the war that it could do this, not only for individuals but also for groups, tribes, and nations. — Elisabeth Young-Bruehl

Forgiveness, reconciliation, and apology—all close relatives—are the lingua franca of our day, blowing through the world as never before. They have always played an essential role in the lives of individuals, but in the last thirty years they have migrated into the political realm and into the lives of nations. Historically, strong nations would neither acknowledge nor apologize for the harm they did, but since World War II and the Nuremberg trials this has slowly begun to change. We live in an age of public apology; some say a tsunami of apologies. For the first time individuals have been held accountable for crimes against humanity. There is a new understanding that nations cannot successfully move into the future without dealing with the dark corners of their past. This awareness marks an extraordinary shift in consciousness.

Psychotherapist Elisabeth Young-Bruehl, the biographer of Hannah Arendt, describes this remarkable shift as "a sea change" and argues how World War II birthed a despair that enabled this new thinking. "The world seemed so outrageous. Not just the horrors of war but the Holocaust and the 'unthinkable' possibility of nuclear weapons. While the treaties, trials, and end-of-war ceremonies were important, how could they address what we had been through? Populations had been eradicated; societies had become so toxic that they looked away while neighbors were murdered. The fear grew that the dark forces released would go on and on and that the survival of the human race was a tenuous matter. There needed to be a dramatic interruption, an internal process of change, rites of expiation, truth, and reconciliation. We needed ways of dealing with each other that could release us from this horrible past, which challenged the whole idea of forgiveness. As the poet T.S. Eliot said, 'After such knowledge, what forgiveness?' And yet it was the very possibility of forgiveness that drew people to think anew."

The Nuremberg trials were arguably a defining moment. It is generally considered that the purpose of these trials was purely punishment, but they also raised profoundly important questions about repair. Once verdicts have been produced and acted upon, what then? What comes after? Or, as the author Thane Rosenbaum frames it, "Can we expect that, simply by punishing wrongdoers, nations will be able to move into the next phase of their history? One of the things we learned from Nuremberg is that it's not enough simply to enter judgment and punish. There also needs to be an aftermath, and this has to include acknowledgments, apologies, and the language of repair, a time when nations own up to what they have done, where they admit and accept collective guilt and responsibility, where they undertake gestures of restitution and reparation. Even that they seek forgiveness. This is all part of the new ethic of our age, and it is very, very important."

It used to be that victims were objects of pity and charity, but the birth of the human rights movement has empowered victims to no longer live in secrecy and shame. On the contrary, they have rights. Paul Van Zyl, who had a front row seat on many truth commissions, notes with visible satisfaction, "No longer do they go cap in hand and say pity me, I want an act of charity, but they are people with distinct rights—and that is something powerful, something assertive. It means that what happened to you was wrong, fundamentally immoral, and you are owed recompense and apology. I think that forgiveness, reconciliation, and apology are the corollary of the notion of rights and they have been quite dramatically birthed into the public arena in the last thirty years."

In Poland, on July 10, 2001, President Kwasniewski apologized to the Jews of his country when he formally admitted that Poles had massacred hundreds of their Jewish neighbors in the small town of Jedwabne in 1941: "For this crime, we should beg the souls of the dead and their families for forgiveness. That is why today, as a citizen and as the president of the Republic of Poland, I beg for forgiveness in my own name and in the name of all Poles whose conscience was shaken by that crime." It was an emotional ceremony that took place at the site of the barn where Jedwabne's Jews had been locked inside and burned alive.

At the sixtieth anniversary of the end of World War II, Japan's Prime Minister Junichiro Koizumi apologized for the great damage and pain Japan had inflicted on their neighbors during the war. "We humbly accept these historical facts and would like to express once again our deep reflections and heartfelt apology." The Emperor expressed "his sincere condolences."

In France, on July 16, 1995, French president Jacques Chirac acknowledged the role that the French state had played in deporting its own Jews to Nazi death camps during World War II. "The criminal acts of the German occupiers were assisted by French people and by the French state ... these black hours will stain our history forever and are an injury to our past and our traditions."

Whether cynical or sincere, coerced or voluntary, enduring or ephemeral, these apologies are proliferating and they play a central role in world events. Thane Rosenbaum underlines this with precision and poetry, "Public apologies that are sincerely stated are knee buckling. They are mystical in their form, completely disabling. When individuals and/or nations undertake true gestures of acknowledgment, contrition and remorse, when one is in the presence of that, it has a truly restorative healing power. It's actually quite magical. It opens a pathway to repair; it's the alchemy of giving a traumatized victim some restoration of their dignity."

Paul Van Zyl, who is critical of the frequent failure of public apologies to move beyond symbolism into the realm of recompense, acknowledges that we should never underestimate their power, even at the symbolic level. "At its best, apology is about a fundamental reckoning with what is right and wrong. It is about the defining line between civilization and barbarity, and apology is what you do when you cross that line. It calls us back to what we ought to be."

Great national apologies require not only will but also humility. Sometimes the most powerful apology is unspoken. In 1970 Chancellor Willy Brandt from West Germany—who had absolutely nothing in his wartime past to apologize for because he had been a fierce anti-Nazi living in exile during World War II—visited the Warsaw Ghetto Uprising Memorial in Poland. In a completely spontaneous gesture he fell to his knees, overwhelmed.

Many people wondered how he could have done this. "The nation of Poland was immobilized by this gesture. Jews around the world were shocked by it. Should he have knelt down?" asks Rosenbaum, especially as there were many in Germany who were not ready for contrition and even vilified Brandt as a traitor. "It was the ultimate expression of penitence on behalf of the collective of the German people, and he was deeply and profoundly aware of the enormity of what had been done. Some historians describe it as the turning point in German-Polish relations and, perhaps, the beginning of Germany's public atonement for the Holocaust. As such, it was an astonishing gesture. In that moment, the chancellor dignified the entire experience of apologies in a national and global way."

Years later, when asked about this moment, Willy Brandt simply said, "As I stood on the edge of Germany's historical abyss, feeling the burden of millions of murders, I did what people do when words fail."

A spoken apology that is generally considered the gold standard and may be the defining moment in the history of race relations in Australia, is the apology made by the Australian Prime Minister Kevin Rudd on February 13, 2008. On that day he apologized in Parliament, "To the Aborigine people for the laws and policies of successive governments that inflicted profound grief, suffering and loss on these, our fellow Australians. For the indignity and degradation of a proud people, we say sorry." He singled out the 'Stolen Generations' of thousands of children who had been forcibly removed from their families. "We apologize for the pain, suffering, and hurt of these stolen generations. We say sorry."

Rudd received a standing ovation inside the Chambers and throughout the country. People watched the speech on huge screens erected on city squares, or listened in on radios, and there were tears and celebration.

This remarkable apology was the culmination of a decade of national debate. Aborigines were invited into local parliaments to tell their stories. Chief magistrates began to apologize, as did heads of churches, welfare agencies, trade unions, parents and teacher organizations. A National Sorry Day became an annual event. Against this tide, the conservative government that refused to offer an apology was voted out of power and it became the first priority of the new government. The day the apology was offered was described as "an historic day in the life of the nation."

Along with everyone else in Australia, Bishop Geoffrey Robinson was watching the apology and attributed its success, in part, to there being no conditions put upon it. "No yes, buts, or ifs. Rudd just looked straight at the Aborigines who were in Parliament on that day and, after the apology was repeated three times, he said these were only words but here also is action in the form of the reimbursement fund, and he spelled out how the government would be held accountable. The only sorry note to the day was that the leader of the opposition got up and tried to place some conditions. This went down like a lump of lead and many of the Aborigines and members of Parliament stood up and turned their backs on him—a story told and retold with great relish."

However, Van Zyl adds a cautionary note, "Yes, it was extraordinarily moving seeing thousands of Aboriginal people watching these television screens, bursting into tears, and the symbolism of the act meant the world to them, but if it stops at that it is insufficient. And that's both the great power of apology and its great danger. It's the famous Archbishop Tutu story about stealing someone's bike, apologizing for having done so, but then riding off into the sunset with it. If it becomes empty rhetoric then it is not the beginning of true amends."

In America, President Reagan apologized to its Japanese American citizens. In August 1988, he said, "Shortly after the bombing of Pearl Harbor, a hundred and twenty thousand persons of Japanese ancestry living in the United States were forcibly removed from their homes and placed in make-shift internment camps. This action was taken without trial, without jury. It was based solely on race. The legislation that I am about to sign provides for a restitution payment to each of the sixty thousand survivors. Yet no payment can make up for those lost years. For here, we admit a wrong."

And yet it has been hard for America to admit other wrongs, preferring to look forwards and not backwards. Like many countries, it has its own dark corners, particularly its tormented history with its native people. Since the first arrival of Europeans on their shores, Native Americans have suffered the appropriation of their lands, broken treaty after broken treaty, forced assimilation, and near annihilation. Unlike Australia, America has never fully acknowledged nor apologized. The Museum of the American Indian bears powerful witness to this ignored past. Theologian Rev. Donald Shriver believes, "One of the important meanings of the museum for Native Americans is that it says 'we are still here and we need to be recognized as part of this country and its history.' This is the least that we owe them as citizens."

Many also feel that we have not yet collectively expiated our guilt for the enslavement of African Americans. The Civil War was fought, in part, to end slavery, but America has not yet publicly atoned, as South Africa has done, for the reality and horror of institutionalized crimes based upon race.

The power of a successful apology serves to underscore the insult of a weak or delayed one. On at least a hundred occasions Pope John Paul II apologized for church injustice, invoking crimes against Jews, women, even reaching back over the centuries to the Crusades and the Inquisition. He spoke eloquently of the need of moral reckoning as the year 2000 approached, and about "the purification of memory" that could come through apology. And yet, he could not apologize for one of the greatest failures of the church: the sexual abuse of children by priests. Finally, his successor, Pope Benedict, apologized repeatedly on his trip to America in 2008 and thereafter. He met with the victims and expressed his remorse and shame for the church's failures, though much of the damage was already done.

Bishop Geoffrey Robinson, who lost his parish by speaking out with brutal candor against such behavior, considers this crisis of sexual exploitation in the church as one of the worst chapters in its history. "This is not an evil somewhere out on the edge, this is right at the heart of the community. These are priests sexually abusing children. It's hard to think of a more complete denial of everything Jesus Christ stood for. And it's about bishops looking away, in some cases even enabling them. We lose all credibility on every other subject until we confront this part of our legacy."

He believes that public apology is central to the recovery of both the institution and the victims, whose sense of meaning and trust in people—and in God—has been shattered. "In all my dealings with victims of sexual abuse in the church, I have found that most of all they want an apology in the strongest sense of that word. They want someone to say: 'What happened to you was wrong. You were not in any way at fault. You were the victim of a more powerful person who abused the authority that the church had given them.' Sadly, this apology has rarely come from a priest, so it has to come from the institution behind the offender and the higher up the better, right up to the Pope. It helps give them back something of value to their lives, it says you matter, you are a person with dignity."

New ways of seeking apology and forgiveness have surfaced in the last few decades. In Latin America and throughout the non-Western world, societies emerging from violent conflict have revived native courts and created commissions searching for the truth of what occurred. They ask painful questions about how best to deal with the demons from their past, and whether forgiveness has a role in shaping a new future. They focus on reconciliation and healing, rather than investigation and punishment.

These commissions are continuing a history of oral testimonies, where both survivors and perpetrators speak out about what happened to them, preserving historical truth. Survivors of atrocities are invited to give evidence at public hearings, often recounting deeply disturbing tales of torture and suffering. In Sierra Leone, for example, a woman bravely testified that not only were her parents and other relatives killed, but that she had to watch her father have his throat cut and was then given his blood to drink.

In 2006 the Liberian Truth Commission was launched at the end of two civil wars in which 250,000 people were killed. Many of the perpetrators refused to testify but one of the worst killers did confess and was, remarkably, forgiven.

Joshua Blahyi was an infamous rebel leader during the Liberian first civil war in the 1990s. Along with his followers he was responsible for twenty thousand deaths. At the end of the war he stopped his rampage, claiming a dramatic conversion had freed him of satanic power. Today, he is a successful evangelist preaching forgiveness and reconciliation. When he testified at the Liberian Truth Commission, however, he confessed to human sacrifice, including draining the blood of living victims and eating the hearts of children before battle. "We would get drunk and drugged up, then sacrifice a local teenager and drink his blood. We would strip down to our shoes and go into battle slaughtering anyone we saw, chopping off their heads and using them as soccer balls. We were naked, fearless, drunk, and homicidal. We killed so many people that I lost count." In an unforgettable moment he was asked by one of the commissioners, aghast, her voice trembling as she struggled for words: "Do you expect the people who hear your confession today to forgive you?" Blahyi paused, looked around the room, and murmured, "I want to say sorry to the nation. I want to say I am sorry." He then covered his eyes and lowered his head.

His weak apology challenged the meaning of forgiveness, pushing it to the very limits and possibly beyond. And, in fact, there are many critics of these commissions who worry that public forgiveness can be shallow and may invite repentance that isn't genuine. They are concerned that too often it preempts prosecution and punishment, thus allowing terrible criminals to go free. For them, forgiveness for a mass atrocity is an obscenity.

As South Africa emerged from years of apartheid atrocities it needed a way to heal the country. It too faced critics who worried that justice would be sacrificed in the name of reconciliation. There was new equality with black and white voting side by side, but the brutality of its past had created a deep hurt and lingering hostility, as well as vast economic disparities that endure to this day. The Truth and Reconciliation Commission was initiated to address this need by creating a public venue where both the voices of those who had committed the atrocities and those who were affected by them could be heard. If the perpetrators fully and honestly admitted their crimes, often face to face with the survivors of those crimes, they would be granted amnesty. As Archbishop Tutu, co-founder of the TRC with Nelson Mandela, explains, "Our objective was to find out the truth in order to assist in the process of healing our land."

The TRC took apology global because it occurred in public and in the fullness of day, not behind closed doors, and it was on the front pages for three years. It brought questions that would otherwise have been dealt with quietly onto the streets, onto televisions screens, and transmitted them across the world. This meant conversations that started in the TRC spilled out into churches, over dinner tables, within the halls and corridors of power, in businesses, and on sports fields. Paul Van Zyl, one the architects of the TRC who was present throughout its proceedings, attests to its ubiquity: "It permeated every aspect of South African society. It gave victims and perpetrators an opportunity to tell their stories in public and brought them into direct contact with each other. And that, more than anything else, caused questions of forgiveness and reconciliation to be thrust into the foreground."

Whereas in South Africa it was one color against another but rarely did the two live side-by-side, in Rwanda the Hutus and the Tutsis lived next to each other as neighbors. It is impossible to imagine what it must have been like to find someone you have grown up with, gone to school with or shared food with, suddenly and viciously killing your family and community. When it was finally over, how was the country to find peace and heal itself, how where the different peoples to live collectively once again?

The government chose to modify an old system of traditional community gatherings known as gacacas, where victims and criminals would share their stories and be judged by the entire village. There were doubts that such an old system could meet the demands of the far more serious and recent atrocities, but in many cases it has led to apology and reconciliation, albeit a fragile one. Instead of wanting revenge, dreaming of it and even planning for it, genocide survivor Celestin Buhundra said, "We can perhaps find forgiveness so that the next generation will not continue to feel the hatred."

Critics voice apprehension that in the urgent need to move beyond the carnage, shattered countries can inadvertently create a culture of impunity.

Especially when the issue at stake is that of torture. There can be no discussion about forgiveness if we leave this out for it has become the coin of our realm. In the words of the most eloquent survivor of torture, Jean Amery, "Torture is the unforgivable, it is the most horrible event that a human being can retain within himself.

Whoever was tortured stays tortured, even when no clinically objective traces can be detected." Over the centuries, there has been mounting revulsion against torture, leading nations to sign treaties declaring it a crime against humanity. For Chilean author Ariel Dorfman, who puts torture at the center of some of his writing, "Our revulsion against torture is a wisdom that has taken thousands of years of tribulation and shame to achieve. A wisdom that we are now being asked to throw away."

For today in America, we are being confronted by the use of torture during "the war on terror." For a while, debate raged about what to do until the financial recession moved any soul searching to the side. But there are still voices—and their numbers grow—who feel that America has lost its way in the war on terror and that at some point we must undergo a moral reckoning with this dark chapter in our history. Patricia Haynor, a scholar of the world's truth commissions and international law, raises this question forcefully: "We have changed from a country that was trying to advocate human rights policies and standards to one that was actually setting standards of practicing torture for purposes of intelligence gathering. Now that just can't be right. Have we really faced up to what we, as a country, have done in the last years, and can we reconcile with our own past?"

The failure to acknowledge and apologize contains another hidden danger, believes Paul Van Zyl. "Once you say that a nation is threatened by a group of ill defined terrorists who pose an existential threat to your idea of what civilization is and to your own way of life, and once you say that you can commit criminal and illegal acts in response to that threat, then you abandon the fundamental rule of law and civilization as we know it. So an apology is not just an acknowledgment to the victims, as crucial as that is, but it is also an insurance policy that we don't do it again."

Perhaps the clearest evidence of the power of apology is what happens when it is withheld, and this is best demonstrated with the Armenian genocide that took place in the last fury of the Ottoman Empire. The number of Armenian that died was over a million. Armenians have not forgotten it; Turks deny it. For the Armenians, this denial is the second genocide. Each year on April 24 in Times Square and throughout the world, Armenians gather together to remember the first day of the genocide in 1915. They vow never to forget.

Her life shaped by this obsession, documentary filmmaker Carla Garapedian raises her voice as she tries to be heard over the gathering. "I can't turn my back on what happened for it would be like turning my back on my grandfather, on my family, and on the one and a half million who were killed."

"From the spring through the end of 1915, more than two million of the Armenian Christian minority population in Turkey were arrested and deported." Author Peter Balakian's grandmother was the sole survivor in his family. "They were put on death marches, women were raped, abducted, murdered. The killing was done with hatchets, axes, knives, and farm tools. It was a slaughterhouse, the first genocide of the modern era, the genocide that was the template for all genocides to come in the twentieth century. The denial, the withholding of recognition, acknowledgment, and apology, strived to create a counterfeit universe for the victims. A whole civilization was wiped out, a 2,500-year-old culture disappeared, all its art and buildings, as well as its people. And to pretend, as the perpetrators want us to, that this didn't happen, is to send a message that this kind of systematic mass killing doesn't matter and demands no moral accountability. Indeed, Hitler was inspired by the fact that the Turkish government was able to mass murder a million people alone in 1915, a million and a half people in total before World War I was over."

There were very few witnesses to this crime. "The ache and the trauma that this has continued to cause in the Armenian people will not go away," says Thane Rosenbaum. "Instead, there is this steadfast denial and defensiveness on the part of Turkey that it never took place, that this was never genocide. Not only does the rest of the world acknowledge it happened, but the only party that we need to hear the words of historical truth from is the one nation that is the most unrepentant: Turkey."

This withholding of acknowledgment and apology has a deeply corrosive effect. Peter Balakian has seen it close up, not only in his own family but also in the community at large. "Some Armenians find themselves stuck in a rut, locked in an endless repetition of grief and anger. The perpetrator is replaying his power, but now it is psychological rather than physical violence. Just imagine what it would be like for modern-day Jews if the Germans denied the extermination of six million Jews with the same aggressiveness with which the Turks deny the genocide? The destructiveness of this on the psyche of Jews and on their relationship with Germany seems hard to imagine, but it's happening today between the Armenians and Turks."

If, as Paul Van Zyl believes, "Apologies were just about symbolism then they would be made at the drop of a hat. But more importantly they are about power. And that is what makes them so difficult to extract."

When asked to describe the ideal response from Turkey, Balakian pauses. "Sometimes I imagine how Turkey could admit that it committed this genocide in a time of its own desperation and that now, looking back, not only does it apologize for the atrocities but wishes to make efforts to preserve whatever pieces of Armenian civilization there still are. If this were to happen I think the walls of rage and isolation and anger would start to dissolve. Forgiveness is that end place you come to when you have acknowledged the humanity of the wrong doer in some fundamental way." Then he quickly shifts into a tone of toughness, wary of sounding naïf, a dreamer: "But that is not an imaginable reality until the Turkish government asks for forgiveness, and right now we are a million miles away from that."

A skeptic in the forgiveness world, Van Zyl sees this yearning as a paradox: both an illusion and absolutely necessary. Having witnessed the aftermath of genocides, he considers these last decades as a time of great trauma and anguish, punctuated by apartheid, military dictatorships, 9/11, terrorism, the fear of nuclear weapons, and environmental degradation. He sees human beings trying to find "some silver bullet that can return us to a safe place, that can allow us put the world back together again." He develops this idea carefully, trying to achieve the right balance between resignation and hopefulness. "When something terrible happens between parent and child, or between husband and wife, we hope we can put back together what has been shattered by saying, 'I am so terribly sorry, I wish it hadn't happened, and I hope that we can go back to where we were before these terrible things occurred.' In the same way the use of apologies in the international community has been a sense of asking: 'Can't we go back to a more simple, innocent, and benevolent time?' That may be an illusion, but humanity is in part dependent on illusions to help us deal with the traumas of everyday life."

Notwithstanding Turkey's reluctance to face its history, many other nations have. And for Rosenbaum, this is significant. "I think that some nations have realized that there is an obligation to admit moral failure and to undertake gestures of acknowledgment, repair, reconciliation, remembering, and forgiveness. We are all better off if truths are not buried and forgotten, then the ghosts of the dead can somehow rest easier. We must listen to survivors and victims and take testimony from perpetrators. And most especially, we must not forget. We may be unable to prevent these horrors from happening again, but the soul of a nation depends on memory, a moral reckoning, and owning what has taken place."

"Everyday we see images from all over the world of bodies being exhumed. From the mass graves of Shites in Iraq, to Jews in Lithuania, to the killing fields in Rwanda, and those who disappeared in Argentina, the victims of civil wars, of states turning on their own, and of genocide." Thane Rosenbaum acknowledges that the impulse to dig up these bodies is often inspired by citizens and resisted by governments. But not always. "What is remarkable is that nations could just let these bodies rest in unmarked mass graves but they don't, and part of their motivation is the recognition that the unearthing of a past, the unburying of these dark truths, is essential to the health of the nation. It is forced to confront the enormity of its misdeeds, as if it knows that these bones tell important truths that are neglected at our peril."

South Africa's Search for Truth and Reconciliation: OWNING THE PAST

Paul Van Zyl

What does it mean for a nation to come to terms with its past? Do nations, like individuals, have psyches? Can a nation's past make people ill, just as repressed memories sometimes make individuals ill? Conversely, can a nation be reconciled to its past, as individuals can by replacing myth with fact and lies with truth? Can we speak of nations working through a civil war or atrocity as we speak of individuals working through a traumatic memory or event? These are mysterious questions, but they are urgent and practical ones too. And when it comes to healing, one is faced with the most mysterious process of all. — Michael Ignatieff PC MP, "Articles of Faith"

In the last thirty years over half of the world's nations—a stunning number—have undergone a transition from dictatorships to democracies, albeit fragile ones. As the old orders fell in South America, Africa, and parts of Eastern Europe painful questions arose about how to deal with the past, especially histories of mass atrocities, apartheid, and genocide. Should the tyrants be put on trial for their crimes? Can the victim's pain be assuaged? Will the perpetrators be held accountable? Will the new society be more or less stable if it searches its soul? Can the country heal and reconcile if it doesn't?

Since the 1970s, there have been more than thirty truth commissions across the world that have struggled with these questions, offering as many different solutions as there are political philosophies and religious thought. They are attempts to grapple with alternative ways to build a sustainable peace that previous political attempts have routinely failed to accomplish. Propelled by two forceful elders of unquestioned moral integrity, President Nelson Mandela and Archbishop Desmond Tutu, the South African Truth and Reconciliation Commission was one of the most extraordinary efforts to deal with a brutal past in a proactive, innovative, compassionate and morally ambitious manner.

Truth commissions have become a powerful part of the political fabric in transitional societies and beyond. Benjamin Nienass, a PhD candidate at the New School, has focused his research on the intersection between forgiveness and politics. "Often, these commissions complement traditional approaches of punitive justice, based on an understanding of the important role a full disclosure of the historical facts can play in building a new life in common. The South African TRC remains one of the most ambitious examples. Many believe that its main achievement rests in the fact that certain truths about the apartheid regime can simply no longer be denied, certain lies no longer be told.

"The TRC was ambitious not only in its vigilant pursuit of truth, but also in stressing its mandate to foster reconciliation in a deeply torn society. It was a multifaceted project with many different actors and locations, and whoever searches for the one guiding principle of the commission is doomed to fail." Nienass is passionate in his understanding of the complexity involved. "The lawyer's view stresses the principle of amnesty, and the psychologist's view emphasizes the individual healing processes and the importance of testimony, while the priest's view explicitly introduces forgiveness and repentance. Within the commission, these different views were constantly renegotiated and, as a result, there was no overarching definition of reconciliation to speak of."

Undertaking a comprehensive investigation into past gross violations of human rights and building on the history of commissions that had preceded it, the TRC developed a sweeping mandate to bring both victims and perpetrators to the table. It granted amnesty to those who came forward to tell the whole truth of their crimes and could persuade the commission that these were political in nature; and it sought out the victims to give them a chance to tell their stories.

More than any other truth commission that preceded it, the TRC brought the language of apology, forgiveness, and reconciliation to the fore and into public debate. While forgiveness was never explicitly stated as the commission's goal nor referred to in its title, forgiveness was very much in the air. It was present in the early discussions that planners had about their mandate; it was present during the televised proceedings that began and ended with hymns and prayer; and it was there when Archbishop Tutu urged witnesses to forgive, praising those who could and expressing sorrow for those who couldn't. In fact, as social anthropologist Richard Wilson remarks, "the virtue of forgiveness and reconciliation were so loudly applauded that emotions and bitterness were rendered unacceptable, an ugly intrusion on a peaceful healing process."

Among some Christian scholars there was debate about Archbishop Tutu's appropriation of the religious language of forgiveness. Sondra Wheeler, a moral theologian and professor of Christian Ethics at Wesley Theological Seminary, recognizes both the cost and the gain. "Tutu was trying to effect a modest political miracle in South Africa after all the atrocities, at this precarious moment in its history. So, with all the best intentions, he used the language of forgiveness and reconciliation very consciously—to a political end. In the process, the language was taken out of its own rich liturgical complexity of repentance, contrition, and self-examination. You can't run a political enterprise with all those resonances intact. However, the great risk is that you cheapen the process. There's a shallowing of the language. The premise of forgiveness in the religious tradition isn't just acknowledgment and truthfulness—and that's a lot—but actual transformation. This is an impossibly high standard politically. So what you get is a promise of amnesty from prosecution."

As one of the youngest architects of the TRC, Paul Van Zyl considers that those moments when the TRC, "sought to force reconciliation and manufacture forgiveness were when we were at our weakest. Forgiveness is complex. It's not switched on and off like a light. And it's not something that should be attempted under the glare of television cameras before a national audience. Rather, it is deeply personal, very intimate, and extraordinarily spiritual. What the TRC did was to create conditions in which people could arrive at those moments on their own. That said, I think that the TRC made a new South Africa possible and it came at a moment when it seemed that we had walked to the edge of an abyss. The very real possibility of South Africa exploding into internecine bloodshed was on all our minds."

At the very least, the TRC helped to prevent the country from walking into that abyss. In fact, many would claim that it did much more than that. Now, fourteen years later, some of the South Africans who helped to create the commission and participated in it share their memories and thoughts, recalling the extraordinary drama of those years and pondering its legacy. While their stories diverge widely on the accomplishments and shortcomings of the TRC, they all reveal the remarkable ability of the hearings to bring perpetrator and victim into a shared and open space, which stood in powerful symbolic opposition to the covert and violent politics of the previous apartheid regime.

"The Truth Commission came shortly after the democratic elections of South Africa. For the first time we all voted, black and white as equals, it was a marvelous moment," smiles Albie Sachs, a judge on the Constitutional Court of South Africa, who witnessed the momentous change facilitated by the TRC. "As the hearings began, in April 1996, of course we all had questions: What about the pain of the past, that unrequited, repressed feeling of extreme anguish amongst so many people who had suffered torture, or lost parents, children or neighbors? Were we going to say nothing about that? Were we just going to say it was all over and let's forget the past? No, that couldn't be. We had to own up to what we'd done, that it was against our values and the very things we'd been fighting for, so we could come clean into the new society. Then we could move forward.

"The strength of the legal process is that it is both dispassionate and outside of the individuals who are involved, but that's also its weakness. It means it is lacking in humanity and concern." Although he supports prosecutions, Sachs also sees them as being fundamentally limited. "You get a guilty verdict according to the law but you can't penetrate into the deeper reaches of their story. You never hear answers to the most essential questions, such as how could you do this, what were the circumstances? The TRC was a remarkably different and more humane alternative to this as it responded to an ache that we reconnect with each other. Often the commission would meet in very poor areas, in a school or church hall, and people would walk a long way to get there. It would start with Archbishop Tutu and all the participants singing together. And then the victims would talk and talk and talk. They expressed the most acute forms of intense anger, the hurt, the pain, the injustices that were not only serious in themselves but were made more serious by being denied. The process facilitated people to come forward and say, 'Yes, I did that, these were the circumstances, this is why I did it.' In this way it lanced the boil.

"It was called the Truth and Reconciliation Commission, not the Truth, Reconciliation and Forgiveness Commission, nor the Truth, Reconciliation and Justice Commission, just truth and reconciliation," Sachs makes this point emphatically, his lined face having witnessed years of truth telling. "There were Muslims, Hindus, Jews, atheists, and agnostics on the commission, so it wasn't related to any particular faith or world view. It was simply a public acknowledgment of what had happened. One of the things about the TRC that astonished and even worried me was that so much truth just came pouring out, the emotion that was involved was volcanic, we just knew, yes, yes, this is real. These things happened. Saying sorry when you've done something that's so unpardonable can seem almost impossible, but in the process you are facing up to the truth and that is what's so important."

The amnesty clause became one of the key and most essential differences with other truth commissions. "The ability for perpetrators to apply for amnesty if they told the truth was remarkable," says Susan Collin Marks, senior vice president of Search for Common Ground and well experienced in conflict resolution. "Sometimes—and these were rare occasions—they expressed remorse, even apologized, and it was profoundly moving. But an apology wasn't required for we knew that if it were coerced then its sincerity would always be in question. Due to its public nature many people, black and white, were able to experience the pain of those who had been victims of the apartheid regime. They truly saw, often for the first time, what this had all meant. It was an unfolding story of horror but also of heroism. As chairman, Archbishop Tutu brought great humanity and humility to the table, he wasn't afraid to weep at what he heard. He showed us how, when we're willing to be in our hearts, we can still have the gravitas and credibility to be seen as a leader."

The hearings were tough to listen to and tough to participate in. And some, as Albie Sachs remembers, were excruciating. "We know people were assassinated, we know people were tortured, and we know cruel and evil things were done, but to see an enactment of a particular form of torture done in the courtroom by the torturer in front of his victim and broadcast across the country was something we were not prepared for. The whole nation participated in that drama. Who can ever forget the moment when Tony Yengeni, the young man who had been tortured, turned to Sergeant Benzien and angrily asked him to demonstrate: 'Just show us how you put wet bags over our heads and smothered us so that we felt like we were drowning and then kept them there until we felt our last moments had come.' Someone lay on the floor and Benzien knelt by him, wrapped a plastic bag around his head and gradually pulled the strings. The entire room was riveted until Yengeni, his anger spent, quietly asked: 'What kind of man is it that uses a method like this on other human beings, and then listens to their moans and cries and groans, taking each of those people so near to their deaths? What kind of man is that? What kind of man are you?'"

There is more to this scene beyond its horror, as Sachs tries to explain: "Acknowledgment is taking responsibility for what happened, and it goes further than just the person who put the wet bag over the head of the one being smothered. Who provided the wet bag? Who gave the instructions? Who turned a blind eye and didn't ask questions afterwards? We watched Jeffrey Benzien crying, this man who had the power of life and death over others. He was defeated; it was a moral defeat for all the torturers. But he had come forward and had acknowledged what he'd done and he wasn't being sent to prison. The sight of him crying, and the collapse of the order he defended, was far more powerful than having a trial that could have gone on for two or three years, had problems with getting witnesses, then an appeal, and then wondering why should he go to jail and not the person who commanded him, and the person above that who gave the instructions?"

Another excruciating moment during the proceedings—that was discussed by the entire nation—came while watching Winnie Mandela, the former wife of Nelson Mandela, unable to ask for forgiveness. She had appeared at the commission to testify about the events leading up to the murder of a young activist, Stompie Seipeid. For Professor Pumla Gobodo-Madikizela, coordinator of the victims' public hearings in the Western Cape, the scene was agonizing: "In some ways what happened was the symbol of contradiction in the entire struggle for liberation. Over the nine-day period of that hearing, the mother of this young man sat in the audience waiting and hoping there would be a moment of truth from Winnie Mandela and her body guards, who called themselves the Mandela football club, about the killing of her son. It never came. Archbishop Tutu implored Winnie Mandela to apologize; he came close to falling to his knees. But the statement she offered, according to most people, was false.

"As the meeting was coming to an end, Winnie strutted across the floor to embrace this woman. It was heartwarming to see this mother respond to the embrace, her openness and graciousness, but she had received nothing from Mandela. No recognition, no truth. And although the mother seemed satisfied, saying later to reporters, 'Winnie was a woman of power and to meet her at that level was rewarding,' still there was such a feeling of loss and failure. Winnie had been the mother of the nation, the embodiment of the struggle for freedom, and instead she used her power to offer a superficial, condescending 'we are all in this together' phrase meant to pacify." Pumla shakes her head, "It is almost too painful to talk about."

There were also some remarkable times of forgiveness that added gravitas to the proceedings. "While I believe that they were the exception rather than the rule, they were powerful and to this day are embedded in our memories." Albie Sachs watched sworn enemies reaching accord together. "One in particular was Dawie Ackerman, whose wife was killed by the left wing organization, the Pan African Congress, during a bombing operation in a church in Cape Town. They had come into the church and shot her right in front of his eyes. Now, three years later, they had submitted written statements to the TRC in the hope of receiving amnesty. At the commission hearing, Dawie wanted the bombers to look at him as he directly addressed them: 'I want to ask who actually entered the church? My wife was sitting right at the door when you came in. Can you remember if you shot her? I would like to hear from each one of you, as you look me in the eyes, that you are sorry for what you have done, that you regret it, and that you want to be personally reconciled.'" One of the bombers turned towards him and answered: 'We are sorry for what we have done. I am asking for an apology as we were under orders. I also say, please forgive me.'"

It was deeply moving. Ackerman's face was red, his voice unsteady, his eyes filled with tears. "As each of these men expressed their apology, Dawie witnessed their remorse." Pumla Gobodo-Madikizela was sitting near Ackerman. What was especially significant to her was when he followed up with another question. "He asked, 'Do you remember my wife, she was sitting next to the door and was wearing a blue coat?' As the memory of his wife sitting next to him on the day of the bombing operation returned, he broke down. Even though the likelihood of the perpetrators remembering the identity of the people in the room was almost zero, he had to ask that question. It was not so much about, 'Do you remember my wife who was wearing a blue coat?' but rather, 'Did you recognize the humanity of my wife? The woman I loved, the mother of my children. Did you recognize her as a human being?' The work of recognizing the humanity of the other begins with remorse; without a feeling of remorse, the perpetrator is unable to recognize. What we see in this intricate dance of witnessing on both sides is an opening that can lead to forgiveness."

Careful to dispel any notion of a quick and happy ending, Pumla continues, "Forgiveness is not a simple closure of the chapter, it doesn't mean that now I forget. Rather, it means 'I am integrating the story of this man who is now facing me and looking broken as a result of his actions. I'm integrating this and the fact that he has done these terrible things and I'm seeing him as a whole person.' Deeds that were rightfully considered to be evil, beyond repair, unredeemable, almost unspeakable, and yet we saw the victims reaching out to the perpetrators with words of forgiveness, and we saw the perpetrators apologizing. This was something very new in a political context. Such a demonstration that people can forgive, even in the context of so much tragedy, was a huge lesson for us all in South Africa, for the world really. When we heard the actual words of forgiveness they exploded into the public sphere.

"The defining feature of the commission was its public nature. We were emerging from a past where secrecy had been official, such as covert operations and the security forces of apartheid. The TRC insisted on exposing all the secrets of the past, demanding the men and women who were working for the State to give full disclosure, to open up, to be truthful about what they had done."

Their actions were broadcast loud and clear for all to hear. "The TRC permeated every aspect of South African society and was covered on national television for three solid years. You would have had to be in a coma to ignore it," laughs Paul Van Zyl, director of the International Center for Transitional Justice and known for pioneering new approaches to peace and democracy. "The commission grabbed us by our throats and hearts because human beings find meaning through stories. Some of the most difficult moral and philosophical questions are made accessible to us by storytelling, and through the TRC we came into contact with literally thousands of stories of unimaginable suffering. Some were stories of great heroism, others of great depravity. We heard the words of people who were tortured alongside the voices of those who did the torturing and the killing. We heard the stories of mothers whose children disappeared and the endless agony of that experience. During my years growing up in South Africa I would sit at dinner tables and hear white South Africans' justifications and denials." He pauses, his face showing the seriousness of having witnessed such suffering at a young age. "Now it became very difficult to describe apartheid as a benign, separate but equal experiment, when the next day on television we were hearing a man tell us about five months of barbaric torture and a woman tell about the assassination of her son."

"White South Africans were discovering a completely new country, because apartheid had been so successful that the white community didn't know what had been going on and, in many cases, didn't choose to know," elaborates Susan Collin Marks. "The daily impact of the commission was profound, but for some people it made them put up barriers and say, 'No this can't be true, I don't want to know it.' Significant sections of the white community would turn off the television, wouldn't read the paper and wouldn't attend the hearings, which was a tragedy." She shakes her head in disbelief. "For others it was the most painful journey into what had been there but hadn't been known, acknowledged, or understood. Many of them were changed forever as they faced the enormity of what had been done in their name and on their behalf. The stories being heard were of a brutality they could barely conceive of: brutality against children who were put into prison because they were caught up in a demonstration, against women who were raped and tortured, against men because they had joined the ANC, and brutality even against citizens who had nothing to do with it but were just in the way. There were also stories from the ANC of violence amongst their own cadre, and there were stories of black violence against whites. It cut every way."

"The TRC opened a door for people across the color line to emerge in the possibility of engaging with one another," says Pumla Gobodo-Madikizela. She pauses, collecting herself, for witnessing these meetings has moved her profoundly. "Often a victim would be telling the story of what happened, how they lost their loved ones, and they would break out into this mournful wail that was heard and reverberated throughout the country over the radio waves and through the cities of South Africa. You were impelled to listen. Other victims were moved to identify with the story because it reminded them of their own pain. Recipients of apartheid privilege were moved to ask themselves, 'Where was I when this was happening? I voted for apartheid, I benefited from it, I lived a life of privilege.' It forced people to face themselves, to confront all the complexity, the guilt, pain, and collective shame. In turn, this created the opportunity to discuss the potential for healing."

The white population was also startled to discover how those who had been tortured by the regime were not, as they had thought, limited to the poor black population. Many professional whites were attacked. "I was about to start work in a new parish in Bulawayo, but waiting for me were two religious magazines, one in English and one in Afrikaans, posted from South Africa to my home in Zimbabwe." At the time Anglican priest Father Lapsley was chaplain to the ANC, the anti-apartheid organization that is now the majority party in South Africa. The memory of what happened next is obviously still painful for him. "As I opened the English magazine it exploded in my face with a bomb that had been placed inside its pages. I lost both my hands, my eardrums were shattered, I lost an eye, and I had a range of other injuries. For months I was as helpless as a newborn baby; I could do absolutely nothing for myself. I knew I was on a South African government hit list and, as a result, I'd lived with armed police guards for years and I was always prepared for the possibility of death. What I wasn't prepared for was permanent physical disability. There were many times when I thought that it would've been better to be dead.

"Some years later, I went to the TRC to give evidence. I said I wanted to know who did this, I needed to know why they did it, I needed to know the chain of command. Three names emerged, men who might have been responsible but, to my surprise, when I was given their names I began to cry. Suddenly, it was not the system but it was three real human beings with parents, children, lovers, friends." Father Michael stops to take a deep breath, then slowly continues: "I would like to meet those who did it, but only if they care; I'm not sure that I could handle meeting someone for whom sending a letter bomb was not an issue. But if the person who did it is a prisoner inside himself because of what he did, then I have a key and I'd be happy to turn it.

"For me the enduring emotion has been grief. It is a permanent part of my life; I can never forget I have no hands. Touch is gone forever." He looks momentarily and wistfully at his missing hands. "Sometimes I feel angry towards the political leaders of the apartheid state and their denial of responsibility for what they did. But I don't spend my days being angry. I am well aware of the danger of preferring unforgiveness, the negative power this gives us over another human being. So, I have struggled to make the bombing redemptive in the healing work I do for others who are trying to leave the past behind and move into the future.

"Archbishop Tutu would call the hearings the crying commission. Tears would flow as we heard the stories of kindness and compassion, of our ability to hold each other and to be gentle and tender." Father Michael has continued to seek a sense of completion. "About three or four years ago I was at a healing of memories workshop in Zimbabwe. At the end of the workshop a white man who was there stood up and said, 'I remember when you were bombed in 1990. And I thought you got what you deserved.' No one knew this was coming and the whole room froze. Then he said, 'I want to say I'm sorry.' It was an extraordinary and very healing moment."

Albie Sachs, who worked for the Freedom Movement and was actively involved in the ANC even when in exile, lost his arm and his sight in one eye when South African security agents placed a bomb in his car. He was also tortured. Today, as he reflects on this experience, his condemnation is fierce and absolute. "Torture is absolutely unpardonable from a moral point of view. There is no context that could ever justify torture. It's destructive to the person who is doing it as well as to the person who suffers. It taints the whole of society. I was privileged: I didn't have electric shocks, I wasn't made to stand on bricks for hours, I wasn't hung from the ceiling with a bar between my legs. As a white lawyer I was given the honor of being tortured politely." He pauses, uncertain whether to go on; clearly he prefers to keep this memory to himself. "Everyone has a worst moment in their lives and I don't even have to wonder which is mine. I was kept up all night; probably a drug had been put in my food. They were working on me, working on me. My body was getting weaker and weaker, until eventually I collapsed and fell on the floor. I felt water pouring down on me and I saw these shoes, black and brown shoes, urgently moving around. This was the moment they were waiting for. They lifted me up and pried my eyes open—I remember those fingers of the colonel in charge—and I sat and sat and collapsed again. The whole process was repeated over and over. They were using me against myself, using my capacity for suffering to destroy my sense of dignity."

Despite his injuries and treatment, Sachs has been unable to hold it against the perpetrators. "How do I feel about those men? While I was detained in such confinement, which was awful beyond imagination, I tried to hate the guards and to imagine myself killing them, but I couldn't. I see them as people doing their work, supporting an evil and racist system that justified treating people as subhumans. I see them as people who took it for granted that whites were superior and saw me as a white person who had betrayed his own, worse even than black people. I can see how tortured their brains were. It's not forgiveness that is so important to me. It's much more, how can I understand why these things happened, who the people are who did it, what drove them, what motivated them? What is it that's going to enable us both to live in the same moral world?

"I was interviewed for the *New York Times* and the reporter asked me if I wanted some kind of accountability, to send the people to jail who had done these things. I said no. Then he told me, 'I've just interviewed Nelson Mandela and Walter Sisulu and Ahmed Kathrader, all prominent leaders of the ANC who had more than twenty-five years each in jail, and they said exactly the same thing.' If we repay the perpetrators in kind, even if we do it through due process of law, we're simply maintaining the same story and nothing changes. Instead, we must find a way to get beyond the cruelty and the evil, a way that involves acknowledging what was done was wrong, not in some pious way begging for forgiveness, but by confirming that human beings needn't do these things to other human beings," Sachs's voice is filled with conviction. "That's not the world I want to live in. These men are my neighbors. They live in the same country I live in. Their children go to school with my children, go to university with my children. How can we end this huge gulf between us? How can we start living in one country? How can we start seeing our shared humanity and not simply punish them for what they did?"

Forgiveness became an integral ingredient in the political shift from the dominance of apartheid to equality for all. "Forgiveness is a living thing, it's not abstract," says Susan Collin Marks, a gentle and eternally optimistic peacemaker in her fifties. "We saw it again and again during the course of the transition to democracy. I remember one occasion when a former ANC activist, who had been detained and tortured by the police during the apartheid era, came to a meeting facilitated by the National Peace Accord along with the very police colonel who had been his torturer; he shook his hand and even sat next to him. It was a dramatic and heroic act of forgiveness for it takes huge courage to do that. Forgiveness is not dependent on apology, remorse, or contrition. It is about each individual digging deep within his or herself to find a common humanity with the other, and the willingness to let go of the resentment, pain, and anger that comes with not forgiving. This cannot be made to happen, it cannot be told to happen, it has to be something that each one of us finds within ourselves. When that is inspired to happen collectively then you get a movement that creates forgiveness as a whole new piece of the structure of our world."

"Part of the ability to heal is the recognition that while 'I remain unforgiving then I am damaging myself' for forgiveness is often a form of healthy selfishness. Forgiveness is for my sake, in order that I may be free," explains Anglican priest Father Lapsley. "I remember meeting a woman in Rwanda and she said that she needed to forgive because she didn't want to carry the burden any longer. It was for the sake of her own freedom that forgiveness needed to take place. I also remember Beth Savage, a white woman who had been attacked. She came to the commission and said that she'd like to meet those who had carried out the attack because she wanted to ask their forgiveness for what she had done in her life that had led them to do what they did. That was remarkable, it shook us all."

Eugene de Kock was the head of covert operations and the apartheid government security forces. His role was chief assassin and it earned him the nickname 'Prime Evil.' The story of the widows of the men killed by de Kock, and their encounter with him, epitomizes the potential for forgiveness that came out of the TRC. "He had earlier appeared before the commission and given a full and truthful disclosure of what he had done." Pumla Gobodo-Madikizela was there to witness this man's admission. "After more than ten years this was the first time the widows had heard what happened to their husbands, so when they later met with de Kock there was a readiness, an openness, they already knew the story. One of the widows said to me, 'Eugene de Kock helped us retrace the steps our husbands took to their deaths, so now we can release them and begin the path of mourning.' This is critical, because without mourning we are unable to forgive. The process of mourning is one of recognizing the pain, anger, and frustration, the desire for revenge, the resentment of the other, all of these emotions that we carry.

"In that meeting with de Kock he said to the widows, 'I wish I could bring back their bodies alive and I could say here are your husbands.' In turn, the widows reached out to him with forgiveness. What struck me most were not only their words of forgiveness for him, but also their unconditional expressions of forgiveness. One of the widows said, 'I want to hold Eugene de Kock by the hand and show him that it is possible to change and that there is a future.'" Pumla shakes her head, incredulous. "I was stunned. I wanted to know what they meant by 'I forgive,' and what he meant by his apology, so I interviewed him in jail over a period of three months. What I discovered was a man deeply broken and remorseful. At one moment in our conversation his body started to shake and I spontaneously reached out to touch his hand. It was not a moment I thought through but later, driving back home, I was troubled by it. Did I cross the line? Did I betray my people?

"If de Kock, the embodiment of evil, can break down and feel remorse to the degree that I was touched by it, then the line that separates evil from what is human is very thin and we are all implicated as human beings. And that's a frightening thought because the people we deem as monsters we want to keep at arm's length;

we're afraid of seeing ourselves in them. I don't mean that we are evil like him, but it means that there are moments when we can be driven to the edge and it's a slippery slope. De Kock is an important person in this whole story of our country trying to reconcile, not only because he led many perpetrators to testify but because he represents for everyone the absolute worst in apartheid, and yet he was able to confront his conscience and express genuine regret and remorse."

On occasion, the lives of victim and perpetrator became enmeshed with one another. "I got a phone call one day and the man identified himself as the security officer who'd organized the bombing of my car that cost me my arm and my eye. Would I be willing to meet him?" Albie Sachs says wondrously, still awed at the courage it took to make this move. "I found myself opening the gate to this man who'd tried to kill me. We sat down and spoke together for a long time as he told me his story. I wanted to hear it; I was intrigued. Who was this person who had the courage to now face me, to come and speak to me? At the end I said, 'Henry, normally, when I say goodbye to someone, I shake their hand. I can't shake your hand. But please, go to the commission and tell them what you know. Fill in the gaps so that we can become a country that knows what happened, knows the processes, so we can recapture our history, and so it doesn't happen again.' To me that was so important as he became a human being by owning up to what he'd done, not just a soldier blindly carrying out an operation."

There were, however, not too many Henrys reaching out to those they had injured. And sometimes during the proceedings the insensitivity of the perpetrators was deeply disturbing. "Not only insensitivity," Pumla Gobodo-Madikizela elaborates, "but contempt. 'This was war' was their rationale and they continued to justify their actions even in the presence of family members of the victims who were crying out for some recognition of their pain. For me, these were the most difficult moments."

Religion also played an important role in the reconciliation process, but it was not always a beneficial one. "Part of the problem is that forgiveness is so central to the Christian teaching that it's led us to speak glibly as if it were cheap and easy, which belies the hugeness, the massiveness of what's involved, the scale of letting go that is required for forgiveness truly to happen. It's a travesty when pastors or laity increase the burden of those who are hurt by saying they should just forgive. My own view is that we in the faith community talk too much and listen too little," believes Father Lapsley, smiling. "Yet, when forgiveness does happen, it can be so liberating. I think of Brian Mitchell, who gunned down people in an African village while they were sleeping. He was sentenced to death, his case was commuted to a life sentence, and eventually he received amnesty through the TRC. He said that he would go to that village and in whatever way was possible he would seek to make it up. He said he was sorry, and he continued to show that by walking a journey of restorative justice."

Such a journey of repentance has, however, rarely been taken by those in power. It was the foot soldiers of apartheid that applied for amnesty and expressed their remorse, not those at the top running the country. "We have not yet had our Willy Brandt moment," Pumla says with resignation inflected with anger. "The image of this man kneeling in front of the Warsaw Memorial captured exactly and exquisitely how victims need to be acknowledged by those in positions of leadership. The power of that apology lay in the kneeling, the gesture of the body, it went beyond words. We cry out for something like this in South Africa as there has been very little expression of remorse at the public level."

South Africa, however, remains a society driven by inequality, poverty, and social unrest. Did the TRC create a new way of thinking about transcending the wounds of grievous violence, or merely another way to forgive by forgetting? Did the focus on forgiveness and reconciliation obscure the need for more rigorous accounting of the past? Did the forgiveness and reconciliation last beyond the trials? And, ultimately, was the TRC a more effective mechanism for national rather than individual healing?

"The number of cases where the TRC led to deep, lasting, and transformative acts of reconciliation was actually very small," says Van Zyl. He suggests that it may not be helpful to see the Truth Commission as the forum for individual acts of reconciliation: "It is more useful to think of it as the symbolic venue in which the nation could have a conversation with itself about what we did to each other and how we can understand that, both in factual terms and in moral terms. It provided very useful fodder for the deeper, more intimate, more personal moments of reconciliation that followed."

The work of the commission also gave rise to the bigger question of how to integrate forgiveness into all parts of society. "If we think of some of the major conflicts up until the end of World War II, somebody won and somebody surrendered, but many of the conflicts since that time have been characterized by negotiated settlements. No one won, nobody lost, and yet the most terrible things have happened." Father Michael Lapsley is a social justice activist and Anglican priest involved in pastoral, educational, and theological work within the South African liberation movement. He is earnest in his quest for answers: "And so we have to ask, how do we create a different kind of future? It's in that context that the whole discourse around truth and reconciliation commissions arose, but enmeshed within that are issues of forgiveness on a communal scale to enable healing the wounds of history and healing memories. Forgiveness is an integral part of how we struggle as a human family to acknowledge what it is that happened in order to create a kinder and more compassionate world."

Susan Collin Marks agrees, as she believes in the quality of compassion the TRC emphasized. "So much that has been done in our world to try and resolve conflicts hasn't worked. We've tried different forms of war. We've tried sanction. We've tried isolating people. But in the process we've missed an understanding of our humanity. We can make a choice to cut through this, to say I'm a human being and you're a human being and let's find our common humanity."

While the commission forced the country to face its dark path, Professor Gobodo-Madikizela wonders sadly, "If we had held that extraordinary moment and decided to maintain and continue that dialogue, to take it beyond the point of feeling moved to the point of really engaging in what it means to have been part of this history, then I think we would be in a different place in South Africa today. But there was something lost after the TRC so that now, years later, that spirit has largely disappeared and from that legacy has been birthed a new anger."

"It's a journey full of jagged edges, and sometimes we took three steps forward and one step backwards." Father Lapsley agrees that many of the most serious criticisms were about the failures of the new democratic state to follow through on the recommendations of the commission, especially those of financial reparation. "Recently, we've had a couple of extremely racist incidences, one with a group of white students at a university, another with a young white boy who went berserk and indiscriminately killed black people. Both incidents have really made the nation ask how far are we on the journey of reconciliation? It brings to the fore that this isn't just about national reconciliation, it's also about the journey of unlearning racism."

And yet, despite the failings, a real change has occurred. "Are we a healed society? No. There's still a lot of pain. There are still many things that have to be encountered and dealt with," concurs Albie Sachs. "We still have massive inequality; we still have huge unemployment; we're ravaged by diseases, the impact of AIDS is enormous; we have crime that's completely unsupportable. But," he pauses for emphasis, "we have human dignity, we have a constitution, we have law, we have a free press, and we can speak out openly. The Truth Commission helped us become an open society. It had a limited mandate and it stuck to that mandate and was more effective for doing so. It wasn't telling the story of South Africa, it wasn't telling the story of apartheid or how we're going to transform our society. It was picking up on extreme examples of grotesque pain that were both cruel and illegal and that were being denied. Apartheid was something monstrous and abominable and totally unacceptable. And so the TRC was extremely important for the nation. No country can exist without some shared truths and we have enough now that we all—blacks and whites—can feel we are living in the same country.

"The commission didn't build houses; it didn't provide remedies for measles, it didn't provide food or jobs for the unemployed, it didn't deal with HIV/AIDS, but it did focus on something of intense significance and meaning." Sachs ardently believes in the humanity of all. "We use the term *ubuntu* to describe what happened on a deeper level: I am a person because you are a person, I can't separate my humanity, my dignity, my sense of self from acknowledging your humanity, your dignity, your sense of self; we are all bound up with each other. We are individuals and it's important to have this recognized, but it's individuality in a community with a sense of connection and responsibility.

"I personally don't like the word 'forgiveness.' I prefer seeing examples of forgiving—the forgiving heart, the generous heart, the embracing heart," explains Sachs, entering into the deeper meaning of the word. "Forgiveness is an awkward term for me. It gives too much power to the forgiver, and it requires too much humility on the part of the person being forgiven. I like to think of humanizing a relationship, of discovering humanity in another on the basis of a shared sense of what's right and wrong, a sense of connection that enables us both to move forward in a liberated way. We've got to be deep enough and willing enough to engage with all these contradictions, and to start discovering a human being in the neighbor you hated. In the process of doing that, the neighbor starts discovering you as a human being. To me, that's marvelous."

Without a doubt there have been mistakes and failings, and, given the devastation left by apartheid, perhaps there will never be a complete place of reconciliation. But change did happen and it still continues to affect the country. "Apartheid was very successful as it divided us in both our psyche and our community, we were separated from each other. We had to rebuild and we had to do it quickly," says Susan Collin Marks, who is pragmatic in her optimism. "As we look back fourteen years after Mandela was signed in as the first democratic president of South Africa it's a mixed story because there hasn't been the development that we imagined would happen. But the National Peace Accord and the TRC were built on the understanding of *ubuntu* and I will always be grateful for what came out of this process, of the willingness of black South Africans to move forward with white South Africans into a new future. For all the mistakes that were made, for all the difficulties, something extraordinary happened that affected everybody."

Most importantly, the years of oppression and torture were witnessed and seen by all so that, as a result, such acts of violence were stopped from happening again. "One could say that the whole process narrowed the range of impermissible lies that one can tell in public," says Michael Ignatieff, the leader of the Liberal Party of Canada, who has written extensively on international relations and nation building. "It is sometimes essential that former regimes are shamed into unalterable moral disgrace, that their inner moral essence is named and defined for all time."

Even those critical of the role of forgiveness in the TRC acknowledge that the process raised fundamental and important questions about forgiveness for both participants and observers alike. "These were questions not only about the possibility of forgiveness in the wake of unspeakable atrocities of a racist regime, but also about the plausibility of forgiveness on the collective level," explains Benjamin Nienass. "Can we make sense of forgiveness in the political sphere? Who acts on whose behalf? And how do the many individual stories of reconciliation become part of a larger national story? The reconciliation process illuminated not only many of the limits of forgiveness, but also its powerful force to appear in the most unexpected of circumstances. If we can reach one conclusion about forgiveness in light of the TRC, it is that it cannot be planned. It emerges from the unpredictable surplus of human encounters rather than from individual determination and conviction."

Germany's Penitential Journey: FACING THE PAST

The Holocaust

The extermination of the Jews was not a sudden outbreak of violence. It was doctrinally founded, philosophically explained, methodically prepared and systematically perpetrated. And so I would willingly say, reversing the terms of the prayer that Jesus addresses to God according to Luke: 'Father do not forgive them, for they know precisely what they do. It is a crime for which an entire people was more or less responsible. — Vladimir Jankelevitch, "Should We Pardon Them?"

"Forgiveness is not the last word in politics. But in its complex combination of our acknowledgment, forbearance, empathy, and will to repair the damages of our evildoing, it can speak an indispensable first word... And we should never underestimate the degree to which the moral posture of individuals is shaped by their leaders."
— Rev. Donald Shriver

Germany is a country that plunged Europe and the rest of the world into two world wars, causing the deaths of nearly fifty million people; it has the Holocaust in its history. It is also a country that has embarked on a long penitential journey. The process of coming to terms with its history has been excruciating, not always voluntary, and it is not yet over. It began in denial with a frozen silence immediately after the war, when not one member of the ruling Nazi elite fully acknowledged the evil for which they were responsible. And although West Germany continued the investigations against national socialist perpetrators initiated by the Allies, only a fraction of these cases ever reached the courts.

The pain of the past lives on in the voices of the people, in their questioning and searching for answers, and in their often-contradictory views:

"It is my duty not to forget." Economist and educator Peter Mayer Dohm

"There should be an end to all this talking about Nazi guilt." An unidentified man at the Holocaust memorial

"We shouldn't ask for reconciliation before we repent." Engineer Helmut Reihlen

"I have never, ever seen one of the real murderers, the real perpetrators, publicly apologize and ask for forgiveness. So how can we ask for collective forgiveness?" Stefan Kramer, general secretary, Central Council of German Jews

"Germany has been historically unique in doing penance. No other country in the world has devoted so much time, money and attention to commemorating the worst parts of its history." Susan Neiman, director of the Einstein Forum

"I still don't understand it… the validity, the legality and the ways of killing an entire people." Nobel Laureate Elie Wiesel

"Germans are trying as a nation to work on being forgiven. There is still a little bit of a dark cloud over all of us and I don't know when it will be lifted." Sabine Reichel, author of *What Did You Do in the War, Daddy?*

After the war, West Germans concentrated on materially rebuilding their country and not on confronting their past. With the help of the Marshall Plan, and with many rehabilitated former Nazis now back in positions of power, the country achieved an economic miracle. They elected a democratic government and became strategic partners with the west in the growing Cold War. But the past would not go away. At home, the questions asked by children were relentless: 'What did you do in the war?' hung in the air unanswered. It was a silence that ruptured families, sometimes permanently, and prolonged the suffering.

Having spent many years in Germany as the director of the Einstein Institute, Susan Neiman was struck by the depth of the damage. "I think it is safe to say that very few people who were born after the war, and whose parents were directly responsible in some way for the Nazi period, had anything resembling a normal family life. You can see the scars, they are like open wounds."

Gottfried Wagner, who bears a striking resemblance to his great grandfather, Richard Wagner, was raised with Adolf Hitler as an integral part of his life. "I am an example of living with someone who did not repent. Until she died, my grandmother, Winifred, publicly glorified Hitler as the savior of Germany. Hitler would sit at our table many times with my grandmother sitting beside him and simply adoring him. This was the atmosphere in which I grew up. After seeing a documentary in school about the rise and fall of the Third Reich I tried to talk about it at home. The images of the dead bodies at Buchenwald and Hitler arriving at Bayreuth being greeted warmly by the Wagner family were shocking. My father would harshly silence me by saying, 'You are nine years old, so shut up and do your homework.' My grandmother, a militant Nazi, told me that 'what you see in this film are all the lies from the New York Jews and one day you will find out how evil the Jews are.' Like so many others in my generation, I led a double life: silence at home, searching for answers outside.

"There really wasn't the slightest form of a penitential journey after the war ended," Gottfried continues, emphatically. "Everything was concentrated on remaking the country economically. What we heard from our elders about the war was that it was our duty, we had been in an economic crisis and Hitler had to respond. We were drawn into the war, we were victims of the allied bombing raids, victims of expulsion and displacement, and on and on."

Historian Hannes Heer also belongs to the generation of children of the perpetrators. "When I asked my father, 'Why did you join the Nazis and what did you do in the party?' he abruptly got up and left the room. He could not answer. I kept asking him and eventually he exiled me from my home." Banging his hands together, Heer expresses his father's outrage at the questioning. "I couldn't have any contact with my mother, my sisters, or brother. But the silence wasn't just at home. As students we raised the question with our professors: 'What side were you on, what was your role?' and their refusal to answer was maddening. It provoked fury, aggression, and demonstrations, an entire movement started at the universities. If our elders responded at all, it was that Hitler and his group were responsible and most Germans were innocent. Looking back, I think I became an historian as a way of reconstructing not only the story of my father and his generation, but my own."

"It's hard for people to understand the power of this taboo subject," says Sabine Reichel, who remembers growing up without ever hearing the word 'Jew'. "As there were none around, effectively, they didn't exist. In this way they killed the Jews twice: once for real and then once in memory." Sabine looks away for a moment before concluding, "We were basically trained not to ask questions, that was their best trick. And it worked too, except for some people. It didn't work with me for long. They thought that when the war was over then after a few years everything would be forgotten. They were so very wrong."

Author Anna Rosmus is an historian who, as a young girl in high school, exposed the hidden Nazi past of her hometown, Passau. Her essay won a national contest but it caused a firestorm at home, alienating her from her family, friends, and community. Ultimately, amidst death threats, she immigrated to America. She frequently returns to Germany to do research for her books and during one these trips she met with a Jewish survivor now living in the outskirts of Passau. For the small number of Jews that returned to Germany after the war, life could be difficult. "Abraham Eiboszycz was a survivor of a concentration camp so I arranged to interview him. I wanted to learn what it was like to live with that past in the very community where he knew the perpetrators. He had married a local woman and for decades he had heard the same hate-filled, anti-Jewish remarks coming from the same people." Her voice grows in intensity as she develops his story. "For all those years it kept hurting him until finally, in the 1980s, he realized he would never be able to change these people and that the only way he could live without committing suicide was to forgive them.

"I was staring at him in utter disbelief. How could he have reached such a conclusion? Abraham anticipated my reaction and told me, 'It wasn't a matter of whether they deserved forgiveness or not, it wasn't about them. If I continued to give in to being pummeled and insulted over and over again, I knew that soon it would kill me. These neighbors were finishing off what the Nazis had not completed in 1945. If I wanted to keep my sanity I had to really accept that perhaps it was not their personal fault. They may have been raised that way; maybe if I had been raised the way they were raised I would think like them. Whatever they had been through in life, if I had been in their shoes, maybe I would be like them. I drew a line: whatever happened in the past stays in the past. Otherwise I could not manage to hang on to my life. From then on I could look forward. I saw that forgiveness is not only to be granted out of graciousness or altruism, but also sometimes in order to sustain one's own sanity, to cut oneself free. This is what worked for me.'" Rosmus pauses. "I often think about this encounter with this extraordinary man when I hear others talking about clearing the slate and moving forward."

Slowly, the Germans started to give up many of the myths about the 'good Germans' and the 'bad Nazis'. The denials of the first generation gave way to discussions of their Nazi past, while Germans' absorption in their own pain and loss deepened into an appreciation of the far greater suffering imposed by Nazi Germany. Their expressions of formal regret for the horrific crimes of their country turned into monetary reparations to survivors and to the state of Israel, totaling $70 billion.

The Bitburg Controversy

By the mid-1980s, forty years of dealing with the Nazi past were enough for many Germans. It was time to move on. In 1985, a meeting of two world leaders in a remote cemetery in Germany—President Ronald Reagan and Chancellor Helmut Kohl—threatened to shatter this fragile, incomplete moral accounting. In the spring of that year, President Reagan announced he had accepted an invitation from the German chancellor to jointly take part in a symbolic act of resolution between the two countries. It was agreed that they would visit the Bitburg cemetery.

"It was one of those occasions in which an anniversary has more dimensions to it than anybody knew," recalls theologian Rev. Donald Shriver. "Ultimately it would become a searing lesson in which we learned much about what forgiveness is and what it is not in international affairs."

Some of these lessons touched on the limitations of forgiveness in politics, as well as the dangers of attempting to speak of forgiveness on behalf of a group or to offer it without proper legitimization and carefully chosen symbols and rituals. The Bitburg fiasco, as it came to be called, also raised questions about the unforgivable uniqueness of the Holocaust, about the conventional wisdom that 'time heals all wounds,' and the critical distinctions between legal guilt and moral responsibility.

"It began with the intention of the leaders of both Germany and Washington to observe the fortieth anniversary of the end of World War II. On both sides of the Atlantic there was a lot of hope that this would be a time of celebration and reconciliation between the countries," Rev. Shriver recognized there were also pragmatic considerations: "Reagan wanted Kohl's support for his Strategic Defense Initiative, while Kohl needed a victory in the upcoming state elections and chose the politics of memory to mobilize his base. It was also decided by both powers that the president would visit the Bitburg cemetery in order to honor the German war dead and as a way of symbolizing that the war was now in the past."

Gottfried Wagner

It quickly became known that members of the Waffen SS were buried at Bitburg. Reagan's proposed visit set off an absolute furor that lasted for months. At its core was the issue that by going to the cemetery as president, Reagan appeared to be giving his official approval to Germany's war past. "Since it was partly an act of reconciliation and, by implication, forgiveness, it meant that Reagan would symbolically be forgiving the SS," explains Walter Reich, former director of the US Holocaust Memorial Museum. And, as Gottfried Wagner clarifies, "These were absolutely the killer troops of Hitler, highly responsible for the Holocaust."

"When we learned about the SS being buried there, everyone in the administration was shocked." Reagan's former speechwriter, Josh Gilder, was appalled by the idea that Reagan would lay a wreath to commemorate these fallen SS soldiers. "Even his most stalwart supporters visited him in the White House trying to persuade him to cancel the visit, including his wife, Nancy. We were used to being slammed in the

New York Times, NBC, CBS, and the entire media, but this was different in that almost everybody except Ronald Reagan thought he was wrong not to pull out of that ceremony. We all assumed that he would change his mind. However, that didn't happen. He stuck to his guns and would not shift his position, despite a firestorm of controversy."

The angry response was from both sides. "At the heart of the Bitburg controversy was the collision between those people who thought we had remembered enough and other people who were sure that we had not remembered enough, and these different groups were in both countries." Rev. Shriver saw a conflicting picture emerge. "In America, people wanted to let bygones be bygones, because that is our culture, and some of the people in Germany felt the pain of their past was something that they were tired of being reminded about."

Mainstream news reporters swarmed over this story. It was on the front pages of all the newspapers, domestic and international. It was the lead story on the nightly news. Political parties jumped on it: "President Reagan has spent another day defending his plan to visit the German military cemetery at Bitburg next weekend," reported Peter Jennings on ABC News. "There has been more pressure from Congress to cancel his visit, because there are soldiers buried there who belonged to the SS." The house voted overwhelmingly, urging the President not to go to the cemetery at Bitburg, and for days there were public demonstrations in front of the White House.

President Reagan's stubbornness was seen as shallow, insensitive, and certainly careless about symbolism. Donald Shriver carefully points out that, "One of the lessons of Bitburg is the importance of symbolism in political life. When two world leaders gather around a graveyard for the fallen war dead something is going on that is deeper and wider than anything these leaders might say. Many felt that just by standing there with Kohl, President Reagan was symbolizing forgiveness."

Lance Morrow, at that time a columnist for *TIMEMagazine*, wrote an impassioned editorial criticizing Reagan for his carelessness. "President Reagan has displayed a curious insensitivity about the past, as if he did not know how important it is and how dangerous it could be. As if he did not know that the past has monsters in it. His eyes accustomed to sunshine, Reagan did not peer carefully into the shadows."

Hannes Heer

Now, thirty years later, Morrow believes Reagan's motives were more complex. "While I still feel he was careless, I think he was working with the idea that there had to be some statute of limitation on always remembering or dwelling upon the trauma. Americans tend to view the past as a wreck on the highway that should be cleared off so that we can get on with the business of the future. The past is an encumbrance and an irrelevance. Or, in the words of our greatest American philosopher, Ralph Waldo Emerson, 'Why drag about a monstrous corpse of memory?'" Bitburg, Morrow believes, emerged from this American view. "Reagan, the quintessential American, wanted to clear off the wreckage—the horrible, grotesque wreckage of the war and the Holocaust. Memory has a tendency to be sacred and has elements of the mystical that American briskness rejects. Americans believed as did Scarlet O'Hara: 'Tomorrow is another day.' Reagan was being Scarlet O'Hara. He was saying that, like all the wreckage of the Civil War and *Gone with the Wind*, Hitler's Germany was yesterday and tomorrow is another day."

In an effort to defend himself, President Reagan succeeded in making matters worse when he spoke out: "I think that there is nothing wrong with visiting that cemetery where those young men are also victims of Nazism, even though they were fighting in the German uniform, drafted in the service to carry out the hateful wishes of the Nazis. They were victims, just as surely as the victims in the concentration camps." This speech caused an incendiary reaction. For many it was a grotesque equation, even if inadvertent. "That statement alone led to a huge rejection by a lot of people, not only in the Jewish community but others as well," Rev. Shriver pauses, shaking his head, baffled. "There's a huge difference between being drafted into an army and being sent off on a train to Auschwitz to be gassed to death.'

If forgiveness was being discussed or intended to be discussed, it was premature. "There's such a thing as forgiveness that comes too late and forgiveness that comes too soon, which was this case," Shriver continues. "It was superficially enacted and superficially talked about when Mr. Reagan smoothed over the differences between Holocaust victims and the men who were draftees in the German army."

The story began to acquire energy and culminated with the occasion of the Congressional Gold Medal of Achievement being awarded to Elie Wiesel, a Holocaust survivor, writer, professor, and human rights activist. Wiesel agreed to accept the award on the condition that he was free to say whatever he wanted. According to Reagan's biographer, Edmond Morris, before they went out to the presentation, Elie said to him, 'Mr. President, you realize that I am going to have to speak out and declare that you not do this.' The President was very angry because he was sure that he was going to be read the riot act and be embarrassed in public. They went out to face the cameras and indeed Elie Wiesel said, 'Mr. President, this is not your place. Bitburg is not your place, you should not go to Bitburg. Your place is with the victims of the SS. I have seen the SS at work, and I have seen their victims, they were my friends, they were my parents.' As Elie talked Reagan's neck and face got very red. He did not respond but became even more determined to go." A news reporter at the time noted his growing intransigence: "An embattled Ronald Reagan dug in his heels today over Bitburg, with a note of stubborn determination."

Wiesel's remark was picked up by the press in Germany. It made the controversy more tangible, for here was a famous Jewish leader and a survivor of the Holocaust, confronting the world's most powerful leader and telling him what not to do. It provoked lingering anti-semitism in both Germany and America, with such comments as 'how dare the Jews object to what the United States President chooses to do!'

Speechwriter Josh Gilder watched the controversy growing from his perch inside the White House. "In the beginning I had the reaction that almost everyone else did, which was shock. He seemed so perversely stubborn, but the more he stuck to his decision the more I listened to what he was saying, especially during our time together while I was taking notes for the speech. I began to understand he really was talking about forgiveness. He would talk about the importance of reconciling after forty years, that it was finally time. He felt there was this incredible burden of guilt being imposed on these people, especially since they had rebuilt their country as a democracy. They had been stalwart allies in the fight against Soviet totalitarianism and they were on the front line of the Cold War. This is where the moral or spiritual issue of forgiveness intersected with the geopolitical one."

Thane Rosenbaum

Chancellor's Kohl's National Security Advisor, Horst Teltschik, remembers Bitburg with restrained irritation: "Look, we had been allies for a long while. The Americans had helped the Germans immediately after the war, we got the Marshall Plan from them, and they had already demonstrated reconciliation. After the war ended in 1945 we had intensively discussed what had gone wrong in our history. Now, decades later, what was the need to question the symbolic act of reconciliation?" He continues, his anger growing. "We couldn't understand why the American Jewish organizations, mainly people at the top, started a campaign against Germany. They were aggressive, fighting hard; there were incredible threats. We were told Holocaust survivors would fly to Germany and would shoot the president and the chancellor if they went ahead with this. At the end I told the chancellor to forget about it, cancel it. But it was President Reagan who said, 'No! We have agreed on it, and we should stick to it.'" But, Teltschik adds: "If President Reagan had not come to Germany because of the threats, it would have damaged German/Jewish relations. Many Germans would have blamed these Jewish organizations who were telling us that we are all guilty, whether we were born after the war or not."

Menachem Rosensaft, founding chairman of the International Network of Children of Jewish Survivors, was born in Bergen-Belsen three years after the war, when it was fast becoming the largest displaced persons camp in Germany. He reacted forcefully to Teltschik's claims about alleged threats by Jewish leaders. "That's idiotic! There was never any suggestion that there would be any kind of violence, any type of non-respectful demonstration." Rosensaft was one of the leaders of the demonstrations. He traveled to Bergen-Belsen, one of the stops on Reagan's visit, with a large group of Holocaust survivors in order to protest peacefully. "If anything, the

Jewish leadership was reluctant to confront Reagan over Bitburg, the president was considered to be a friend of Israel and not in any way anti-Semitic. I think he was a fundamentally decent man but he was prepared to use the symbolism of forgiveness for political purposes. And that was unforgivable, because in doing so he was exploiting and desecrating the victims and survivors of the Holocaust."

Teltschik sees this as a misunderstanding. "Neither Reagan nor Kohl thought that they were offering forgiveness—such things can never be forgiven. If I were in a concentration camp I would never offer forgiveness. There was only one idea, which was to demonstrate our close friendship." He pauses for a long while, considering. "Looking back now, clearly there was a misperception, for out came all the memories of the Holocaust and the fear that the top politicians wanted to forget what happened. It was never our intention to do so or to confer forgiveness. But, today, I would say BItburg was a mistake, we could have avoided harming the feelings of so many people."

In reality, the word forgiveness was in everyone's thoughts and in most of the letters, speeches, and press accounts. Reagan's belief that Germany wanted forgiveness was clear in the mind of his speechwriter, as well as in the analysis of the event by Walter Reich: "West Germany was trying to grapple with and face its history so it was understandable that it wanted to get past it, get over it, and be forgiven for it. In Ronald Reagan they found somebody who, presumably for his own spiritual and principled reasons, wanted to confer some level of forgiveness."

This became the essential issue as Gilder prepared to write Reagan's speech. "Originally this was a drive-by speech in a foreign graveyard, perfect for the junior writer just out of college. And then it exploded. It became hugely important, every word a landmine. To this day I don't know why it wasn't given to someone else to write. Perhaps no one wanted it." He chuckles, remembering his friends in the speech-writing division: "They'd see me coming down the hall and would duck into doorways. Everybody was waiting and talking about how this speech was the only thing that could rectify the situation. There was a lot of pressure on me, but I was young and enjoyed the challenge. It was even more exciting when I began to understand that forgiveness was the central point. I had a theme, and as a writer with a theme I was all set to go. I bounded into the office of Marshall Breger, our Jewish liaison, filled with naïf excitement. I said, 'Marshall, I've got it. The speech is about forgiveness. It's also about forty years after the war, our two nations finally coming together and reconciling. That's what the president wants to talk about.' Marshall is very kind but he brought me up short by saying that really it was not going to work, that for the Jewish community this was the one unforgivable fact: they do not believe that forgiveness is possible where the Holocaust is concerned. And of all the issues the president might talk about, he certainly should not talk about that. At first I was uncomprehending and then somewhat shocked, because I realized that I had to write a speech about forgiveness but I couldn't use the word forgiveness anywhere in it."

President Ronald Reagan arrived in Germany in April and was greeted by his host, Chancellor Helmut Kohl. Their first stop was the concentration camp, Bergen-Belsen, several hours away from Bitburg. Demonstrators greeted them, among them American Jews who were survivors of the Holocaust. The protests turned ugly and it was a painful sight to see elderly Holocaust survivors being led into police vans, some of them resisting and screaming. Stefan Kramer, general secretary of the Central Council of German Jews, questions the right of the president to be there: "Forgiveness can only be given by those who were victims themselves to those who were perpetrators and murderers. Who gave the legal power of attorney to either President Ronald Reagan or to Chancellor Helmut Kohl?"

The main accusation leveled against President Reagan's handling of this event was that he was being sentimental rather than realistic. It was not a profound appropriation of memory, of understanding the past, or of the cost of getting over the past. "In that very same month of April 1985, veterans of the SS were holding a reunion in Passau." Rev. Shriver describes how little remorse they showed. "Some of them were quoted as saying, 'We never committed any war crimes.' They were very resentful that any Jewish person should try to prevent Ronald Reagan, the president of United States, from coming to Germany and going to the cemetery. There was much anti-Semitism in these remarks, but even more noticeable was that there were many Germans alive from World War II who did not believe they had done anything wrong, even members of the SS."

Walter Reich

The city of Passau was both the cradle of National Socialism and Anna Rosmus's hometown. "When Ronald Reagan came he probably meant very well, that finally Germany should be forgiven, that this messy past should not stand between the countries. Unfortunately, what it really did was to embolden old Nazis and new Nazis alike to hold gatherings and spread their ideology. Year after year, Passau has hosted Europe's largest meetings of Nazis. I cannot imagine that Ronald Reagan could have envisioned thousands of Nazis marching through a town, flooding an entire city. Our bakers were baking pretzels in the shape of big swastikas. When you walked through the inner city of Passau at that time, you would see thousands of people marching through the town and greeting each other with the forbidden Heil Hitler salute, wearing swastika pretzels in front of their chests, and openly bragging about the crimes they had committed. Ronald Reagan did not create any of these ideas, but he enabled the organizers of such events to show themselves openly, proudly. There was certainly no sense of penitence. There was no sense of, 'Oh my God, I was blind; Oh my God, I was involved in this horror and didn't realize it in time.' No, there was no shame."

The Bitburg fiasco confirmed for Susan Neiman how complicated it can be to talk about the Holocaust or the Nazis. "In the second half of the twentieth century they have become the symbol of evil, the gold standard. I think there is a tendency to stop thinking when one refers to the Nazis, rather than to actually analyze what is going on. Reagan should not have gone to Bitburg, but not because stepping into a German cemetery is a way to make peace with evil, I don't think that makes sense or helps to prevent future evils. The mistake made was in not seeing that many Germans did not want to forget, and that German politics from 1947 had been driven by a desire to confront the past."

"Bitburg was a most necessary grief," wrote William Safire in the *New York Times*, "because it showed how many people were, in fact, hungering for an honest facing of the past rather than gently skipping over it. It signified something of great importance."

For Donald Shriver, at the heart of the situation was a question of what the acts of a political leader mean in regards to the evils of the past. "Has that evil really been given public notice? Have we stared at that evil enough to know what it is, and said what it is, and refused in any way to excuse it? The important thing about forgiveness is that it's not an excuse. Forgiveness involves the facing of an evil and then asking, if by facing it, is some reconciliation still possible?"

West Germany's president, Richard von Weizsacker, was acutely aware of how, throughout the world, people were unsure whether Germany was ready to deal with and repent its past, and that the visit to Bitburg had actually served to intensify their fears. So he decided to speak to and for the nation. "It was a long speech, composed mostly of agonizing details of the specific crimes of the Nazi era. It was a catalogue of crimes almost without precedent in any speech given by any politician that I know anything about. It took courage to stand in front of the whole country and say that this is the past we must confront, this is the past that many of us helped put into practice." Donald Shriver uses language close to the original speech as he paraphrases the climax when President von Weizsacker took responsibility, along with his country, for the crimes of the Third Reich: "'I, as a member of the Wehrmacht, and the rest of us as bystanders to an evil that was going on that we knew about, but didn't do anything about...'" Shriver pauses, moved by the memory. "As an example of repentance in politics, this speech is almost without equal. There is not a word about forgiveness in it, but there is an abundance of words about what it is that Germans have to regret in their political past. What was so great was that it nailed down public repentance, which at last opened the door to the possibility of public forgiveness. The hope of reconciliation was not a vain hope. The world can live with a repentant Germany; it could not live with a forgetful Germany."

It was a speech of enormous complexity and power. "When people heard it they fell silent, both because of von Weizsacker's impeccable standing and his social position as president." Anna Rosmus smiles joyfully, remembering its effect. "I don't think I ever heard a single person, from beer drinkers to culprits, opposing him or debating his speech. People listened. All of a sudden it sunk in, its reality struck home. I was so grateful to this man. From that moment on I could see society opening up, it was a turning point, even Bavaria finally moved forward in the right direction."

The dam had burst. The 1980s saw a flood of articles, books, and films about the Holocaust. There were open debates about the Hitler years. Was that time a temporary aberration or a catastrophe with deep roots in German culture? There were youth exchanges between Germany and Israel, and obligatory day visits to concentration camp sites. German cities invited survivors to return. There were, however, some lingering myths that were especially hard to relinquish. In 1999, a museum exhibition traveled throughout Germany that explored and depicted war crimes committed by the ordinary German soldier. Wherever it went it generated both huge audiences and massive protests. Some of them turned ugly, and images of screaming and fighting demonstrators outside the museum were a disturbing reminder that the past, for some people, was still very much alive.

"It wasn't just Hitler and the SS, it wasn't a few major culprits. Now we knew that the vast majority of soldiers either witnessed or participated in war crimes." Rosmus describes the contents, "These were pictures that families had at home in their family photo albums: Daddy in a uniform, Daddy with a gun, Daddy with corpses. This was nothing unusual. But it shattered the myth that only a very few had been personally involved while the rest were ignorant and innocent. Now we knew they were not."

"All the legends and stories that soldiers told when they came home simply collapsed because this exhibition showed the facts," agrees Hannes Heer, the curator of the first version of the exhibition. "The whole exhibition was like a private photo album. We used the pictures that the soldiers had taken and sent back home and all of a sudden the public saw what their relatives had done. The number of perpetrators skyrocketed into the millions as the gap narrowed between the small soldiers and Hitler and his generals. This material became the beginning of a process of purification and self-enlightenment. A great number of people visited the exhibition and, combined with the number of people who participated in debates at home, it showed a growing and collective effort to come to terms with the past."

Hannes carefully makes an important distinction: "Collective guilt is a term that no longer describes Germans today because many of the people who committed or enabled crimes by turning their backs on what happened are dead. We now have generations that biologically and politically have nothing to with that time. However, we are collectively responsible. As long as I live in Germany, I'm responsible for my history, all of it, its glories and its crimes."

Shaking her head, Sabine Reichel gently disagrees. "Although Germans are adamant about saying there is no collective guilt, I do think their hearts tell them something else. The Holocaust shaped our collective soul and I think it injured our soul very deeply, much more than Germans ever thought. Something of the souls of the German people went up in smoke in the chimneys of Auschwitz."

Donald Shriver

Germany has built numerous memorials to its worst atrocities; the landscape is filled with libraries, museums, monuments, and plaques dedicated to the Holocaust, testimonials to their civic shame. In the very heart of Berlin, the Holocaust memorial spreads over five acres, equivalent in importance to Times Square in New York.

There are many voices that question these memorial *mea culpa's*, worried that their massive size creates both an emotional distance and a superficial closure. In response, artists have created more intimate remembrances that surprise and provoke, while throughout the country resident communities have memorialized what happened in their own locale.

One of the most remarkable and talked about memorials is, in fact, very small *and local*. It's a cobblestone, a stumbling stone made of copper that shines in the distance, and it is placed in the pavement right outside houses where the Jews were rounded up and deported. On these are inscribed the names of the Jews who lived there and the camps where they were killed. Throughout the streets of Germany you can see people stopping or 'stumbling' over these stones. Mothers and children bend over them talking, reflecting. As Hannes Heer explains: "They force you to pause, to look down and think, 'they lived here, and this is where their neighbors lived and looked away.' It's like an electrifying shock."

Or, as Donald Shriver speculates: "Imagine what it is like to live in a house which you can't enter or leave without stumbling over one of these stones, which proclaims that this house used to be inhabited by a Jewish family murdered by my government. That's getting repentance down to a truly local level."

"Maybe Ronald Reagan was a head of his time when he tried to open up the cellar in which the buried Germans were trapped—locked up by themselves—when he called out the collective shame of the Germans," considers Stefan Kramer. "Then and now we face the urgent problem of Germany's broken identity, because what we are facing today is an uprising of right wing extremists who are using this vacuum that exists, filling it with old hatreds and a new nationalism. We have two groups among Germans today. On one side we have a destroyed personality saying, 'We're guilty, we've done it all.' On the other side we have youth who are saying, 'Stop it, we can't hear it anymore.' Perhaps our Holocaust education of the last thirty years went totally wrong?"

Pastor Christian Staffa, managing director of ARSP, a German peace and volunteer service founded in the aftermath of the war, remembers a rare moment of public patriotism: "Such a sea of flags at the 2006 World Football Championship has never been seen in Germany since the war and it was both thrilling and scary. I was at the VIP lounge at the stadium in Berlin and the fervency of the crowds brought up all those old images from the Third Reich. Now, I know it is not the same thing as at the Nazi time, but what I was seeing was our collective yearning to be German, to sing 'Deutschland! Deutschland!' It showed a need to be proud of it, to say it over and over, to love it again: Yes, we are proud and we want to be normal. Please, let us be normal."

But feeling normal can be difficult and elusive. Throughout Germany, Jews, and Christians have come together in small groups similar to Pastor Staff's Aktion Suehnezeichen, trying to confront their fears and the divide between them. At a small conference of young Germans and Israelis meeting in Berlin, a German man in his early thirties haltingly expressed his fears about not being "normal." He said: "This is so deep inside me, as a German man. It is a very subtle dread that at some point the monster will come out of me, that which has caused the horror. The fear is that I can't trust myself, that because I am German there is something within me that one day will burst out and cause destruction."

Sabine Reichel has sought out these encounters, though without much hope until recently. "I have wondered, will we ever, the Jewish people and me, overcome this divide? Overcome the millions of bodies between us? I always thought it's not possible; it's too overwhelming, too big. Nobody said to me, 'I forgive you,' though, of course, you don't need to hear those words. But now I think, yes it is possible. Definitely. We can move towards each other and find a place to live in the middle."

Such resolution and forgiveness touches on years of conflict and does not come without inner torment. "Most of my extended family was gassed in Poland. Just saying I forgive, or it's okay, or I've gotten past it, is something that we continue to wrestle with." Walter Reich shares his ongoing struggle in a measured tone that builds slowly in intensity. "Everyone has his or her own approach to resolving extremely painful relationships with those who have harmed us, our families, our parents, our children, our people, harmed our interests and our civilization. We have to do this not only as a group, but also as individuals. Sometimes we can genuinely forgive. Certainly, as time passes, most of us have less need to think about the harm, to obsess about it, or to feel the hurt; we can move on, time does do that. But it doesn't necessarily take it all away. One of the hopes is that forgiveness will short-circuit the process and make it possible to do it in less time. Maybe sometimes it does. But maybe we're only fooling ourselves."

Not only have Germans and Jews moved towards each other, but so also have members of families torn apart by the war. Such reconciliation is rare and sometimes requires a lifetime, as was the case for Hannes Heer, whose Nazi father had banished him from his home. "Our whole life we had conflict, we had debate, I could never forgive him after those battles. I couldn't see that there was a father behind this old Nazi. I always wanted to deny the political side of him, and in so doing I forgot that he had two sides—the political side, yes, but also the father. I was able to dialogue with him much better when he had dementia and he became like a child. Then it was possible for me to forgive and make my peace with him." Hannes pauses, collecting his feelings. "I was holding his hand when he died, it was a very peaceful moment. He was no longer the old Nazi; he was just interested in what was happening with his son. It was not the Nazi and the anti-Nazi but a father and a son moment. You can't force it, you are not the master of this process, you cannot know which direction it comes from or why it comes, it happens spontaneously. For me it was like a miracle, and I am not religious. I saw him, this man who was once very strong but was now so weak. When he came nearer and nearer to his time to go, we lost all the anger, lost all the memories of our attacks. He pauses, overcome with feeling, "It was just a father and his son. And that was very powerful."

To think about the transformation of Germany in the last fifty years is to be astonished. This was a country that was at the heart of the twentieth century's most bloody wars, a nation that hatched genocide in the middle of Europe. And now, fast-forwarding to the Germany of today, we find a modern and prosperous European nation, which, objectively, respects all human rights.

There are, however, also reasons for skepticism. Germany still has the scourge of racism and neo-Nazism in its midst. And, as political scientist Ben Nienass, who has closely observed Germany's recent debates about the Holocaust, states: "Germany has managed to find ways to make the memory of the Holocaust all about themselves. Too often we end up with a language that describes Germany as the first casualty of the bestiality of the Holocaust, a view that once again reveals the peculiar absence of the victim in much of the memory talk."

But, as Paul Van Zyl believes, Germany has transformed itself in the last fifty years in one of the most profound ways. Van Zyl has spent his life examining countries struggling to come out of brutal pasts. "This would not have been possible had there not been an absolutely relentless process of reckoning with its past, of acknowledging the barbarity, of apologizing to its victims, of engaging with Israel, of staring into the inner psyche of the German character, or of Germans' attitude towards their neighbors. I am utterly convinced that the only way that deeply abusive nations transform themselves, in the way that Germany has, is though such a process of soul searching, of moral anguish, of deep reckoning, of relentless apologizing, and through supplementing those apologies with tangible committed political action to ensure the scourge is removed from the heart of the nation. Germany has done this."

Rwanda Emerges from the Darkness: FORGIVING THE UNFORGIVABLE

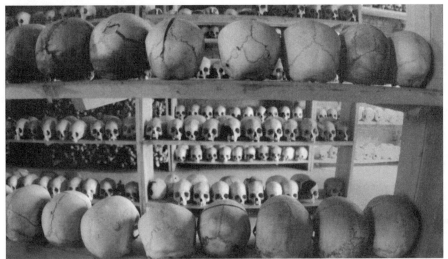

Rwandan Genocide

Forgiveness is especially difficult for the survivors of genocide. They are being asked to forgive the very things that are so unforgivable. It is a burden, a sacrifice for the future of their country; it is the most difficult thing you can ask of another human being...Some of them feel they are being forced into it, and in some sense they are right. — Pastor Antoine Rutayisire, former vice-president of Rwanda's National Commission of Unity and Reconciliation

The blood of the genocide in Rwanda is barely dry and the country is still struggling to recover. In the space of a hundred days between April and June 1994, an estimated one million Tutsis were massacred, alongside moderate Hutus who did not share the extremists' plans to annihilate the Tutsi. Unlike South Africa, where the black and white populations live in distinctly separate areas, or Germany, where Jews were either killed or fled, in Rwanda the killers and the survivors live side by side. The issues of reconciliation and forgiveness are urgent, difficult beyond comprehension, and the outcome unclear.

On April 6, 1994, a plane carrying the president of Rwanda was shot down by a surface-to-air missile as it descended on Kigali airport. The assassination of the president was used as a pretext by Hutu extremists to secure power by commencing a systematic plan to exterminate all Tutsi in Rwanda. Their plans had long been ready: all Tutsis were targeted along with opposition Hutu groups. Within hours the borders were closed and the killings had begun. Once called "the tropical Switzerland in the heart of Africa," Rwanda exploded into murder and chaos after decades of tension in the wake of colonial rule. Tutsi men, women, and children together with moderate and protective Hutus were killed in schools, in their homes, and hunted down throughout the countryside; they were killed in churches with clergy often colluding in the crime. Doctors, nurses, and teachers took part in the slaughter. In their last moments the victims were faced with an appalling realization: their cold-blooded killers were people they knew—neighbors, work-mates, former friends, even relatives through marriage.

"If the Rwandan genocide were to happen in the United States, thirty million people would have died in the course of three months," explains peacemaker and co-founder of the Truth and Reconciliation Commission, Paul Van Zyl. "That's ten thousand 9/11s happening, and recall what 9/11 did to America: how it traumatized the country, how it shaped and continues to shape national and international politics, how it completely transformed the discourse in this country. And that's for an act that was one ten thousandth of the number of people who died in Rwanda."

Those who survived the genocide describe that time as beyond human comprehension. Their voices are many, and come from both sides.

"You cannot imagine that your neighbors would come one day and start killing you, but they did." Genocide survivor Beatha Uwazaninka lived near the river where her mother drowned in broad daylight, with people watching. "My uncles and cousins were all killed with machetes. I was hiding in my uncle's bedroom when I heard him begging the killers: 'Do whatever you like, but don't kill my children in front of my eyes.' I fled out the back door." Beatha remembers peering through a little hole in the gate and hearing women who were being raped, shouting, and pleading: "'Please forgive me, please forgive me. No, I won't be a Tutsi again. I don't want to be a Tutsi again.' It's so horrible to hear people asking to be forgiven for being themselves. It is a grotesque distortion of the word. And the killers said, 'No, we are going to finish all of you.'" Beatha was just fourteen years old when this happened. "After the genocide I was alone, left on my own. Nothing that I knew before was left for me, all my family and friends were gone."

"I stood on the hill around my home and saw people chopping and killing this man with a machete." That is when genocide survivor Immaculee Ilibagiza knew something terrible was happening. "When they found my brother, they stripped off his clothes and surrounded him, laughing and tormenting before killing him. He was calling out their names as he recognized them. He was a friend to everyone and yet the whole village came to watch him die. What went through the killers' minds? A million people died. Their bodies were everywhere." Her face reflects the shock and horror of that time. "I asked myself, is this the end of the world? Am I dreaming? Is this a nightmare?"

When the killing began, Immaculee found refuge along with seven other Tutsi women in the home of their neighbor, a Hutu pastor. He hid them in a four-by-three-foot bathroom where they lived for ninety days without speaking or moving.

When she emerged, a 65-pound skeleton, she discovered that her entire family had been murdered. Today, her formerly emaciated body filled out, she is a tall, striking woman for whom the genocide and the future of her country are intensely present.

"Holy week, the most holy week of the Christian calendar, was when the killing started in one of the most Christian countries of the world." Father Petero Sabune, the Chaplain at the Sing Sing Prison, New York, found it beyond comprehension that, "the priests and the nuns, the pastors and the ministers, were all part of this carnage of killing."

"All the Tutsis I met, I killed. Those who worked with me knew that I loved what I was doing. Those whom we killed used to say forgive us, but forgiveness meant nothing for our minds were on the killing." Genocide participant Elie Musabyimana is often asked how he killed so many people. "It wasn't with a machete, because that would have meant using the same weapon to kill the animals for my food as for the killing. No, I used a big club." His face is impassive, lined, and his voice is muffled; he is clearly not proud of what he is saying."Once we took some Tutsi's down to this mining hole. One of them, a businesswoman was begging, please don't kill me. She gave me twenty-eight thousand francs to protect her from the people who wanted to cut her into pieces. So I dropped her and some others into this hole while she was still alive. It was a very deep hole where they used to mine cobalt, maybe thirty-meters deep. We knew that no one would come out alive so when we finished dropping them in we put soil on top of them."

The killings ended when Tutsi rebel forces, lead by Paul Kagame, entered Rwanda in June 1994. They swept through the country and drove the former regime from power. There were reports that these Tutsi forces committed many revenge killings against the Hutus during this bloody period. The country was in ruins. Those in power fled or had been killed. In a country of eight million, one million were dead, mainly Tutsis. Three million Rwandans sought safe haven in refugee camps in neighboring countries, among them many Hutu perpetrators, thereby coming under the protection of the United Nations High Commissioner for Refugees. Close to one million were displaced within their own county. At most, only four hundred thousand Tutsis survived.

Slowly, slowly, people started to return to their homes. Over the next fourteen years the Tutsi-led government struggled to rebuild the country. In 2003 Paul Kagame became Rwanda's first elected president since the genocide. The international community that had abandoned Rwanda during that time now sent human rights monitors and billions of dollars in aid. Buildings started to go up, roads were being repaved; tourists began to visit the capital and to take organized treks to see gorillas in the Virunga Mountains in northwest Rwanda. But the new wealth in the country's capital has not yet spread to the countryside and rural Rwandans remain desperately poor, surviving on subsistence agriculture.

The government has promoted reconciliation throughout the country, but how deep does it go? And in the face of so vast a crime, what does justice and reconciliation really mean?

The most urgent question after the genocide was what to do with the perpetrators? "Everybody who took part in the killings had to be punished." Senior pastor of St. Etienne Cathedral, Kigali, Antoine Rutayisire, has spent many years working for unity in his war-torn country. "The consequence was that we ended up with one hundred and fifty thousand people in jail. No prosecution, no investigations, sometimes one accusation was enough. Our criminal justice system had been destroyed but, even if intact, how could we try all these people through a normal court process? It would take generations. Moreover, these prisons, built for seven-thousand men, were so crowded that the prisoners had to sleep in shifts. Many died of cholera and malnutrition. It was a huge crisis.

"We had to help those living in jail so that's when the prison ministries started. People started going with humanitarian aid, distributing food, clothing, and blankets, and slowly the process shifted from justice to reconciliation." At this time, the government put in place a law stating that all people who confessed would get minimal penalty and would be released from prison. "That encouraged churches and social workers to go inside the prisons and preach repentance."

Father Sabune was invited to do pastoral work throughout the prison system. A lithe, intensely expressive man, his hands constantly moving as he talks, he considered himself well prepared through his work in American prisons, but the devastation he encountered in Rwanda, both inside and outside the prisons was overwhelming, leaving him exhausted and grief stricken. "When we arrived there were some prisoners who didn't want to talk to us. There are people today who still think, 'If I hadn't done it, they would've done it to me. I had to do it; it was a civil war. They were part of the gang that was coming to attack us.' These men would look at us with curiosity: you don't know what you're talking about, why are you here, what are you doing here? Many would not talk to us. Totally unrepentant, given a chance they would do it all again. But we slowly learned that others were curious about us and did want to talk.

Beatha Uwazaninka

"We started to ask them some tough questions. We wanted to know how they could have killed so many people. 'How could you do that? How many did you kill? And when did you kill them? Everyday? Didn't you get tired?' I remember the first time we spoke with one young man, he told us, 'Well I don't know how many people I killed.' We were appalled. 'What do you mean, you don't know? You have to know.' He said, 'When you are doing it everyday you lose count. It's like hunting. You get up, you hunt, you run after them, you cut them and they drop, and then you run to the next person and you cut them and they drop, and then you go to the next person. You don't stop to count. The children were the hardest because usually they didn't die right away so you had to look in their eyes, and they look at you. That was hard.'" Father Sabune pauses, experiencing again his original shock. Out of all the brutal stories he heard in the prisons, this young man stood out.

"Some of the prisoners were desperate for reconciliation, were aching to be cleansed of this evil they had done," he slowly continues. "They wanted to know if they could ever live again with the survivors of the families they had killed. Was it possible? This wasn't just, I'm sorry or I feel bad, it was: Can I ever be a human being and live among people again? So our job became one of spelling out the steps of repentance, confession, and restoration. And it is step by step, it's not something that just happens. The first step is to examine one's own conscience. I would ask them: What did you do that day and the day after? You have to admit that you were there and participated in this thing—this horrendous horrific killing. This can be very painful; it's something we call the healing of memories. But we can't guarantee that just because they confess that they are going to be forgiven. They may not be forgiven. In truth, they have to live with it for the rest of their lives.

"On my last visit to Rwanda, I shared with the prisoners my own story for it goes to the heart of how difficult it is to forgive, how long it takes, the anguish involved." In 1976, Sabune's beloved brother was tortured and killed in one of Uganda's jails. A friend of the family, Yosa, had turned him over to Idi Amin. "For the next twenty years my family and I were consumed. We plotted revenge, we even thought of contracting someone to kill him. We obsessed about the betrayal; I lived with unrepentant, unremorseful rage. Here I am, a pastor, I use the language of forgiveness in church, I counsel people how to forgive, and I wasn't forgiving. I realized my obsession was hurting my children and carving out chunks of my life. I carried the guy for twenty years, but I knew I had to let it go. It was a long, slow, painful and complex process, and it is not completely over."

Sixteen years later, Pastor Rutayisire reflects on the damage to the body and soul of his country. During this period he worked for the government as the vice chairman of the Unity and Reconciliation Commission, and developed a reputation for rare, sometimes bracing candor. "Every person we lost left behind a trauma in the heart of someone. When you have a neighbor whom you trusted and depended on, somebody to whom you did good but he repaid with evil, then the wound is proportionate to the intimacy of the relationship you'd had. And that's what happened in our country. The trust that we lived with was gone, because the neighbor you shared with yesterday has today turned against you and killed your children, your husband, or killed your wife. This was the depth of the problem: the mistrust and animosity that came out of the treachery created a deeply wounded nation. I often tell people that it's very easy to rebuild a school or a hospital as long as you have enough money to do it. But if you don't rebuild hearts and relationships then you're in trouble, because it's like a landmine planted in the soil. At some point in the future it's going to be detonated and will destroy so many things again."

Reconciliation became an imperative, not just an option, if Rwanda were to build a new country. But how deep could the reconciliation go? And was it possible for forgiveness to become a part of the process? "Forgiveness is so difficult, especially for the survivors of the genocide," Pastor Rutayisire concedes. "They are being asked to forgive the very things that are so unforgivable. It's a burden, it's heavy, it's a sacrifice they have to make for the future of the nation, but it's the most difficult thing you can ask of another human being." He pauses, reflecting. "Some of them feel that they are being forced into it and in some sense they are right. "

The government decided to reach back into Rwanda's past to revive and revise the gacaca courts. They had once served as a judicial system at the local level for settling disputes about civil rather than criminal matters. This was Rwanda's most ambitious and innovative tool for reconciliation, a bold experiment in restorative justice that was born out of tragic necessity. Tens of thousands of prisoners were released and returned to their villages where they awaited their trials in these traditional community gacacas, rather that facing many years going through the court system.

Antoine Rutayisire

"The model of gacaca presumes that there can be reconciliation at the individual level," explains Priscilla Hayner, director of the International Center for Transitional Justice in New York. "It's not a court process but a community gathering at which the accused person comes forward and the community talks about whether this person was or wasn't responsible for the crimes that, in most cases, he is accused of. In the past this was never applied to serious crimes, such as killing or rape, so now they were taking the core ideas of a system and trying to change them to address genocide. It was very hard, a huge challenge. There have been critiques of it, there has been frustration around it, but it was an essential part of the process to at least try to find some way to reconcile with over a hundred thousand people that are in jail accused of having taken a direct part in the genocide. How could we ever try them in a normal court process?"

To begin with the gacaca system was welcomed enthusiastically by Hutus and Tutsis and over a million people participated. But problems have also emerged. "Does gacaca lead to reconciliation? It can, but I think it is still unclear," concludes Priscilla. "Hutus began to feel that it was a one-sided justice for the Tutsi government would not allow its own army to be tried in the gacaca for killing Hutus after the genocide. And for the Tutsi survivors, the experience can be difficult and dangerous."

"The gacaca is another way of a survivor being asked to do too much. We are suffering the burden of forgiveness." Beatha Uwazaninka criticizes the law that says everyone has to attend gacaca. "How would you like someone to take you back to your worst nightmare, to the most horrific time? The victim is not allowed to respond, to express any emotion; you attend literally and figuratively with your hand held over your mouth. This person cut your father into pieces or your mother, so to you this person is the face of evil, and yet the law says you have to go there and face him again. This is very difficult."

As if that were not enough, the victims are putting themselves in danger. "Survivors are scared of testifying because there are threats being sent to their houses," Beatha continues."Let me give you an example. This man who had killed people in the village was standing in the court and nobody was there to testify against him. Then a young woman stood up, a brave Hutu, and said, 'I see that no one is testifying against you because they are scared or didn't see you, but I did. You killed four people. I saw you with my own eyes.' He gave her a very hard look and just walked away. The next day her infant daughter disappeared. When her daughter was returned, she was dropped on her doorway dead, tortured, with a note attached: This is what will happen to you if you do that again.'"

Pastor Rutayisire knows full well that it can be dangerous for the survivors. "Because of the genocide against the Tutsis, it means that there are very few survivors and they are pitted against the families and relatives of the murderers. There is intimidation going on. Survivors are booed and beaten, and in extreme cases they are killed." He pauses and spreads out his hands, emphasizing his disappointment, before lifting his face in hope: "But still we hear people giving testimonies they had never dared to give. It is a very powerful moment when you have somebody confessing evil, when they stand up and say, 'I'm so sorry for what I did, and I repent, and I ask for forgiveness.'"

There appears, however, to be a missing element in the gacaca courts, and for Antoine Rutayisire this is critical. "We utilize the gacaca as a judicial system, but we don't use it as a reconciliation process. We go for investigation, we find information, we get an admission, we go for a verdict, but it hasn't created a sense of forgiveness, of 'we have forgiven, we've been forgiven, we are together again.' In our traditional system of the gacaca, apology was always due; it was part of the process to cement the new relationship. Both parties and their families would come and sit on the grass together, as would neighbors and witnesses. Everyone would talk and argue and finally come to an agreement. And when the perpetrator accepted and confessed, he would apologize. At that point, the injured party is supposed to say, 'I forgive you.' The objective was to restore the good climate and relationships in the community. I look forward to the day when we move to the next step where we go from justice to forgiveness. This is where we sit together in the community and the people of integrity on the Hutu side stand up and say we are so sorry for what our group did. For me, that would be the culmination of healing the nation in the gacaca system. At this moment we have peace, but we don't have reconciliation."

Paul Van Zyl was part of a delegation from the South African Truth and Reconciliation Committee that came to Rwanda after the genocide. The visit was intended as the start of an ongoing conversation between the two countries, a sharing of ideas and a discussion about the lessons learned from the TRC. Paul remembers these meetings vividly. "I was immediately struck by how radically different their situation was from ours. Rwanda had experienced a deep, intense period of genocide in which those in power had a very clear sense of who was right and who was wrong. They also had a very justifiable outrage that the international community had stood by and let it happen. So the Rwanda government was not in the mood for any sense of moral equivalence or seeing things from someone else's perspective. This was something that we in South Africa had labored to do when the TRC looked at the ANC's human rights abuses. The Rwandan government wanted the deep wrongfulness of the genocide to be acknowledged in unequivocal terms and the perpetrators be punished. But the government was not prepared to accept responsibility for any of the violent acts of their own troops as they brought the genocide to an end. And so the conversation was very different."

Paul does, however, express considerable sympathy for their situation. "The Rwandans are faced with an impossibly complex and difficult task and it is important that outsiders neither be moralistic nor judgmental in evaluating their efforts." He pauses significantly, for he does have reservations about the gacaca courts as a realistic vehicle of reconciliation. "First of all, I'm not sure that one ought to engineer individual acts of reconciliation, and by that I mean I'm not sure it's helpful to bring a hundred thousand perpetrators into contact with three hundred thousand victims, for they can easily feel forced to reconcile while dealing with impossibly difficult and painful episodes."

He continues, anticipating criticism, "Don't misunderstand me, I am in favor of countries seeking to achieve reconciliation. The South African experience tells of the enormous importance of having a Mandela or Tutu exist at a crucial transitional moment when the country could have gone up in flames. So I know the value of reconciliation, but I don't think that it is something you can impose on the hearts and minds of individual victims. If you do, you invariably offend and re-traumatize. I believe it is better attended to at a societal level by creating circumstances to ensure that it will never happen again."

Pastor Rutayisire wouldn't disagree but argues that his country is trying to think through such questions. "What do we owe the victims? What laws can we pass that will protect them? How do we make sure we acknowledge their suffering? In an impoverished country, what resources, if any, can we provide them? How do we deal with the next generation? How can we best change our national curricula? What national language policies can we implement? How do we deal with monuments and sacred places?" For example, he explains, "As a tool of remembering the evil in its magnitude, many of the churches where people were killed with the active collaboration of their priests have been turned into genocide memorials to tell us that real people were killed in those places. The skeletons and the bodies remain."

Although these memorials are important they are difficult for the survivors. "The bones are carefully placed and piled up on shelves." Beatha explains. "But this is hard for us, because you wonder whether that dead body could be a member of your family, even your mother or father? In Rwanda, we believe it's important to bury the dead, not to expose them, so this is another sacrifice we make for the future of our country. These memorials make a very clear statement. If the children of the perpetrators are not told the history of the genocide at home, their schools will tell them. Denial is not possible."

Immaculee Ilibagiza

There are other reconciliation efforts. The government encourages national unity through a new flag, a new anthem, and a new constitution. Identifying oneself as Tutsi or Hutu is now officially discouraged, the mantra is that 'We are all Rwandans.' The government also promotes active reconciliation by bringing survivors and perpetrators together in healing groups, peace villages, and in mass forgiveness ceremonies held in stadiums.

On his days off from working in the prison ministry, Father Sabune travels through the Rwandan countryside and is astonished by the pervasiveness and openness of the conversation about reconciliation. "Wherever I go there is something reminding people of the importance of reconciliation. If you switch on the radio there are plays, popular soap operas, and songs about reconciliation and forgiveness.

People talk about it on the streets, in restaurants, my taxi driver from the airport talked of little else. Pastors preach it non-stop from the pulpits. In memorials, the names of the dead are read for hours. You see giant posters describing the gacaca courts and explaining how this kind of justice will reconcile us. It's an odd, almost surreal feeling, knowing the darkness of what happened and then hearing these sunny upbeat conversations swirling around you."

The radio soap opera Father Sabune hears is a weekly drama series that tells the story of two villages in conflict. It has been hugely successful, capturing 92 percent of the radio population and has been inspired by the work of Ervin Staub, a Holocaust survivor and professor at University of Massuchusetts. He has spent most of his life developing approaches to help healing and reconciliation in the aftermath of great violence. Since 1996 he has worked in Rwanda. His overriding concern is that former victims will become perpetrators and so his programs focus on changing the psychological orientation toward 'the other.' Like Ervin, outsiders with skills honed through experience and fierce commitment to moral and spiritual repair have come to Rwanda to help the reconciliation work, operating independently of the government and church groups.

There is also growing concern regarding the youth and the next generation of Rwandans, those who were young at the time of the genocide or have been born since then. "Balancing reconciliation and forgiveness with justice and retribution is a struggle taking place at unbearable depths within each affected person. But when we talk about these challenges we are usually thinking of Rwandan adults, whose moral and spiritual development was already shaped or misshaped before the genocide. What about the young survivors of 1994 and the children born during or in the early years afterwards?" asks Associate Professor Richard Neugebauer, who has worked with bereavement and trauma for the past thirty years and led a multinational team evaluating children and adolescents traumatized by the genocide. "Left alone and unformed in the morally devastated and pathless landscape of the genocide, what becomes of the child's development of self, of the capacity for empathy, attachment, and love, all of which are fundamental to reconciliation and forgiveness? An awareness of this and answers to these questions are urgently needed as the new generation of Rwandans come of age."

However, there are worrying signs that certain government policies and practices may undermine these efforts to stimulate reconciliation and justice. Alison des Forges, the leading American voice for human rights in Rwanda and author of a definitive account of the genocide, summarized these omens. "The government is increasingly authoritarian: it punishes dissent, it reserves positions of power almost exclusively for Tutus, it protects its own soldiers against charges of war crimes and refuses to publicly acknowledge the suffering of Hutus who died in the genocide." Alison's depth of knowledge and love for the country was unmatched by any other outsider, yet she was barred from Rwanda because of her critique of the post-genocidal government of President Paul Kagame. "In the early years I saw remarkable things and heard stories of forgiveness and reconciliation. Now, it's different … and yet your ears will be filled with how happy everyone is."

Paul Van Zyl agrees that the political situation is troubling. "Not unlike 9/11, the genocide in Rwanda is increasingly deployed for political ends. While there is a real and legitimate way in which Rwandans want to recognize the victimization and horror that occurred, there is also a deeply unprincipled, strategic, and cynical deployment of the genocide and the notion of victimization that is being used to shut down dissent and to support an increasingly authoritarian strain of government. And that is profoundly dangerous. In addition, because they were victims, no one can impugn the motives or question the legitimacy of individuals who employ their own sense of victimization against others. I think that Rwanda will have to have an honest and more open reckoning with the conflicts of their past if it is to avoid returning to an unhealthy and dangerous place."

Antoine Rutayisire is sensitive to these criticisms, but he would diagnose the problem more as spiritual and psychological rather than political. He does not question the legitimacy or sincerity of his government and rebuts claims that it is dangerously repressive. At the same time, he is not naïf about the rising discontent nor does he gloss over the problems. "The danger is that we confused peace with reconciliation. We have accepted the minimum: I hate you, you hate me, but as long as I don't step on you that is peaceful cohabitation. We are not digging deep enough or looking at the negative emotions that sprang from the evil. We don't have just the anger of the survivors but also the guilt of the genocidaires and it is an explosive mix. These wounds are transmitted from father to son, they continue through the generations. So when you are wounded, your children will be as well, but even worse because the second generation wound is emotional, it doesn't have any rationality to it. They hate without justifiable cause."

Rwanda is not alone in dealing with such difficulties arising from years of conflict. Kenya has always been presented as progressive and peaceful but one tiny spark during the elections and it was in ruins. "The Balkans conflict goes back to the fourteenth century." Journalist Lance Morrow remembers a trip he took to the Balkans with Elie Wiesel when the wounds of the past became a visceral reality to him. They were in Sarajevo when the Serbs were trying to drive out the Bosnian Muslims. "Within ten minutes of checking into the hotel in Prague, someone had slipped a brown envelope under my door full of ghastly atrocity pictures. The only way I could tell whether they were taken in 1940 or 1991 was whether they were in black and white or color; it was the same decapitations, the same burned bodies. Nothing is forgotten there, not since the Battle of Kosovo in 1389. Grandmothers give their grandchildren the bloody shirt in which their father had been killed: 'You must avenge!' It comes out of this obsessive rancid memory and a refusal to forget anything. So when I think about forgiveness, I also think about the dynamics of forgetting. Is it better, as Elie Wiesel tells us, to never forget, or is it better to forget?"

For Antoine Rutayisire, both are true. "We have to remember this so that it doesn't happen again, but in order to get on, day by day, we also have to forget." He believes that the crucial part, however, is that hatreds must be lanced and healed before they can be forgotten. He speaks from personal experience about how difficult this process can be, as he had to struggle with it himself. "Getting rid of your anger is like giving away a part of yourself. When your anger lives in you, slowly it melts into your blood and your emotions, it shapes how you think about people, about life, and so relinquishing it is like losing a part of your body, your character, a part of who you are. You have come to feel that it's your right to hate. Giving it up means you lose your cutting edge, you become vulnerable, and feel like a victim again. When you keep your forgiveness from someone it can be as if you are exerting some revenge. And so you have to recreate yourself and this isn't easy."

Ultimately, a government can promote reconciliation at the national level but it cannot legislate it. Reconciliation happens between individuals and, in this overwhelmingly Christian nation, it is frequently guided by a faith that has survived the failure of all the religious institutions during the genocide. Pastor Rutayisire's own faith is private, intense, and only survived after considerable struggle. "I look at Jesus hanging on the cross with nails in his hands, with a crown of thorns on his head and his whole body bleeding, with the people who did it just staring at him. He is looking at them and saying, 'Father, forgive them.' How do you do that? How do you forgive the people who are crucifying you? You should be cursing them! I had a long list of people who took my job, who kicked me out of school, who killed my father; my life was entangled in a whole maze of people I hated with good cause and I couldn't forgive. One day I sat there and asked: 'God, are you telling me I can forgive this?' And Christ said he did it so I too can do it. That's when I started weeping, 'God, but I can't, I can't,' until finally I was given the grace to do it. I call it the grace of forgiveness because forgiveness is not purely from human power, at least not for me. If you are going to forgive, if you're going to let go, you need extra power. I had to open up and say, 'Lord, I can't, but you did, so help me do it.'"

During Immaculee Ilibagiza's ninety days of hiding in the pastor's bathroom, she too entered into an intense struggle with God whom she believed was personally calling out to her to forgive. Meanwhile her rage was consuming her, eating her alive. "I didn't feel sorrow, only anger." Her voice rises as the memories return. "I was angry at the government for unleashing this holocaust. I was angry at the rich countries for not stopping the slaughter. But most of all I was angry at the Hutus, all of them. I had never done anything violent before, but hiding in that bathroom I wished I had a gun so that I could kill every Hutu that I saw. Not just a gun, but a machinegun, grenades, a flamethrower! I wanted to be like Rambo and set the whole country on fire. If I had an atomic bomb, I would have dropped it on Rwanda and killed everyone in our stupid, hateful land. I never would have guessed that I had such a capacity for rage and knew that I'd have to do a lot of praying to rid myself of it."

After the genocide, a Tutsi rebel commander challenged Immaculee's fragile faith and her belief in forgiveness. She had gone to the prison to confront her father's murderer. It was a life-changing moment. "The jailer told me I could spit on him, kick him, kill him, anything I wanted. My father's killer shuffled in. He had been a friend of the family, an important dignified man in our village, but now he was a thin scarecrow, dirty in rags, his eyes avoiding mine. And I instantly felt pity and compassion, not anger, so I touched his sleeve, expressing my forgiveness. When I tried to explain this to the commander he was uncomprehending and angry. He took me to a church filled with decomposing bodies and rebuked me for my cheap forgiveness. It was then that I realized I needed to find a place to breathe where I could sustain the peace that I had found." Immaculee moved to New York where she lives with her husband and children, but she often returns to Rwanda.

Perhaps as a sign of repentance for their massive failures during the genocide, many church groups are actively bringing killers and survivors together in an effort to promote reconciliation. The results can be startling and inspire great hope. For instance, before the genocide the following two men lived in the same village and knew each other well; after the genocide they were bitter enemies, until last year.

"I started with killing the family of Celestin. I went on and there was another relative of Celestin's family and I also killed him," admits genocide perpetrator Elie Musabyimana in a flat, affectless voice. His eyes are bloodshot and his words chilling but his manner is remorseful. "After the Presidential decree of 2003, I was released from prison. I got out with a very hardened heart. But I discovered the essence of being forgiven when I attended the Evangelical training. On the first day of the session I looked out and saw relatives of the families I had killed. I saw Celestin. He was the in-law of the first family I killed, there were six of them. How was I going to face these people?"

Softly spoken, shy, and slightly withdrawn, genocide survivor Celestin Buhanda had been asked to attend a reconciliation program that was a collaboration between an African evangelical organization, AEE, and the employees of World Vision. "They called us to attend the training, and to my surprise I found Elie and Samuel there, who are the people who killed my family and my village. When I saw Elie I was so traumatized. I started to question how that training could possibly help me, I felt so bad." Celestin has a slight tremor in his quiet voice. "During the genocide all acts of evil were committed, women were gang raped and got HIV/AIDS, others had their private parts destroyed, it was beyond human. I never wanted to see Elie again because of what he had done.

"But with the help of the professional teachers and ministers, slowly, slowly, I started to feel okay. They preached the first day and I felt no change, then the second day, but as time passed I started to feel that God was changing my life through their words. Then came a lesson that was entitled 'Let us bring our troubles together.' Each of us had to write down on a piece of paper whatever was hurting us, but without saying it out loud. We each took the paper to the cross and burned it. Then came the lesson about taking away our fears and that we should speak out everything we had written on the paper." Celestin's voice grows stronger as he shares the power of that moment. "It was a difficult process but some, like Elie, took courage. Elie said that what he had done was wrong, that he had killed, hurt, and betrayed others. Kneeling down, crying, he said, 'I hunted them and I killed their families and relatives, I did wrong to them, but I humble myself, and I kneel down in my heart. I ask forgiveness from the survivors and from their families.'"

Initially Celestin felt that he had no choice. "I felt that I had to forgive him. I hated him, I feared him, I never wanted to share anything with him, I had all these emotions, and yet at that moment we were able to hug each other and express our forgiveness. As people got up and spoke, we all cried, we remembered what had happened and we heard remorse from those who did wrong to us. We saw the strength it took for them to ask for forgiveness. And that's how the miracle happened, how our heavy hearts were no longer burdened. After the training, Elie and I reconciled and we started to build a new relationship. Today we have a good friendship with each other; we have moved forward."

"On the third day everything turned around," remembers Elie, his hardened face becoming softer, more relaxed. "The counselors told us to stand up but I went down on my knees. I said, 'Before I ask for forgiveness on behalf of all my fellow Hutus who killed Tutsis, I am asking for forgiveness for myself.' Celestin and the others came to me and hugged me, saying that as I had asked for forgiveness so I should be forgiven. They could not believe that I asked for it; it was the first time they had heard someone accepting his role and begging for forgiveness. From that day, I respected the forgiveness they gave me, I felt reborn. Even today, when I think about what I did, I always ask myself why did I kill people? Why did any of us do it? I hated myself so much I felt that I deserved to die. In prison I felt worthless and I would constantly think about death. My life changed when they gave me forgiveness. I no longer condemn myself, I am a new being."

These two men, whose lives were enmeshed in the most unfortunate way, became friends. "After the training we became so close that our neighbors were shocked at our good relationship," confirms Celestin. "They see me with Elie and ask, 'Don't you fear going with that killer?' I say to them, 'No. He asked for forgiveness and I forgave him.' We have a lot of houses to build so that the victims have shelter and the widows get some place to sleep. When we work together we get close to each other. If one lifts a brick and gives it to the other without thinking of him as an enemy then it's another lesson taught to the community who see that we really have forgiven each other. When he got married I was his best man. Now we have formed an association of victims and perpetrators in order to teach unity and reconciliation. Forgiveness is the only way to have a peaceful mind as it creates a new relationship. Instead of wanting revenge we can find forgiveness so that the next generation will not feel the hatred. That is the big difference I see between reconciliation and for-giveness or just punishment. But," he adds somberly, "it is important to say that, given a chance, many of the genocidaires would go back and kill. They ask for for-giveness because they know it will get them out of prison. Sadly, those who have genuine repentance are rare and the government still has a lot of work to do. But for us, it is real and it has worked."

Such a story is remarkable in its sincerity and honesty. But is it sufficient? "When you are in the business of healing a nation, one story, two stories, three stories, a thousand stories, or even two thousand stories are not enough," insists Antoine Rutayisire. "You need more than nine million because Rwanda has more than nine million people. Or, you aim for a critical number of people who are going to be healed and you say, 'Now I see signs that this country is healing.' It would be very naïve to believe that all the wounds are going to heal because some people have been wrecked beyond recovery, so we are going to live with this for many years."

Rwanda remains a work in progress. Many people worry whether the forgiveness and reconciliation are paper-thin and that any anger denied will return with greater ferocity. There are those who feel pressured to forget and are unable to do so, while there are others who have forgiven deeply and been transformed in the process. Whether or not the gacaca courts lead to enduring reconciliation will only be revealed through the passage of time. Unconditional forgiveness—Immaculee and Antoine's solution for moving forward—may be the most effective solution for the thousands of victims whose suffering and losses cannot be redressed through official or quasi official means, but it is fiercely resisted.

For some, forgiving the perpetrators is another way of betraying those who died. "How far can I go to run away from genocide?" asks Beatha. "I can't. It's something I live with, I eat with, I sleep with. One day during the massacre I passed through an area where these three men were digging their own graves. On the other side there was a woman who looked like she had just been killed, probably half an hour earlier, with her arms chopped off. I didn't know these people, but I feel a relationship with them because I witnessed their last time in the world. So I'm part of their lives. Can you tell me, if you forgive the person who did this, what that woman would say to you if she could speak? It's not that I don't want to forgive, yet how can I forgive when those images are still talking to me, they're telling me no? We still have our lives and our arms and our legs, and we're fine. That's why we survived; we survived for them."

"Those who are dead are never gone," sings the Senegalese poet Birago Diop. "The dead are not under the earth… they are in the flowing water… in the still water… they are in the hut, they are in the crowd… the dead are not dead." The internal struggle created by the genocide includes settling accounts with both the living and the dead in order to move forward. "Among our many relationships are our relationships with the dead," observes Dr. Richard Neugebauer, currently engaged in health research designed to advance the social and psychological reconstruction of Rwanda. "When their loss comes through atrocious violence, the beloved dead make powerful, intimate, and legitimate claims on us: to remember, to bear witness; maybe to seek revenge. For many survivors of the Rwandan cataclysm, continued engagement with the world entails a harrowing, not always possible task of renegotiating their ties with the deceased. For some, the new terms permit reconciliation and forgiveness as their gift to the future, not as an act of desecration or a rupture in their hallowed bond with the dead."

"There are times when we say, 'I can't forgive. I prefer to live with my ulcers, I prefer to live with my sleepless nights, I prefer to live with my anger despite the bad effects it's going to have on me.' Wrong. We are not dead." Antoine Rutayisire offers us his final thoughts. "We have to let the dead sleep while we start living. I remember one person asked me, 'Don't you think that by forgiving we are desecrating the memories of the people who were killed?' And I said, 'What do you prefer, to die twice or to forgive and live?' It's a matter of living with the tension, living with this faithfulness to the dead or faithfulness to yourself and your life. It's a choice."

into the collective soul of nations, and into the lives of its citizens. He adds, "Forgiveness is above all a personal choice, a decision of the heart to go against the natural instinct to pay back evil with evil."

And though the world's vast burial grounds are on a whole other scale when measured against individual suffering, nonetheless personal betrayal can cut as deeply as a machete. These wounds, if not tended to, can destroy lives, ravage families, and stain generations to come. Forgiveness has the potential to heal these intimate woundings of the soul. No less than any nation, an anguished heart cries out to forgive and to be forgiven. In the end, forgiveness begins and ends with one person facing another: mother and child, father and son, husband and wife, friends, strangers, enemies. The decision to forgive—or not—is a choice at the heart of our shared humanity.

HELEN WHITNEY BIOGRAPHY

Helen Whitney is an acclaimed writer, producer, and director who has more than thirty years of experience producing dramatic features and documentary films. Her subjects have stretched across a broad spectrum of topics, including youth gangs; a portrait of the 1996 presidential candidates; a Trappist monastery in Massachusetts; the McCarthy Era; Pope John Paul II; and photographer Richard Avedon. "Faith and Doubt at Ground Zero," arguably Whitney's best-known film, was a PBS two-hour special on 9/11, which explored the spiritual aftershocks of this horrific event. Her film "The Mormons" was a four-hour PBS series, the first collaboration between American Experience and Frontline. In her feature films Whitney has worked with many distinguished actors, among them: Lindsey Crouse, Austin Pendleton, Brenda Fricker, and David Strathairn. Among Whitney's many accolades are an Oscar nomination; two Alfred I. du Pont-Columbia University Awards; a George Foster Peabody Award; an Edward R. Murrow Award for distinguished journalism; an Emmy Award; and awards from The Writer's Guild of America, The Director's Guild of America, The Hamptons International Film Festival, and The San Francisco International Film Festival. Whitney is a sought after lecturer who frequently speaks at universities, divinity schools, museums, and art institutes. She has served as director of the Board of Film Forum in New York City. She has been artist in residence at six universities and is a member of the Woodrow Wilson Visiting Fellows Program.

Now available on DVD and Digital Download from Docurama Films.

DVD bonus features include two never-before-seen extended sequences.

Available wherever DVDs are sold, or order now at WWW.NEWVIDEO.COM

CONCLUSION

Monsignor Lorenzo Albacete

From the beginning of time humans have committed brutal acts against one other. In this last century alone historians estimate that despotic tyrants and their armies, inflamed citizens, and even neighbors have murdered at least a hundred million civilians. We have been producers and consumers of hatred, violence, injury, injustice, bigotry—the list is endless—and in the process have become lessened in our humanity. The enormity of these numbers numb us and can lead us away from a melancholy truth: that for civil war and genocide to take place, it is individuals who conduct the atrocities that so stun the mind and take us to the very limits of comprehension.

At the same time, we yearn for a trace of redemption, for repair, and to break free from addictive cycles of violence. We crave some kind of absolution. Is it because we cannot escape the horrors of living in a world of total transparency? Is it an informed cry of despair? Or of spiritual exhaustion? As our world faces increasing problems of guilt, as horror done to us yesterday becomes terror we inflict on others tomorrow, has forgiveness become our last hope from the endless recurrence of blame and failure? And, finally, is this new language of repair enduring and transformative, or is it fleeting and ultimately of little significance?

In the resonant words of John Paul II, it was his belief that forgiveness can purify memory; it can travel through time and history breathing life into the killing fields,